Divine Light and Fire

OTHER BOOKS BY PETER ROCHE DE COPPENS

Ideal Man in Classical Sociology

Spiritual Man in the Modern World

The Nature and Use of Ritual

Spiritual Perspective II: The Spiritual Dimension and Implications of Love, Sex, and Marriage

The Nature and Use of Ritual for Spiritual Attainment

The Invisible Temple

Apocalypse Now: The Challenges of our Times

The Sociological Adventure: A Holistic Perspective

Lo Sviluppo dell'Uomo Nuovo, Volume I

Lo Sviluppo dell'Uomo Nuovo, Volume II

Lo Sviluppo dell'Uomo Nuovo, Volume III

The Art of Joyful Living

Divine Light and Fire

Experiencing Esoteric Christianity

Peter Roche de Coppens

ELEMENT

Shaftesbury, Dorset ● Rockport, Massachusetts
Brisbane, Queensland

Published in the U.S.A. in 1992 by
Element, Inc.
42 Broadway, Rockport, MA 01966

Published in Great Britain in 1992 by
Element Books Limited
Longmead, Shaftesbury, Dorset

Designed by Roger Lightfoot
Cover design by Max Fairbrother
Typeset by Colset Ltd
Printed and bound in the U.S.A. by
Edward Brothers, Inc.

Library of Congress Catalog Card Number 91–222123

British Library Cataloguing-in-Publication Data available

ISBN 1–85230–262–3

This work is dedicated to Marian Karpacz who suggested it and encouraged me to write it, many years ago, and who gave me back my freedom, when this was the last thing that I wanted, so that I could have the necessary experiences and freedom to write it. She suffered more than most, but always with great courage and dignity, and it is she I consider to be the true Muse of this work both on this side and on the other side of Life.

About the Author

Peter Roche de Coppens was born on May 24, 1938, in Vevey, Switzerland. He was educated in Switzerland, Argentina, and Italy through secondary school, and in the United States, Germany, and Canada at the university level. He graduated with honors from Columbia University and Phi Beta Kappa. Recipient of two Woodrow Wilson grants, he received his Ph.D. in Sociology from Fordham University in 1972. In 1978, he received an M.S.W. from the University of Montreal with a specialization in humanistic psychotherapy. He has studied with Pitirim University of Harvard University and was trained in Psychosynthesis by Roberto Assagioli of Florence, Italy.

He practices psychotherapy using personal and transpersonal Psychosynthesis with a particular interest in existential crises due to psychic and spiritual awakening. For the last twenty years, he has been teaching at East Stroudsburg University of Pennsylvania where he is a professor of sociology and anthropology.

In 1980 he was knighted "Knight Commander of Malta." He is a member of the Board of Directors of the International Institute of Integral Human Studies of Montreal, Canada, and Vice-President of the U.S. branch. He is also a member of the International Institute for Educational Excellence of New York and a past Field Faculty member of the Humanistic Psychology Institute of San Francisco. He is a Fellow of the American Orthopsychiatric Association, and is listed in most standard directories. He is also a member of the New York Academy of Sciences, a spiritual consultant at the United Nations in New York, and a lecturer at various universities and institutes of the U.S.A., Canada, Italy, France, and Switzerland. He is a member of Doctoral Committees at several universities and travels to Europe to give regular lectures and workshops at the Sorbonne University, the French Institute of Psychosynthesis, and various other centers. And he makes frequent appearances on television shows in various countries and, particularly, on the Maurizio Costanzo Show in Rome.

A productive researcher, pioneer, and writer, Dr. Roche de Coppens has dedicated the past thirty-five years of his life to the study of spirituality and to the investigation and the development of spiritual consciousness. For these studies and investigations, he has traveled widely to meet scholars, scientists, mystics, and spiritually awakened persons who have provided him with "living models" for his investigations. He belongs to, and has held high offices in, several esoteric and spiritual organizations. Finally, he considers this present work to embody the very best of his personal spiritual investigations and experiences, and to be the "crowning jewel" (or mature synthesis) of the previous three trilogies he has written on spiritual subjects.

PERSONAL STATEMENT

"The essence of Life is LOVE—of the Creator and Supreme Intelligence, and of our fellow humans—which leads to the awakening of spiritual consciousness. The 'heart of the Art of Living' revolves around someone to love, something to do which one truly enjoys, and hope in a better future. True wisdom is not 'not making mistakes' but never giving up—and stopping to learn."

Contents

Preface

A fundamental question has been my constant companion for many years and has motivated much of my work. What is Christianity and how can its essence be experienced here and now? In this book I hope to answer that question from my own personal experience but with a view to what in that experience is objective and might possibly help others, to make religion—any religion—come alive from within. Like a knight declaring his true intent before his quest, let me state here at the outset my most fundamental conviction:

Christianity is the Primordial Tradition of spiritual vision and insight, the "Philosophia Perennis" or Ageless Wisdom expressed in simple and practical terms that can be understood and lived by all generations of human beings, on all levels of consciousness and being. As such, it is not another religion amongst the many religions, nor is it the only way to salvation. Rather, the ecclesia is a community: it is a Brotherhood and Sisterhood and a pathway to Initiation, to the realization of true spiritual consciousness.

This view was expressed long ago, and perhaps best, in the famous statement of St. Augustine: "That which is called the Christian religion existed amongst the ancients and never did not exist, from the beginnings of the human race, until Christ came into the flesh at which time the true religion, which already existed, began to be called Christianity." If Christianity is the perennial Holy Wisdom and the quintessence of the ancient initiations, then it can continue to be perceived and lived on *many different levels of consciousness and being.* In its nature it is not a closed theology or philosophy, but an "open system," a companion for human beings on their spiritual journey, however differently they may interpret the means and end, however diverse their levels of consciousness and being.

Human consciousness and the human mind, heart, and will are not static and fixed but alive, dynamic, unfolding. Thus each age, each culture, each country has its own particular focus, central preoccupations, and tasks, which change in time, meet challenges, and evolve as they pass through major qualitative metamorphoses. Today, we are witness to such a qualitative transformation, a paradigmatic shift in human consciousness.

Religion is itself composed of a trinity—body, soul, and spirit. The body contains the basic symbols, images, archetypes, rituals, and practices. The soul represents the fundamental meanings, implications and applications that these symbols, images, archetypes, rituals, and practices have for human beings. The spirit is the power, energies, and Life-force that stand behind the body and the soul; it is that which the body and soul of religion are designed to awaken and render conscious to the individual who practices that religion.

Seen in this light, Christianity as experienced today lacks nothing fundamental in its body or in its spirit, to the extent we can comprehend the former and thus achieve or reconnect with the latter. It is the soul of the Christian experience which we must free from the burdens of the past so that it can speak to the multidimensionality of modern individual consciousness. While science and technology, the arts, education, politics, economics, and the whole sphere of human culture—which is really a projection and reification of human consciousness—have undergone radical changes, religion, the Christian religion in particular, remains unexplored along the strata of this informing and unfolding of consciousness. Thus it is the soul, the link between the body and the spirit, that each Christian must rediscover, opening and healing it so that a new life can circulate in the whole. We can then truly understand and thus participate in creating whatever necessary correctives are needed to the cultural changes we have witnessed in the post-Enlightenment era, particularly in the last ninety years.

This book is an attempt to share a sense of Christianity that speaks in a special way to us in our time, when many feel that they have lost touch with the life of the soul, the kingdom within, the inner spirituality that moves us to live the outer life. Thus we must seek to climb with our human will, aware that extended to us, in loving gesture, is the hand of Christ to direct our steps on this ladder of consciousness.

There is a very vital and important work to be done: Religion, science, and philosophy are to be reunited. They are the three essential pathways into reality, and they complement and complete each other. Together they will work to integrate the past, the present, and the future, the many religions with the one Religion (which has never been and never will be fully incarnated in the material world). Together they will speak the one language of the inhabitants of the global village, reflecting our developing planetary consciousness, addressing our deepest problems, anxieties, aspirations, difficulties, and challenges. This work starts with each individual and in each individual heart and life. And it can begin in very simple and practical ways within one's present religious orientation.

I am well aware that the traditions in esotericism, in general, and of Christian esotericism in particular, are many and varied. Here one finds, among many others, Boehme, von Eckartshausen, Paracelsus, Flamel, Ficino, Pico della Mirandola, St. Germain, Fulcanelli, Saint-Yves Alveydre, Le Comte de Gabalis, Paul le Cour, Johann Valentin Andrea, Rudolf Steiner, Blessed Anne Catherine Emmerich, Papus, Sedir, Maitre Philippe de Lyons. The purpose of this work is not to produce an exhaustive and comprehensive treatise of esoteric Christianity; rather it is to share with the readers some possible means to a direct personal experience of it.

Let me give you a very simple and concrete example of what I mean. At one time (and in the Eastern churches this is still practiced, but not explained), we were told that upon entering a church we should align ourselves with the altar in front, bow our heads, and make the Sign of the Cross three times. Today, in the Roman Catholic churches no one practices this, not even the clergy, who should know better. In the Eastern churches, many people still practice this, but they generally do it out of imitation and custom, and thus mechanically and rapidly, rarely putting all their hearts, minds, and souls into the process—which would make it come alive for them and enable them to reap its benefits. It is my hope that, after reading this book, people will again do this and do it consciously so as to reap maximum and tangible benefits from this ritual. At that point, they should be more aware of its deeper meanings and implications.

What is the spiritual and living meaning of this ritual? For people who have eyes to see and the sensitivity to feel, there are always two angels working in polarity at every functioning altar. They receive, transform, and beam the spiritual energies (the divine Light, Fire, and Life) from the center of the altar outwardly to the whole church, congregation, and world. By bowing to the altar, we align our psycho-spiritual Head Center with it to open up to and receive the energies that are projected from the altar. By making the Sign of the Cross three times, we distribute these energies through the "Cross of Light," first in our mental, then in our astral, and finally in our vital and physical bodies, filling them with Life. And what human being does not need a "booster" at the mental, emotional, and vital levels? It enables us, first, to know and be a little more ourselves and thus to live a more conscious and constructive life, and, second, to participate in a more conscious and alive way to the religious service we generally go to church to attend. This is what living and practical esoteric Christianity is designed to do by focusing again upon the Christian Mysteries.

The Christian Mysteries, like the Mysteries of any religion or tradition (if it is authentic), aim at affecting and transforming the *whole person* and his *whole life*. In a modern word, they are truly "holistic" in their approach and intentions. Now to affect a whole person and his or her whole life, they must touch and affect the *mind*, *heart*, and *will* of that person. That is, they must bring Wisdom to affect the thinking and perspective, awaken Love to affect the desires and aspirations, and activate the Life-force, or creative energies, so that the person may *act upon* and *live* what he or she now knows and loves.

When we look at human anatomy, we see that a human being has a head and a heart, as well as limbs. All of the organs form an essential integrated whole, an indivisible physical human body. Yet, the heart is the central and predominant organ of the human person, as the sun is the center of the solar system. Thus, in the Christian Mysteries and Initiations it is LOVE that is truly fundamental, the wellspring and motive force for both *knowledge* and *action*. Without Love we might understand the phenomena but never the *noumena*, the outer but not the inner parts. Moreover, as some well-established traditions have shown, Love is itself both form and substance of knowledge, a means of cognition, a way of true knowledge that comes from "communion" and "union" with the object of that knowledge, as well as with the end, what then is known. From the center to the limbs, we can say, too, that without Love there is no true will, no sustained action, that one cannot really *live* and thus *become* what one knows and desires without it.

The problem, however, is that knowledge can be described and analyzed, organized and systematized in a cognitive framework and philosophy. Not so with Love, who must be felt, as Action must be lived. As for philosophy, let the reader bear in mind that the philosophy and esoteric interpretation of Christianity proposed in this work have as their true and final aim to awaken a greater and more conscious Love for God. From this will follow accord with God's Laws, so another aim is to know how to *live them* more passionately and fully, to realize them in our own consciousness and being. These Laws and the basic rituals themselves will reveal their "practical and living Mysteries" to those who will meditate upon them, who will practice them, and who will LIVE them; and this increasingly as one's conscious level of being is lifted, attuned, and thus inspired by the Spirit of God within.

Another very important question that presents itself at the beginning of this work is the notion of Becoming and Being, of evolution, devolution, or of "a varying participation in what already IS." In other words, is there such a thing as progress and evolution, moving from a lower to a higher level, from a primitive to a more advanced state? Is there such a thing as physical, emotional, mental, and spiritual evolution or growth? The answer has elements of an unanswerable paradox: Man is ever encouraged to seek, to become perfect in all he is, and thus from the standpoint of the personality the answer must be yes; but for God who dwells in eternity, who is perfect and changeless, the answer must be no. What we can experience is God reaching out to us as human beings, who likewise seek this contact, this communion, and, ultimately, this union—in ways that differ and change with personal, historical, and cultural circumstances.

Both Becoming and Being exist, spanning the different levels of consciousness. The process of salvation, or initiation and illumination, deals with the *actualization of potentials that are preexistent*, that are already there but not yet realized. This is the same problem that we encounter with the notion of "time" and of "eternity." At the human level of consciousness and being there is definitely time and thus evolution—which is polarized into both *progress* and *regress*, for if one can move *forward*, one can also move *backwards*. It is a strange paradox that, since the Renaissance, and the Enlightenment in particular, we have witnessed a great deal of material, economic, and technological progress but must question whether this has been at the price of human, moral, and spiritual regress. Perhaps this is due to the fact that the collective consciousness of Western civilization has opted for "knowledge" in order to obtain "power"—but at the expense of Love. It is primarily to rekindle the power of Love in the human heart and in daily life that this work has been conceived and written. In conclusion, no better words can be found to express this than the passions and aspirations of the final stanzas of Dante's *Divine Comedy*:

> O Everlasting Light, you dwell alone
> In yourself, know yourself alone, and know
> And knowing, love and smile upon yourself!
>
> That middle circle which appeared in you
> To be conceived as a reflected light,
> After my eyes have studied it a while,
>
> Within itself and its coloring
> Seemed painted with our human likeness
> So that my eyes were fully focused on it.
>
> As the Geometer who sets himself
> To square the circle and who cannot find,
> For all his thought, the principle he needs.

Just so was I on seeing this new vision;
I wanted to see how our image fuses
Into the circle and finds its place within.

Yet my wings were not meant for such a flight—
Except that then my mind then was struck by lightning
Through which all my longing was at last fulfilled.

Here powers failed my high imagination:
But by now my desire and will were turned

Like a balanced wheel rotated, evenly
By the Love that moves the sun and the other stars.

This work was originally conceived and written as one volume entitled *Living and Practical Esoteric Christianity* which formed an integrated and sequential whole. Subsequently, however, it was renamed *Divine Light and Fire* and is now coming out in two volumes, possibly to be followed by a third to form a trilogy. Why was it renamed? Because *Light and Fire* stand at the very core of this work. They represent the two "polarizations" and "manifestations" of the spiritual energies when these are apprehended by people who have awakened spiritual consciousness. Those who are more in tune with Wisdom and with their psychospiritual Head Center perceive it as Light; whereas those who are more in tune with Love and with the psychospiritual Heart Center perceive it as Fire. In the present version and publication, each volume is an independent unit that can be read by itself or in conjunction with the other, for each volume further elucidates and completes the other.

Throughout this book, I have used the word "man" to mean, of course, both men and women. For the sake of brevity, I have used the pronouns "his" and "him" implying also "her." In selected places, I have also used the form "he/she" and "him/her" to anchor and emphasize the former. In dealing with the "Divine Spark," the "Self," the "Holy Spirit," and various manifestations of the Divine, I have used the pronouns "he/him" and "it/its" implying also "she/her." This I have done fully recognizing that the Divine Essence, or God, is Androgynous, above and implying all genders, masculine and feminine, personal and transpersonal, singular and plural.

I wish to thank my many teachers and students who have all, directly or indirectly, contributed to the creation of this work. I particularly want to thank Richard Payne for the many hours he put in reading the first manuscript, for his very constructive criticism and additions, and especially for the love and hospitality that I received in his home when an unforecasted accident prolonged my visit.

Introduction

Today, you and I are privileged to live in very remarkable times, but this last decade of the twentieth century is remarkable, ironically, because it is a particularly troubled time. We have seen tremendous changes, massive quantitative and qualitative transformations, and what is at stake is momentous and compelling. Dangers are very real, opportunities great, and challenges imperative. Heaven and Earth do truly seem to be "opening their gates," beckoning us to "enter in," and thus they are accessible to our consciousness in new ways.

We are living in an *expanding material universe*, both quantitatively and qualitatively, objectively and subjectively, as science has exhaustively and empirically demonstrated. Galaxies and star systems are moving away from each other at incredible speeds and have been since the "Big Bang" or "Original Beginning." But, far more important for us, *our own human consciousness is also expanding*, heightening, and actualizing its faculties and potentialities. This is the truly crucial and most meaningful event for us, since it touches us to the very core of our being and has very significant implications. In a few words, what does this mean?

What it really means is this: it brings about, and involves, a *triple transformation and expansion*. First, to make the Deep Mind (the preconscious, subconscious, unconscious, and superconscious) *conscious*—to become aware of and understand things that before we were not aware of and could not understand. Hence, it involves an opening, enlarging, and growth of our consciousness. Second, it means to vitalize, intensify, and vivify our emotions, to make our emotions *come alive* (by making our present emotions more acute and developing new ones). Hence, it involves an opening of the heart, a transformation, amplification, and intensification of our capacity to love, of our inner sensibility and receptivity. Last, it means a powerful dynamization, awakening, and intensification of our creative energies. Hence, it makes us more vital, alive, and powerful—to do good or to do evil, to create or to destroy, to move towards greater Life, Consciousness, and Freedom or towards Death, Unconsciousness, and Slavery!

These possibilities impel us to discover how to live in a *conscious* and *responsible* way. Moreover, our world now demands of us a conscious involvement, and that means if we want to see something done, we must *do something about it* or it will never happen. We must become *engagé* as the French say—that is, give and involve our whole being and consciousness in *whatever we do*. Creation continues to unfold, but part of this unfolding is left to our *human consciousness*, individually and collectively, to complete this process and become what we are meant to be.

At this historical juncture, therefore, it is important to develop a philosophy of life and become wise in the art of living that philosophy. In doing this we are guided by our purpose on earth: the realization of happiness in the service of God and each other. Along the way, some fundamental questions will arise: What role do the established sacred, religious, philosophical, and cultural traditions play? What role does our own sense of the present and future play in developing such a philosophy and art *ex novo*? How can they together suit contemporary needs, aspirations, and conditions? How can we *combine* the old and the new, the past with what exists and those with what is yet to be born? For all the uncertainty we must bear with respect to the future, we can still behold its beams across the dawn horizon.

The creative answers to these questions will be in making a loving *synthesis*, one which provides a true *continuity* expressing God's perennial design. It is a continuity which will not cut the roots of a tree from which we might hope to gather fruit. And it is a synthesis of bark and core; that which is external and exoteric with that which is internal and esoteric.

In practical terms, what does this mean? It means that we can freely choose a point of reference or tradition which we want to connect with and use as a springboard. It may be a reference point which already exists objectively for all human beings: the family, the religion, the state, the race, the socioeconomic status, or historical period into which we are born. For every human soul is not born into a male or female body, into a family, religion, or nation—into a given set of conditions—by chance or hazard. Rather, it is born into the overall situation which best suits its growth, development, and spiritual realization. So choosing to reconnect with the religious tradition one was born into, whether Christian, Judaic, Islamic, Hindu or Buddhist, is not a question of regression dictated by the forces of heredity but rather a conscious awakening to providence: Has one learned all that can be learned in that primary, given spiritual context?

Christianity, like other religions or sacred traditions, reveals itself according to our level of consciousness and being. It is in the nature of tradition to offer us essential, practical yet efficacious, time-tested means by which to unfold higher energies, faculties, and potentialities, and move towards spiritual realization. Thus in Christian tradition we find, in its basic formulations and expressions, an inherent range of possibilities for the different levels of consciousness. How these are experienced in the present yet further individualizes and universalizes Christianity. This is so because, as stated earlier, Christianity rightly understood bears within it the stimulus to grasp all religious creeds and tendencies.

This can be realized experientially. And such is the purpose of this work, to encourage and inspire those who would know this to give their whole *minds*, *hearts*, and *wills* to unlocking the universal truth of Christianity, but this can be done through an intensification of practice in any particular tradition or confession.

And so a purpose here is also to enable people to raise their consciousness to the point where the images, symbols, and rituals of many of our sacred traditions will again come alive, will again speak to them, revealing and unveiling each mystery in progressive degrees, and finally will lead them to be motivated and guided from *within* and from *without*, experiencing these mysteries and truths *inwardly* and *directly* rather than only outwardly and indirectly. For the esoteric, by its very nature, can never be revealed from *without*—however pure a ritual, a sermon, a lecture, or workshop might be—but only from *within*, from one's *personally lived experience*. Yet, a few keys, a few evocative images and explanations, a few functional "tools," and the embryonic fragments of a "spiritual science" can go a long way. They can be a catalyst leading to the *lived experience*, the life of inner faith and understanding. At least, such has been my experience and is my hope for you.

The first breakthrough is that of awakening, stirring up, and making alive something in our consciousness when we use each of the sacred rituals, prayers, or exercises. In other words, it is to make each gesture or act *come alive in us* and *change something, make something happen*. For once this has occurred and we have lived it, then we know, through our direct, personal experience, that the sacred science is alive, that prayer is alive, that religious rituals are alive, and that when we do certain things, as prescribed by tradition or religion, *things happen and we do change and are transformed*.

It is at this point, and perhaps only at this point, that we truly become self-motivated to give the time, the attention, and the energy to the efforts and sacrifices necessary to allow religion to come alive in our consciousness and to become the Power of God for us. It is also, perhaps only at this point, that we begin to live as adults, as mature, responsible *children of God* who can consciously continue to complete their evolution and realize their destiny, by truly encountering the person of Christ.

All my life, in one way or another, in one form or another, I have been fascinated by the fundamental questions of Life and obsessed with the vision of and need for, a comprehensive philosophy of life and of an integral art of living. This has really been the *leitmotiv* of my life, my very *raison d'être*, and what I might call my Grand Obsession! Having crossed the threshold of the fiftieth year of my life in this material world, I have been blessed, many times, in spite of myself and of my short-term goals and objectives, with the traditional three-fold injunction of the genuine orders of Chivalry:

"Let us be worthy of great adventures!"

"Let us be worthy of great battles!"

"Let us be worthy of . . . great suffering!"

The time has now come, for me, to reflect upon and take stock of my life and work. During this half-century, I have traveled much and far, and have encountered many different types of people, including spiritually awakened persons who have taken me into their confidence and who became my friends. I have also suffered much and experienced great joys and rewards; I have been pushed to the very brink of the unconscious—and of the superconscious. I have been very ill and exhausted, as well as full of life and tremendously energized and vivified. In short, I have been blessed with exploring both the depths and the heights of human nature and human experience.

I have taught most of my life in universities and centers of higher learning, and given countless lectures and workshops in different countries and in different languages. I have also written many articles, essays, and lecture-texts, as well as over a dozen books, published in several languages. Hence, now I look forward to the very best decade of my life—towards the harvest period during which I will reap what I have sowed during my adult years and, especially, towards the most alive, creative, productive, and fulfilling years of my life.

In one way or another, I have always been concerned with three basic dimensions, or elements, of human nature and life—knowledge and thinking, love and feeling, power and willing. My first love and concern was, undoubtedly, *power*, or the ability to express myself and to create in this world. This concern ranged from muscle power, as compared to that of my classmates and friends, to will power, the ability to do what I wanted or not to do what I did not want, the power to express myself. Then came knowledge and thinking, which lasted for many years, for I soon realized that there could be no real power without knowledge. This came to the foreground quite early and clearly in my clashes with my father. He was much stronger than I was, and, besides, he was an adult as well as my father, so he could have his way with me whether I liked it or not. I had but one thing left to balance this situation and still be able to do what I wanted and to express myself—thinking and knowledge of the overall situation, which I spent a great deal of time obtaining, to then use, like in a chess game, in my clashes with my father.

By the time I first came to the U.S. at the age of seventeen, I had gotten a reasonable amount of both knowledge and power, and I was now in a situation where I could, indeed, for the first time in my life, really do what I wanted and not do what I did not want to do, because I was truly alone for the first time. After the first moment of great elation and freedom, caused by the novelty of the situation and by finally obtaining my heart's wish, I realized that I was still not happy and that something vital, essential, was missing. What could that be? I thought about this and searched for a long time before I discovered that it was "love," that my affective nature was starved—and that this part of my being and consciousness had to be fed and nurtured if the other parts were to function properly and to enable me to work efficiently with them. But, here, I was in for a shock and for a major change of outlook.

To gain power and knowledge, I had used the male aspect of my personality and ego—thinking and planning, willing and acting—and I was always in control, getting from a situation in direct proportion to what I had put into that situation. Now, however, I learned that I had to let go, that I was no longer in control, that I had to wait, to be patient, receptive—to change myself (that is my consciousness and attitude) rather than the world (things out there). I had to become acquainted with and develop the feminine aspects of my consciousness and being, learn patience, obedience, humility, as well as pass through the school of suffering, loneliness, poverty, and deprivation (of what my ego wanted and felt I should have). It is as though the three cardinal rules of monasticism, poverty, chastity, and obedience, were suddenly imposed upon me, even though I was not a monk!

I also learned that a human being is not a machine and that life is not a linear progression of work and achievements, of successes following other successes, but, rather, a spiral of ups and downs, of conquests and failures, and an alternation of many cycles, many levels, and many activities. I learned the lessons of illness and handicaps, as well as those of solitude, aloneness, and despair: to stand fast and continue even when things did not work out the way I thought they should. But I continued my studies, growth, and self-actualization according to the plan laid out by my Higher Self rather than by the agenda of my impatient and limited lower self. When I took the higher and more global view and put events and developments into their right perspective, I realized with hindsight that things did work out very well for me.

I succeeded in completing my education in the U.S., in making the right contacts in the spiritual as well as in the professional areas, both here and abroad. I became a professor of sociology at a small American university (East Stroudsburg University of Pennsylvania) and was able to do the research, teach the courses, and give the lectures and workshops, as well as attend the conferences, that were essential for my life's work. I also formed various human and spiritual groups with whom to test out and live the core ideas, insights, and principles I was reflecting, lecturing, and writing about. Finally, I also succeeded in publishing several books which contained, described, and analyzed the essence of the comprehensive philosophy of life and integral art of living I was thrusting towards, thus giving objective and external expression to my deepest intuitions, ideas, and ideals.

What I was always seeking and thrusting towards, more or less consciously, was really a way to *become more alive*: an ''art of living'' and a set of tools and exercises which would enable me to know more and become more aware, to love more and feel more intensely, and to express myself more fully and creatively. If Life is the sacred thing par excellence, then, indeed, the central question of life on earth is *how to become more alive*—how to live more fully, consciously, and passionately. And the next most important question is *how to realize this*? These were the fundamental questions which, together with the Riddle of the Sphinx (the question of identity), haunted me all of my life and provided the motivation and the fuel for my long quest. This quest, spanning now more than thirty years, took me to many lands, to many schools, to many teachers and sages, and to the most fascinating adventure—*the spiritual adventure*, or the adventure of self-transformation and of psychospiritual metamorphosis.

The specific task of this work is to apply the assumptions, teachings, conclusions, and perspective of the Spiritual Tradition to one of the major world religions, Catholic Christianity. I consider this book to be the culmination of all my writings up to now, because my conception of Christianity (seen in an esoteric or spiritual light) is that it is none other than the incarnation and full realization of the Great Work and the attainment of true spiritual consciousness and Initiation in the world.

This is what Christianity, as lived and exemplified by Jesus and his Apostles, was before it became a world religion, and what it *still is* for those who are spiritually ready and have ''eyes to see and ears to hear''—a human brotherhood and a practical path to spiritual Initiation. Beneath the many layers of its symbolic and analogical sheaths, which cover its central teachings, rituals, and practices, what we have is the *simplest* and most *practical* path to enable the Divine

Spark to become activated and manifest its attributes in our consciousness and being. To become a "real" Christian for me is none other than to become a "Christed human being," a human being who has achieved true spiritual Initiation. A human being in whom it is the Lord who is King and who Rules; a human being in whom the spiritual Self has become the unifying and integrating principle of the psyche and of the thoughts, emotions, desires, words, and actions; a human being, then, who *becomes another "living Christ."* This perspective and approach to Christianity may seem far removed from, and even alien to, what most Christian Churches officially teach and preach. This is not surprising to me since the language of the Bible, of the old Liturgies, and of the Fathers of the Church is not the analytical and descriptive language of everyday speech or of science, and cannot be interpreted in the same fashion, that is *literally*. It is the symbolic and analogical language of the Sages, used to describe visions, intuitions, and ecstasies obtained in altered states of consciousness, in a state of Illumination or spiritual consciousness; it is the forgotten language of the Deep Mind, the language of images, archetypes, and myths which have as many different meanings and possible interpretations as there are different states of consciousness, levels of evolution, and personal biographies.

Hence, the central images, symbols, myths, and rituals of Christianity, as well as those of any other faith, have a limitless number of meanings, correspondences, and applications, which grow and expand, deepen and brighten, with the growth and unfolding of our human consciousness—which is the *mirror* through which both inner and outer reality are reflected. To put it succinctly: what happens to our consciousness happens to the interpretations we give to the symbols and myths of the sacred traditions—*they move up and down the inner ladder of our consciousness*, changing their meaning and message as our field of consciousness is raised towards the superconscious or lowered toward the unconscious. For me, therefore, it is the linkage between various levels of consciousness and the various meanings and interpretations given to the Gospels, the old Liturgies, and the basic teachings of the Christian faith which account for the historical unfolding, vicissitudes, and splintering of the Church.

CHAPTER ONE

Christianity in the New Era: The Spiritual Life in Contemporary Society

The end of the century is fast approaching. To look at what has happened in over ninety years is to be confronted by massive change, both external and internal, physical and spiritual, quantitative and qualitative. Our times are characterized by wars, hot and cold, civil, national, and international; by economic affluence and depression; by increased urbanization and industrialization, but also by pollution and ecological imbalance. The face of our planet has been transformed by science and technology, by the cure of old diseases and the appearance of new ones, by social, economic, and cultural revolutions. The family, both its structure and its functioning, and our educational institutions have been remolded and reshaped. And through it all our consciousness has metamorphosed.

The year 1955, standing as it does about halfway between the beginning and end of the century, was also the year I came to America, to begin my adult life. I made the journey in eleven days, from Genoa to New York City. On the boat were several classes of people, the wealthy, businessmen, students, and immigrants, all coming to the country that was the political, economic, and military leader of the world. The U.S. dollar was pegged to gold at thirty-two dollars per ounce. In New York, the area surrounding Columbia University where I was a student was relatively safe, and apartments could be rented for ninety dollars a month. There were plenty of jobs, both part-time and full-time, and students who worked in the summer could support themselves during the rest of the year. The main topics of conversation then were how to contain Communism, how to choose the right profession, and how to have fun. After the great cataclysm of World War II, life had again settled into a solid, stable, and relatively slow pace. But one could not speak about spiritual experiences or spiritual training without being considered more than a little odd, given the materialistic, rational, and liberal outlooks of the time.

Today, some thirty-five years later, we live in a very different world, with different fears, aspirations, and parameters. I recently returned to Columbia University and only with difficulty recognized the neighborhood and life there. Finding an apartment in New York is now a very expensive proposition, as well as a herculean task. Finding a meaningful job, before or after graduation, is another major task. The journey that took me eleven days now takes less than ten hours by jet. The dollar is no longer pegged to gold, which is now worth around four hundred dollars an ounce. Communism is crumbling, but so too is the American economy, and so too, throughout the world, is the environment. But spirituality and parapsychology are in vogue. Here, though, the best and the authentic are mixed with the worst and the fraudulent. Schools, courses, and symposia have sprung up like mushrooms in the spring, purporting to convey spiritual teachings, to awaken one's spiritual consciousness, or to actualize one's higher potentialities and faculties.

Today we live on a "new earth" beneath a "new heaven," in a global village with planetary consciousness, in the midst of what is perhaps the greatest period of transformation in the history of humanity—a period of crisis, challenge, and opportunity. On the horizontal axis, which is material, external, and empirical, this is readily apparent; but it is equally true on the vertical axis, internal and psychological. Can these dramatic changes have occurred in our external world without concomitant changes in our consciousness? Surely it, too, is transforming and expanding both quantitatively and qualitatively.

This massive transformation of our outer and inner worlds, of human society and human consciousness, must bring about a new paradigm, a new synthesis of human knowledge, love, and will. This new paradigm will ultimately, I believe, culminate in a convergence of the three core faculties of the human psyche, a reintegration of human consciousness. Touching as it does every aspect of life, this transformation will bring an increase in our sense of personal responsibility, personal freedom, integrity, and self-worth. It will open us to new and deeper ways of loving and of serving others. This transformation will profoundly affect, first by destabilizing and disintegrating and then by re-equilibrating and reorganizing, all aspects of our being, consciousness, and life. Of particular interest for us, in this present work, is the impact of this ongoing metamorphosis on Christianity.

We can intuit that the time has come for a major synthesis to take place—the synthesis first of the exoteric and the esoteric aspects within Christianity, moreover, of Christianity and all the religions of the world and, finally, of Christianity and secularity in all its forms. This work primarily addresses the first of these, for the difference between the conception and practice of religion of the "average person" and that of the Initiate lies at the level of the "soul" of religion rather than at the level of its "body" (the level of its meaning and interpretation, of its value implications and applications). It is the exoteric and the esoteric aspects of the *same* "body" which are perceived, defined, and utilized in a different way.

It has been said, and rightly so I believe, that the Western spiritual tradition, embodied and lived in its social, historical, and cultural expression by Christianity, will go through three major phases: The first is the religion of the *Father*, embodied by the Jewish people and the Old Testament, focusing primarily on knowledge, law, and will. The second phase is the religion of the *Son*, embodied by the New Testament, with its emphasis on feeling, love, and grace. The third phase is the religion of the *Holy Spirit*, now about to be born. It will bring about the grand synthesis mentioned above, as well as the realization and the incarnation of the promises of the first two phases, in the conscious life of each person, and to each in a distinctive way. For the religion of the Holy Spirit is a *scientific* and *experiential* religion (though not in the sense in which science is understood today) wherein each individual realizes and becomes that which was taught at earlier times.

It is also my basic conclusion that the development during the Renaissance of the scientific method, which sought direct personal observation and experience rather than reliance upon indirect authority, was a precursor to what can be experienced today in this phase of the Holy Spirit. For, in fact, today's science is the seed-form which can, eventually, give birth to the mature tree. It is true that until now this scientific revolution has brought in its wake a great deal of confusion, suffering, disorder, and the impression for many that human beings have been cut off from the "Great Chain of Being," from the spiritual hierarchies, and from their very Source and Essence. But this was the necessary dying of the old to give birth to the new—the death that prefigures resurrection. Formerly, an individual was far more limited to his or her place in the social and historical hierarchies, and one can wonder if this also reflected degrees of freedom in the spiritual realm. Are then the increased possibilities here below not reflective of those above, so that each can more and more realize himself or herself as a Great Soul, and a true Child of God?

To realize the Divine Plan of the Celestial Father, major transformations, crises, and metamorphoses were necessary—cataclysms that brought about the restructuring and reforming of social institutions and value systems, including our relationships with the spiritual world, the hierarchical beings, archangels, angels, saints, prophets, and heroes, all who had guided and led humanity in its infancy and adolescence. (They have never ceased to exist but must now operate in the shadow, so to speak, of present-day science.) Without socio-cultural affirmation of these higher creative and spiritual rela-tionships, many have felt abandoned, thrown back on their inner consciences alone, albeit lit by the Divine Spark, as guides and points of reference.

But this was why materialistic rationalism and the development of the ego were necessary, along with the eclipse of Faith and of the earlier forms of spiritual consciousness. In this truly democratic era, authentic teachers and spiritually realized beings *hide themselves* and *turn off their "lights" and their authority* so as to force each person *to look within himself or herself*; they do not wish to become "centers of attrac-tion." Those who do not recognize this profound truth of our times, and who set themselves up as the new gurus, teachers, masters, or authorities are, in fact, whether consciously or not, seeking to reacti-vate the old dispensation. Without this intuition of the nature of our time, they can, in the end, act as a retarding force in evolution, rather than furthering and facilitating it.

In the coming age, according to one of my publishers Carl Llewellyn Weschcke (in a private letter), the central tasks of educators and teachers will be to

reveal the "secrets," i.e. the actual technology for psychic and spiritual development, in practical, step-by-step procedures suited both to the single person and to group working, and we also motivate *action* by telling—as much as our own vision provides—what it is that is happening as a result of such working and why we feel it should be done. The respon-sibility for action, and hence for discipline and growth, remains (always) with the "student."

For me, it is the *assumption of responsibility* by the student. It is this internalized sense of responsibility that characterizes the age of Aquarius. This in contrast to the age of Pisces in which the role of authority was primary. This reflects the shift from an involutionary flow to an evolutionary one—a true passing of the Ages. With such a shift (of orientation and) in energies, we see not only the passing of the Philoso-pher King (whose Vision and Power was God-inspired!) but the (very actual and) modern reality that we *can no longer trust the vision of our leaders* (because, having arrived at a certain point of evolution and level of consciousness and personal development, we have to *personalize* and ren-der *unique* our own being, path, and talents). We have removed the capstone of the pyramid and must ourselves, *each of us*, **build the Temple anew** upon the firm foundation of past experience. Again, in my own interpretation, this is one of the meanings of the American Vision—Novus Ordo Seculorum: A new Order for the Ages.

In my publishing philosophy, it is our job, then, to turn "Power" over (i.e. authority and responsibility) to *the people* and make it truly meaningful and effective to have Power and to know how to use it, and why. In essence, that is the distinction offered both in our evolution of *Free Enterprise* economics to include the capitalization of both Labor and Skill, and of Democratic politics' emphasis on "Grass roots" and "Local Option." People grow only through the *exercise* of moral and ethical responsibility, or mental development and refinement of the emotional and physical vehicles through the more mundane responsibilities we find in modern life. Everyone is (knowingly or not!) a *practitioner of Karma Yoga.*

With respect to karma yoga, each age and each tradition has a certain set of essential truths and assumptions that it makes about reality and life. A perennial truth, one which we can say epitomizes the spiritual tradition in general, but which is increasingly felt in our age in particular, is that: Whatever happens in this world and in our lives has a spiritual meaning and purpose which it is our duty and challenge to discover and integrate—in our consciousness, life, and identity.

Having embarked on an early spiritual quest through an "Eastern Channel," I was to discover that all the great religions do come from the same Source for the purpose of helping evolving humanity on its path of self-actualization. I realized then that before I could definitely leave behind the religion I was born into, I should truly understand it and be able to integrate it into my cognitive universe. Any other way would have meant contradicting my own conception of the world. The fruits of that investigation and analysis are found here with respect to Catholic Christianity, but the approach can equally well be applied to other traditions. In the heart and roots of each, I believe, one can find God, the Source and Essence of all, acting by various means but with the same fundamental purpose—to bring about the incarnation, evolution, actualization, and redemption of human beings in this earthly life.

One of the problems in the past, and thus a challenge for us now and for the New Era, is that many received and lived their traditions in an *unconscious* way, whatever the tradition. It could be a stage of imitation that was never outgrown, or a confusion of certain emotional needs and desires with what authentic religion truly is about. Now the question and challenge is to *live* one's religion, whatever it happens to be, *in a conscious and internalized fashion*. This will lead to our own personal realization and *experience* of a tradition's fundamental mysteries and its arcana of the Kingdom within. This is a matter of grace but also of work, a work which this book hopes to further.

Today we witness many young people and many sensitive and spiritually oriented people of all ages who leave the Christian churches and turn to Eastern yoga, occult, magical, and mystical groups, the human potential movement, the New Age movement, the "new therapies," or secular philosophies. And yet, worldwide, there are millions of people who are affiliated with some kind of organized religion, who give to it their time, energy, and financial support, making many efforts and a number of sacrifices to live by its precepts. There are also millions of people who experience a profound psychological, existential, and spiritual hunger—a need for something more and something deeper— but they no longer believe that organized religion can provide soul-satisfying answers to their fundamental questions. Finally, there are thousands who have joined, or organized, the increasing number of cults, spiritual "families," brotherhoods, or New Age communities. And yet is the goal not the same? Is it not simply, I wonder, seeking spiritual Initiation, a conscious loving union with God? This is what it is to find oneself, and thus to love oneself and to express this love for another. It is what leads us finally to living in the Spirit.

Some observations can serve here as an overview of the historical process of Christianity. The early Church, while retaining the liturgical structure, incorporated many of the writings of the early Church Fathers (whom we would likely call today seers and initiates) and the early monastic traditions, as well as those pre-Christian Mysteries discerned as compatible. The Western Church, in time, assimilated as well the Aristotelian rational philosophical framework. This was set within as a centralized theological doctrine and consolidated without, eventually in economic power and political organization. Thus, more and more, to rise on the ladder of the Western Church's institutional hierarchy, one was helped by being gifted as an accountant, administrator, and diplomat. Often these worldly skills took precedence over the gifts of a saint, seer, or sage.

The Eastern Orthodox Church had, as well, great sensitivity to the old liturgical structure, certain of the writings of the early Fathers, and a unique monastic structure of its own, but it did not integrate a Thomistic, Aristotelian "worldly" philosophical framework with its "otherworldly" Platonic and intuitive philosophical framework. The Eastern Church was thus linked more closely with the esoteric approach and the Mysteries of Jesus Christ, but its exoteric connections were undermined in that it remained more nationalistic and decentralized, adapting itself to the country, the culture, and the customs of the people who embraced it. Finally, its authority was based more on the Cosmic Christ than upon the historical figure of Jesus Christ, and it affirmed the autonomy and final authority of the *personal conscience* of the individual. The Western Church based its authority on the human (worldly) applications of the Divine Order in the context of the common good.

With the Reformation in the West, the sacramental structure, the mystical priesthood, and many of the oral traditions of the early Church were rejected (along with genuinely degenerated, superstitious, and corrupt practices) to make way for a rational, empirical, and "stripped-down" version of Christianity. Thus, the orientation of the Reformation was to effectively remove much in the esoteric and mystical traditions of Christianity and the Christian Mysteries. They rooted their new approach to the tradition in a stricter moral code, a more active mission in the world, a more literal faith in the historical Jesus, a transcendence over nature, and in belief as the path of salvation. It should also be mentioned that a mystical esoteric tradition was preserved within a minority of Reformed Christianity called the Pietistic movement. Its teachers and members included, among others, Arndt, Boehme, Law, Wesley, and the Quakers. This is to say that true saints, seers, and sages have existed and do exist in *all branches* of the Christian Faith—as in all religions as well.

Let us draw together and make explicit several key notions at this point: First, the major world religions are the central and living conduits for conveying spiritual tradition, teachings, and a practical way of life or path to spiritual initiation. However, today the great world religions remain *unconscious vehicles*, in large part, for preserving and carrying forth the theory and practice, the truths and treasures of Holy Love and Wisdom. Yet, they are preserved and carried forth until such time as those who are spiritually ready will rediscover them, reinterpret them, and begin to apply them in their own daily lives. For more and more people, this time is now, at the end of the Piscean Age and the beginning of the Aquarian Age.

Second, within the major world religions, all churches and denominations have evidently developed out of and in turn reflect a certain sociocultural heritage, perspective, and consciousness. Hence, they all fulfill basic needs, ideals, and aspirations of different types of people.

Finally, a modern man or woman *in the West*, who seeks a healthy, balanced, and practical spiritual life, one which can be fed, unfolded, and incarnated in daily life, will perhaps ultimately find it not so much in Eastern religions, or in occult, magical, or mystical organizations (and even less so in the new therapies of the human potential movement), but in what can be rediscovered in the practices, rituals, ceremonies, and symbols of Christianity. This provided that one is able to penetrate through to their "inner core" of meaning through lived experience. For what can be discovered, both in what is brought forward from within and in what is latent and waiting to be revealed from without, is the living synthesis of East and West, of the esoteric and exoteric.

In my own life, even as a child, the spiritual quest has been the deepest wellspring of my being, becoming as I grew older more and more of a conscious objective. The many hardships and contradictions of my early life found both meaning and worth in this deeply felt sense of a quest. From these early experiences, I began to seek both in the world and in books for some philosophy which could explain and put into perspective what I had seen, felt, and lived in those early years. But it had to give, I began to realize, explicit directions and training for developing further my human and spiritual consciousness.

The first "living" philosophy and tradition I encountered, then studied and practiced avidly, was Hindu Yoga. For several months, I bought all the books on yoga I could find, adapted my lifestyle to the teachings of yoga, and finally looked for and found a yogi who could act as my guru. Very soon, I did experience results, becoming very sensitive to other people's thoughts and emotions, and developing a yen to live a pastoral and monastic life—much to the dismay of my family and, I had to admit, against my other ideals.

A few months later, I met a Christian mystic in Paris who became a lifelong friend and teacher, and she had a deep impact on my thinking and on my life. Through her, I came to know the spiritual, mystical, and mystery traditions of the West, in general, and of Christianity in particular. Later, I joined an Esoteric Order which taught me a great deal about the Spiritual Tradition. While working along the lines outlined by the Order, I also studied and became acquainted with many other esoteric schools and traditions.

One day, in New York City, I met the archbishop of an Orthodox Church who was, I have come to believe, a Christian Initiate; he was able to help me make the connection between the Great Work, spiritual Initiation, and Esoteric Christianity. With him, I gathered treasures and a model which I have never forgotten and which come back again and again to my consciousness with increasing depth, beauty, and meaning. When the archbishop passed away, I again began to look in many directions, particularly along the lines of the human potential movement and humanistic and transpersonal psychology.

My chief objective, at that time, was to find or develop a framework in which to integrate the psychosocial and the spiritual dimensions. With one of those extraordinary synchronicities in life which shows we are guided from the higher planes, I met an Italian psychiatrist who was, besides a scientist and a teacher, also a true Initiate. From him, I learned much and did a great deal of work which eventually led me to organize my own groups.

After forming many groups and training many people in different countries, I found myself subconsciously focusing more and more upon the esoteric and mystical side of Christianity and working with Christian rituals as the most practical and efficient tools for training the personality and achieving higher states of consciousness. In the last decade, my experiences have convinced me that the culmination of my spiritual quest, at the practical and living level, lies in the rediscovery and esoteric interpretation of the Christian Tradition and in an experiential approach to the Christian Esoteric Mysteries. These are "buried" and "hidden" in the materials and practices of the Christian Churches in general, and in the Catholic and Orthodox Churches in particular, and they are carried forward today.

I can perhaps further summarize some basic insights and conclusions concering "Christianity in the New Era" in an allegory. Suppose we were to gather together a "council of sages" who represented the most advanced and experienced students of all the present religious, scientific, philosophical, and spiritual traditions of our times, the initiates, adepts, saints, and seers of our various races and countries. Suppose that these were to represent the true Heart and Soul of the real United Nations and that they were commissioned to develop a theoretical and practical *synthesis* of our current knowledge and wisdom. Suppose, further, that they were told to do it in such a way as to meet the following essential criteria:

1. This "living synthesis" has to be simple yet essential, practical yet efficacious, and, most important, *significant, manageable,* and *livable* for the widest possible number of people—ranging from children to older persons, from a simple to a very well-educated person, and from a "common person" to a "saint."

2. It should aim at the most important knowledge and objectives for incarnate human beings—leading specifically to a comprehensive and applicable *self-knowledge, self-mastery,* and *self-integration.* It should particularly be able to answer the most fundamental questions of human existence, such as: Where do I come from? Where am I going? Why am I here? And how can I live the most productive, creative, useful, and happy life? What should I study and do with my life? What value system and ethical system should I adopt? Whom should I marry and what criteria should I use in selecting my life-mate? How can I face the basic challenges, crises, and rewards of human life? Finally, whom and what should I serve? What is my mission in the world? What is my divine calling and gift? It should, in other words, provide the "core essentials" for the development of a comprehensive philosophy of life and of an integral art of living.

3. It should include the very best of human culture, the highest and most profound insights and discoveries of the most creative and inspired persons. To achieve this, it should provide a simple but

practical and livable synthesis of the deepest revelations and visions of the sacred traditions of the past and present, and the most recent advances of the modern sciences. It should integrate the teachings and practices of the hermetic, alchemical, mystical, occult, and magical traditions with the latest findings of the new physics, humanistic sociology, transpersonal psychology, and holistic anthropology, and medicine.

What do you think? How should they go about it? There are, of course, many answers to this ponderous question, this "thought experiment," ranging from stating that this is an impossible, utopian vision, a dream of unpractical idealists; that it would take a very large number of people, striving for a long period of time with practically unlimited means; that it would imply creating a new religion or spiritual tradition, which would, in turn, require the coming of the Messiah, or of a modern avatar.

My own conclusion is both that it can be done and that it is, in fact, being done—if we but had "eyes to see and ears to hear"! We can find this most essential knowledge, this sacred loving, in each one of the great living religions, because each of them has one central and overriding purpose: to bring about a conscious communion and then living union, both internal and external, with God, the Ultimate Reality. What is required to accomplish this is to be able to reconnect *consciously* with the Source and Essence of our being, the Divine Spark, the Spiritual Self, the Christ within, *and* with the Holy Spirit who will act as our ultimate Teacher and Initiator, revealing and providing whatever is most important for each one of us *where we are and in our present condition*. (For more on the Spiritual Self and its relation to other functions of the human psyche, see Appendix A.)

Suppose now that we were to colonize (or should I say "humanize"?) a planet found to be capable of sustaining human life and that we dispatched a select group of persons to "plant the seeds" of human culture, civilization, and spirituality. What would they take with them, at the highest theoretical level and at the most practical level? Would it not at least seek to resemble the living synthesis suggested above, which is found and expressed in the *images, symbols, myths,* and *allegories* of all the world religions. But, and this is a significant "but," there are certain keys which are essential and which one must understand and be able to apply in order to make this synthesis come alive and reveal its treasures, mysteries, and wonders, to make it operative. These keys are:

1. The language to be used cannot be the descriptive, analytical, and static language of our everyday speech or of conventional science; it must be the "language of the deep mind," the "forgotten language," as Erich Fromm called it, of *images, symbols, and archetypes.* It

must be the analogical language of saints and sages, the symbolic language that operates as a function of the *level of human consciousness*, containing as many basic meanings, implications, and applications as there are different states of consciousness—and which can, therefore, be meaningful and alive for the child or the adult, the novice or the adept.

2. This philosophy and art of living must have a *universal foundation and appeal* for people of all races, religions, and countries as they move towards planetary consciousness. For the days of familial, tribal, or racial consciousness and religions in an exclusivist sense are over.

3. It must be anchored in a *sound and unfolding metaphysics* which is in tune with the teachings of the sacred traditions of the past, the latest discoveries of modern natural and social sciences, and the visionary and ecstatic experiences lived in altered states of consciousness.

4. It must operate as a genuine *religion* or Yoga in its basic etymological meaning of "reconnecting" or "uniting." But what does this mean? First, human nature uniting within itself, also the human being reconnecting with God, as well as the human being uniting with others and with nature—that is, human nature uniting with its Creator and with all Creation.

5. It must articulate a cogent theory of human nature, a model of the psyche, describing the nature, structure, and functions of human consciousness. Also how it can be experienced and developed, using elements—I call them "muscles"—like concentration, meditation, devotion, visualization, and invocation and evocation.

6. It must embody and present the inner *anatomy* and *physiology* of our subtle or "energy" bodies, contained in the Tree of Life, its various "Centers" and "Auras." (See Appendix B.)

7. It must provide both a way of life and specific exercises designed to promote and activate the unfolding of higher consciousness, its energies, centers, and faculties.

8. It must provide an overall sense and vision of human origins and human destiny. These will especially provide for a *theoretical* and a *practical* way of coping with the fundamental dualities and vicissitudes of incarnate life—joy and suffering, health and disease, good and evil, life and death.

9. Lastly, but in no way less significant, it must provide a *fellowship* of other beings, in history and at the present time, on the physical and on the spiritual planes, who can offer a *living model* for what one is trying to achieve and become—a fellowship of like-minded persons who share the same values and goals, who have trod the same path and are treading it, and with whom one can do "group work," both in the visible and in the invisible worlds.

When one looks at, interprets, and lives Christianity with an *esoteric spiritual perspective,* one will find the above and more, the more being that which can only be *personally experienced and realized* within one's own consciousness. Thus "Christianity in the New Era" simply means two basic and fundamental things: *to unfold a modern, living soul* of Christianity in developing this perspective, with specific implications and applications, and to *live and embody* in a personal, conscious, and holistic fashion the essential principles of the love of God (or prayer) and of the love of one's fellow human beings (or effective service).

As a postscript to this chapter, and before we begin to build anew our inner Temple, let us clarify some terms which have already been used and which will arise throughout this book:

Levels of Consciousness: We have a separate chapter on this, but since it is an underlying concept, let us give some early definition. The field of consciousness and human self can move up or down various levels of consciousness. Each person is born with sensory, emotional, and mental levels of consciousness which can be more or less developed and coordinated. The sensory level is simply the capacity to have sensations, the emotional level is the capacity to have emotions, and the mental level the capacity to have thoughts. In addition to these, a human being can also develop and awaken a spiritual level of consciousness, which is a capacity to be discussed throughout this work, but includes having genuine intuitions and, often, supersensible perceptions.

Aura: the aura is the "energy field," or "luminosity" around a human being, which is visible to clairvoyants and other "sensitive" persons. It can also now be rendered visible by various mechanical means, the best known of which is Kirlian photography. All living things have an aura or auras, as the case may be. For example, plants and trees have an etheric or vital aura; animals have an etheric and an astral aura. All humans have etheric, astral, and mental auras, while those who are spiritually awakened also develop a spiritual aura. Kirlian photography picks up the etheric and the reflection of the astral aura (rendered visible by the flow of electricity), but not the mental and spiritual ones. The auras are connected with the "energy bodies" and can be compared to the skin, or outer boundaries, of the physical body. With the development of spiritual consciousness, the auras will become increasingly visible to more and more human beings.

Spiritual Energies: Just as there is physical energy manifesting as kinetic energy and electrical energy manifesting as electromagnetic force, so there is human energy manifesting as consciousness, and Spiritual Energies manifesting as Light and Fire, which engender Life. Spiritual Energies are the Source and Essence of all energy which can affect our consciousnesses as well as our physical bodies and behavior.

Energy Bodies: In addition to our visible, physical body, the sacred

Figure 1.1   The statue of St. Joseph at St. Joseph's Oratory in Montreal, Canada, showing the different "energy bodies": the one closely following the outline of the physical body is the etheric body; the larger "egg-structure" represents the astral body; the broken rays represent the mental body; the unbroken rays represent the spiritual body.

traditions and direct clairvoyant perception and investigation have revealed that we have other "bodies" or "vehicles of life and consciousness." There are seven energy bodies: the ones which, at the present stage of the evolution of humanity, we will speak of most often in this work are the etheric, astral, mental, and spiritual bodies. The first three constitute the personality and the fourth, the spiritual body, makes up the Soul. These are related to the four Elements and to the four Planes of Creation. Notice that if the spiritual, mental, and astral are subdivided into a higher and a lower then, with the etheric, we have seven bodies, as frequently mentioned in the sacred traditions. Beautiful symbolic representations of the etheric, astral, mental, and spiritual energy bodies can be seen in the mandala surrounding the stature of St. Joseph at St. Joseph's Oratory in Montreal (see Figure 1.1).

Spiritual Self: This is the Divine Spark, the Christ within, or part of the Ultimate Reality we all have within ourselves, but of which we are normally not yet conscious. The human self is the conscious ego, the center of pure consciousness and will located at the center of the personality. The Higher Self, as used by the sacred traditions, generally refers to the Spiritual Self and the Soul, our higher consciousness.

CHAPTER TWO

The Christian Church: Temple of the Holy Spirit

From the beginning of human history man has been a religious being, aspiring to discover and consciously reunite with his Source, the Essence of all that is. As such, he has built countless and diverse temples, churches, and houses to the Divine. In the Primordial Tradition, the Spiritual Tradition, the Sacred Traditions, or by whatever name the Holy Wisdom has been known, it has always been a cardinal principle that the Temple of God is built as a direct homologue or a replica of God and the Universe.

The Temple represents, therefore, a *projection and objectification in stone and other physical materials of man and his soul, the microcosm, made in the image of God, the Macrocosm*. For he who has the proper keys, therefore, the temple is an external blueprint of the human being made in the image of God. The Jewish Temple of Solomon and the classical Christian Church in the West represent an externalized picture and blueprint of man's psyche, of his psychic and spiritual anatomy and physiology, and of his psychospiritual Centers and their interrelationships which are collectively known as the "Tree of Life."

Thus, when we stand in awe of a classic Cathedral what we are really looking at is *ourselves* as created form made in the image and likeness of God. What we see are the inner and subtle levels which cannot be recognized with physical or psychological eyes alone. Yet, this Cathedral is not only ourselves, but the union of microcosm and macrocosm, man recreated in the image and likeness of God, and God in Creation as known through man. Thus, in meditating upon these magnificent "symphonies in stone," can we gain further understanding, the shapes, symbols, cosmic geometry, colors, all activating certain conscious energies and states of consciousness.

The Living or Inner Church, the "Temple made in heaven not by human hands" is what is within man, and this includes his psyche, the personality plus the soul. The Outer Church or Temple is the external symbol and a map of the former; the compactness and

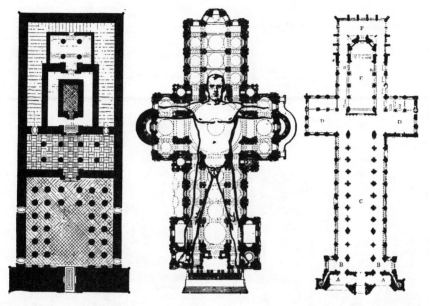

Temple of Khonsu at Karnac.   St. Paul's, London.   Plan of Peterborough Cathedral.

Figure 2.1   The Ancient and the Modern Temple
An Egyptian Temple and two examples of Christian Cathedrals. These plans show the threefold division of the Human Temple. The plan of Peterborough Cathedral shows the average type of strictly cruciform cathedral, while the plan of St. Paul's shows the cruciform type adapted to the classical style of architecture; the circular feature at the crossing of the nave and transept has elements of Rosicrucian symbolism. The cuts show Man to be the archetype of all Temples (George Plummer (Khei), *Rosicrucian Fundamentals*. New York: Flame Press, 1920 p. 322.)

multiplicity of possibilities in the symbol can stir us, open us imaginatively, intuitively, and the map gives us orientation and direction in the spiritual world. When entering a Church what we really *enter is the Temple of our own consciousness*. We enter into our inner Tree of Life and psyche, where whatever we encounter externally corresponds to something that exists internally. And, as we will see, whatever the Priest does in the Church, one can follow within oneself with the help of the human functions of will, thinking, feeling, creative imagination, and intuition. For then the Divine Light and the Spirit of God will pour forth upon us, transform our consciousness, and enable us to commune with the Lord, with the Christ within or the Divine Spark.

From the standpoint of this perspective, let us now see concretely and specifically what the Church building and its various symbols and rituals can represent in the microcosm and how they can be

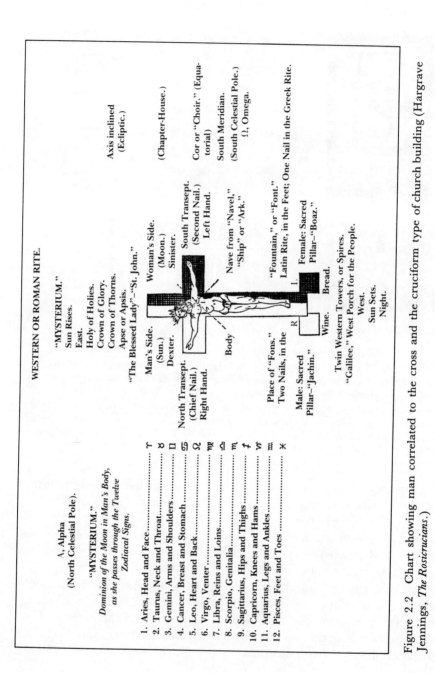

Figure 2.2   Chart showing man correlated to the cross and the cruciform type of church building (Hargrave Jennings, *The Rosicrucians*.)

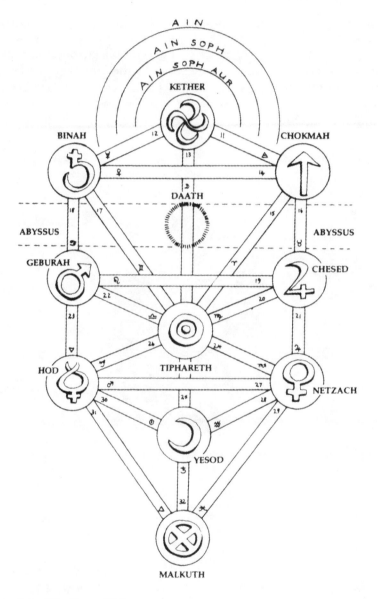

Figure 2.3 The Tree of Life
For further correspondences on the Tree of Life and the psychospiritual Centers, see Appendix B. (Melita Denning & Osborne Phillips, *The Sword and the Serpent*. Llewellyn Publications, 1975.)

entered by the aspirant to the Mysteries. In the physical plan of the Church, one can envision a human being lying on his back with his arms outstretched forming a Cross. Here is the symbolic depiction of the human body with its subtle vehicles of consciousness, but it also contains, in depiction, as we have said, man's psyche, that is, his personality and soul, his aura and "sphere of sensation." At the inner core of the Church's architecture and symbolism, described in the language of imagery and analogy which is the language of the Deep Mind and of the Sages, we find a blueprint. It is *a complete blueprint of man's psychic and spiritual anatomy and physiology*, of his Tree of Life, of his different "vehicles of consciousness" and psychospiritual Centers.

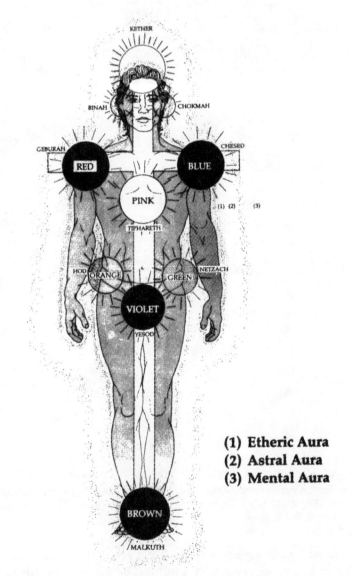

(1) **Etheric Aura**
(2) **Astral Aura**
(3) **Mental Aura**

Figure 2.4   The Human Aura in the Tree of Life
(Peter Roche de Coppens, *The Invisible Temple*. Llewellyn Publications, 1987.)

Therefore, as we enter a physical Temple, we enter the Temple of our inner consciousness where we can focus upon inner psycho-spiritual events and processes. In this aspect of our total experience, we are conscious of leaving the external world behind and of moving, as we cross the threshold of the Temple, from profane into *sacred space*, from profane into *sacred time*, and from profane into *sacred events*. By a great effort of introversion and concentration, we seek to leave mundane cares, thoughts, and emotions behind in order to focus upon the work and activities about to be engaged in. We are aware that the Temple in which we now find ourselves, the physical Temple and the Temple "not made with hands, eternal in the Heavens," the psyche, is sacred ground, the place where one stands in the *living presence of God*. Volumes are written and yet to be written of all that can be experienced here, but one helpful awareness which the esoteric perspective brings forward is that in this place where the Divine Light, Fire, and Life are present, one also can become aware of the *axis mundi*, or the ladder of consciousness, which leads from the field of consciousness to the unconscious and the superconscious, from microcosmic "earth" to "hell" and to "heaven." (For the fuller description of the field of consciousness, the unconscious, and superconscious, see Appendix A.)

Finally, we gain a sense that we are within the Temple to engage in a most important work, *the Great Work*—that by working within oneself, mirroring internally what the Priest does externally, we can connect with the Divine Light and Fire, commune with it and become suffused by its Consciousness, Love, and Life. In so doing and in the degree to which this is possible, we perfect ourselves, offering our inner Temple to God to thus accomplish his work through us in this world.

Many statements in the Bible and in other Holy Scriptures point out clearly and explicitly that the physical Temple, Cathedral, or Church is an external, objectified replica of the Living Temple of God and reflects the human body, soul, and psyche. In the Christian tradition, we have these statements:

> Jesus answered and said unto them, Destroy this temple, and in three days I will raise it up. Then said the Jews, Forty and six years was this Temple in building, and wilt thou rear it up in three days? But he spake of the temple of his body. (John 2:19–21)

> Know ye not that ye are the temple of God, and that the Spirit of God dwelleth in you? If any man defile the temple of God, him shall God destroy; for the temple of God is holy, which temple ye are. (1 Cor. 3:16–17)

When we look at the fundamental features of religious Temples and architecture throughout the ages, we find two distinguishing characteristics in the Temples of many religions. These are the *cruciform* and *threefold subdivision* of the Temple structure. Thus, from *Rosicrucian Fundamentals* by George Plummer:

> The Egyptian Temple had its Outer Court or Court of the People; its Middle Chamber of Hypostyle Hall, and its Sanctum Sanctorum or Holy of the Holies into which none but the Hierophant entered.
>
> The Greek Temples had their Pro-Naos or Outer Court; the Naos or Cella, or Middle Chamber, and the Sanctuary or Holy of the Holies, containing the shrine or statue of the God or Goddess.
>
> The Hebraic Temple had its Outer Court or Place of the People; the Middle Chamber, or Holy Place, and the Sanctum Sanctorum or Holy of the Holies to which similar reverence was paid by the High Priest.
>
> The Pyramid has its Unfinished Chamber on the Ground Floor; its Middle or ''Queen's Chamber'' and the Sanctum Sanctorum or ''King's Chamber'' although no King has ever been there.
>
> The Gothic Cathedrals besides being cruciform in plan, which is simply the Cosmic Man under the Sign of the cosmic Cross, have the Nave, or Place of the People; the Choir or Chancel for the Singers and minor clergy, corresponding to the Middle Chamber, and the Sanctuary or Holy of the Holies into which only the highest ecclesiastical dignitaries and the Celebrant and assistants at the Altar enter.[1]

Made in the image and likeness of God, a human being is made in the form of a Cross and a Trinity. So the Temple or Church must also be made in the form of a Cross and a Trinity. The Cross lies embedded in man's physical form, but the Tree of Life also forms a symbolic skeleton of man's inner being. We can recall the repeated aspects of the Trinity in the threefoldness of human existence, whether of man's structural being (body, soul, and spirit) or in the expressions of his consciousness (conscious, unconscious, and super-conscious; etheric, astral and mental bodies; consciousness, love, and creative energy; and thinking, feeling, and willing).

Entering the Church in the sense of entering our own Inner Temple of consciousness at the conscious level, we enter at the foot of the Cross; on the Tree of Life this is also represented as the level of *Malkuth*. There, through an effort of introversion and concentration, we can leave behind the world, the past and the future, and all worldly concerns and pursuits to focus on our ascent from the foot of the Cross, the level of *Malkuth*, to *Tipphereth*, the Heart Center where one can commune with the Divine Light, Fire, and Life. The three Pillars of the Tree of Life, those of Form, Force, and Consciousness, or Severity, Mercy, and Equilibrium, are clearly depicted and represented by the Church's aisles and naves. The central aisle is the pillar of Equilibrium, the left that of Mercy, and the right that of Severity. The door leading into the Church likewise corresponds to *Malkuth* with the baptismal font; the beginning of the rows of pews corresponds to *Yesod*, and the altar, *Tipphereth*, the Heart Center. The Dome above the altar or the rose window bringing light on the altar corresponds to *Kether*, the Head Center. In this symbolic correspondence, the statues of the Blessed Virgin Mary and Saint Joseph, with their respective blue and red colored lights and garments, on the two side aisles can be seen as reflecting *Chesed* and *Geburah* respectively on the Tree of Life, the Pillars of Mercy and Severity. The rose windows on both sides of the Church present to us what can be experienced as mandalas or composite symbols depicting *Netzach* and *Hod*, *Chesed* and *Geburah*, and *Chockmah* and *Binah*. Thus we discover embedded in the physical structure of the Church and represented there, analogically, and, of course among much else, the complete Qabalistic Tree of Life.

Another aspect of awareness which can emerge from these considerations of the Tree of Life is that it is not without significance where one chooses to sit in the Church. This can have a profound effect and bearing on the internal consciousness we bring to the ceremonies within the Church. Thus, if we sit on the *left side* of the Church not too far from the altar, that place on the Tree of Life is close to that point which corresponds to *Netzach*, the emotional center, and lies on the connecting path between *Netzach* and *Tipphereth*, also known as the intuitive center which, as we said, corresponds to the altar. To consciously choose to sit here is to acknowledge a conscious working on "opening the Heart Center," purifying the emotions, and connecting with God through a more passionate, pure, and devoted love. Were I to work on "opening my Mind Center," I would sit on the *right side* of the Church, a little lower than the above, and roughly in the space that corresponds to *Hod*, the mental center. Rather than *feeling passionately*, I would then be concentrating on *thinking clearly* and on meditating on the meaning and various correspondences of the different aspects of the ritual. The important thing is both to decide what aspect of the Great work you now want to focus upon and develop, and to experiment with sitting in different parts of the Church to see what happens and how *your own experiences* change as you change places. For it is truly in *doing* and in *living* that we learn and grow.

In Churches and Temples that have retained some of the ancient symbolism of the Holy Wisdom, we invariably also find veils between the sanctuary with the altar and the main body of the Church; this can be a veil of cloth, an elaborately carved screen or *iconoclasia*, or an enclosure. Likewise, at the other end of the Church we find a veil or an enclosure setting off the choir, the crypt that may be there, or an enclosure with baptismal fonts or confessionals. Might not these veils be seen as corresponding to the "separations" that exist within our consciousness or between different levels of consciousness, veils which enclose and separate the conscious from the unconscious or from superconscious? (See Figure A in Appendix A.)

The various rose windows, paintings, statues, or other symbols one can experience in the Church have archetypal elements which can help focus our consciousness upon a certain psychospiritual Center, a certain level of consciousness, or a specific energy, whereby we may be stirred to activate our intuition and inspiration through active imagination and visualization.

The four elements are also prominently displayed and used in the Church through the use of candles (fire), incense (air), water and wine (water), and bread and salt (earth). In the Holy Eucharist, we again find the four elements present in the Bread (Earth), Wine (Water), the spoken Words (Air), and the candle in the sanctuary and on the candelabra (Fire).

The Priest, or Officiant, with his assistants, represent humanity and the human functions of willing, thinking, feeling, imagination, and intuition, which all work in synchronicity to bring through the Divine Light, Fire, and Life to the altar. This then is given to the communicant so that he or she can, indeed, commune consciously with the Christ. This spiritual Light, Life, and Fire are present and can be seen and felt by all who seek it earnestly, with sensitivity and consciousness.

During the services we can become aware that whatever the Priest does at the altar, we can mirror within as a conscious act, specifically, in our Heart Centers. For whatever happens in the Church can be experienced within our own being. In approaching the altar, we truly approach the Throne of God, but this is also in our hearts; we will carry It away with us, inside of us, into the world, into our everyday lives as a Living Presence.

Each prayer and petition mentioned by the Officiant can be repeated inwardly, focusing all our attention, thoughts, and feelings upon them. This is so that they may be repeated theurgically, flooding our whole consciousness, awakening and stirring to life many different states of consciousness, energies, and vibrations, opening the channel for intuition and inspiration to manifest themselves. Ideally, every word, formula, and passage of the liturgy should be meditated upon at home to discover the treasure of inner meanings and correspondences. With preparation then, one will find how, during the service, each word and each sentence of the ritual begins to resonate in one's being and consciousness, awakening new intuitions, new thoughts, new feelings, new images, and new energies. The further step is to allow our consciousness to fuse with the words, so we become

them, live them, that they may be "flesh" in ourselves. Then are we
and our lives "living prayer."

At the heart of worship is the mystery of communion between the
heart of the worshiper and the heart of God. In the words of the great
Christian mystic Richard Rolle:

> So I can declare that contemplation is a wonderful enjoying of the love of
> God, and this joy is (a way of) worshiping God which cannot be
> described. And that amazing worship happens within the soul, and
> because of the overflowing joy and sweetness, it rises up to the mouth, so
> that the heart and the voice combine in unison, and body and soul rejoice
> in the Living God.[2]

Therefore, we can participate actively and consciously in the unity
of the Temple's or Church's Body (that is, the physical place, the
words and gestures of the rituals) with its Soul and Spirit—in
experiencing both what lies without and what lies within, in our
understanding, interpretation, and will to reconnect the one with the
other. It is the unison of these three, Body, Soul and Spirit, within
and without, that prepares a ground in our transformed being to
commune with God and to realize his and our Great Work. In life, the
body must serve the soul as the soul must serve the Holy Spirit; this
circle turns the other way as well, the Holly Spirit clarifying the soul,
the purified soul healing the body. So, too, in the life of worship do we
see this wheel in motion: the physical Church or Temple serves the
Mass or ritual which feeds the soul and connects it with the Holy
Spirit. So, too, in the healing reversal, the external Church and ritual
is ever renewed and invigorated through the deepening and clarifica-
tion of the life of the soul, made possible by the gifts of the Holy Spirit.
Recognizing this and living this is what we know as the Great Work
and what should also be the Great Love.

Figure 2.5   Rose Window
Rose windows can be experienced as symbolic of our psychospiritual Centers as
represented on the Tree of Life. The light of the sun ("the Light that shineth into the
darkness") will be altered by the form and the color of the window and by the
openness and conscious functioning of that Center. If the window (or the Center) is
dirty and "clogged up" the light of the sun cannot shine through it, though it is
shining outside; in like fashion, when our psychospiritual Centers are dirty or
"clogged up" the Light of the Spiritual Sun cannot shine through or is "distorted,"
refracted by the imperfections, the presence of psychological debris.

CHAPTER THREE

The Christian Mystery Tradition: Exoteric and Esoteric Aspects

Every religion, like all aspects of human knowledge and all living beings and things, can be said to have an "exoteric" and an "esoteric" aspect. As soon as we bear in mind the holistic and spiritual structure of reality, of the world, and of human nature, we come upon what may be termed their outer or exoteric and their inner or esoteric sides—which are made even clearer and more meaningful by the image of "Man the Skyscraper" and the related insight of the "vertical axis of consciousness."

Long ago, Plato warned us that, if we wanted to communicate in a precise and meaningful manner, we should define accurately all the key terms we are using. For the purposes of the present work, it would, therefore, be very useful to define, clearly and precisely, what is meant by the fundamental terms *exoteric* and *esoteric* that will be used repeatedly in the course of this work. We can begin with the dictionary definitions of these two terms. *Webster's New World Dictionary* defines the word *exoteric* as: Outside, external. 1. Of the outside world, external. 2. Not intended for only a chosen few or inner group of disciples; suitable for outsiders or the uninitiated. 3. That can be understood by the public; popular. Opposed to "esoteric." The word *esoteric*, on the other hand, is defined as: Inner, within. 1. Intended for or understood by only a chosen few; of or for only an inner group of disciples or initiates. 2. Confidential, private, withheld. Opposed to "exoteric."

In the sacred traditions of the past, we can find a holistic structure of creation and of human nature (also interesting in light of modern theoretical physics), and this is a sevenfold structure related to the four elements.

Planes of Creation	Element
1. The Higher Spiritual	Fire
2. The Lower Spiritual	Fire

3. The Higher Mental	Air
4. The Lower Mental	Air
5. The Higher Emotional, or Astral	Water
6. The Lower Emotional, or Astral	Water
7. The Physical and Etheric/Vital	Earth

The sacred traditions and clairvoyant vision alike affirm that each human being is made in the image and likeness of God. Each has a "Divine Spark," or Kernel of the Ultimate Reality, around which is gathered and organized *form* and *force*, matter and energy, from *each one of the seven worlds*. Further, with our physical eyes we can see only the matter aspect of the physical world, but we can *experience*, but not normally see, our own vitality, emotions, and thoughts, which together form what has been termed the "personality" or the "lower self." As our evolution and personal growth continues, we shall also awaken and "coordinate" a Higher Mental or Lower Spiritual and, finally, a Higher Spiritual Body. Then, we shall also have the ability, at first, to *experience* real intuition, inspiration, and "revelation" and then, later, to develop a "psychic" and a spiritual *vision* which will enable us to *see directly* into the Etheric, Astral, Mental, and Spiritual Worlds.

My own image of Man, the Skyscraper, with its core insight of the vertical axis of consciousness, tells me that *all consciousness* (whatever I perceive, conceive, define, and react to) is, ultimately, a *function of my level of consciousness and being*. Thus, there is a quantitative and a qualitative *expansion of understanding, loving, and acting*—of human fullness—with concomitant paradigm shifts, conversions, or transformations of Reality.

What do these basic insights tell us about the terms exoteric and esoteric? How can we, now, define them concretely and precisely for our present purposes? The exoteric aspects of religion are the *perceptions, conceptions, definitions, and reactions* to religious images, symbols, myths, and rituals of people on a *lower level of consciousness*, as well as the faith, love, and ability to act that these responses inspire. These people may be said to be located on the lower floors of the human skyscraper. The exoteric aspects are, therefore, open and accessible to all human beings—even to those who are not "initiated" and, therefore, especially *trained* and *prepared*. Essentially, these aspects compose the "body" of religion, lived and experienced at the personality level. They are what we can perceive with our five senses, apprehend with our reason, and learn from books and written documents.

The esoteric aspects of religion, on the other hand, are the *perceptions, conceptions, definitions, and reactions* to religious images, symbols, myths, and rituals of people on a *higher level of consciousness*, people who are located on the higher floors of the human skyscraper. These perceptions, conceptions, and definitions are, therefore, accessible only to a few human beings—those who are especially *trained* and *prepared*. Essentially, they involve something that must be learned "from within," from direct inner vision, experience, and contact. While some aspects of the esoteric side of religion can be conceptualized, taught, and transmitted to those who are capable of functioning on the higher floors of their consciousness, other aspects, the essential heart of the esoteric mode, are strictly *personal* and cannot be communicated or imparted to others since they can only be revealed through *direct personal experience*.

In the material world of the earth-experience, there are human beings at different stages in the development of consciousness and being. The great world religions, in their universal appeal, have evolved exoteric and esoteric aspects, both in acknowledgment and reflection of successive stages of initiation within what is universally available to all. With respect to Christianity, Jesus Christ often spoke in parables and in metaphors, using the universal human experience compacted in *symbolic* and *analogical* language, but that there are degrees of perception and thus conception in the understanding of these is also indicated when he says repeatedly, "Let those who have eyes, see, and those who have ears, hear." That there are right times and circumstances, certain preparations and training needed in and for the teaching of spiritual truths is also indicated in the stern dictum "Cast not pearls before swine." We can also recall that historically the early Christians made a sharp distinction between the "catechumens" (the neophytes, the unprepared and non-initiated) and the "faithful" (the properly trained and prepared, the initiates).

Thus, we can say that the exoteric aspects of religion are the outer and external forms which can be seen and heard by all; the esoteric aspects are what lie within, and these are discerned with eyes and ears opened in the multiplicity of ways intrinsic to that religious tradition. The key, here, is to perceive the ongoing spiritual dynamic in movement between the inner and the outer life in religion, the one informing and responding to the other, interdependently both in an historical sense but also in our personal experience. Thus we can have the inner experience of God's Grace which manifests itself in our outer, practical living; we then carry back into our further inner development the results of those outer experiences. The movement of spiritual development thus increases the inner life of union with God, so that the outer life can manifest, and become more *transparent* to, the Divine seeking to be more and more present in the world.

In conclusion, then, we can say that the exoteric aspects of religion are the outer forms of ritual, teaching, and authority. The esoteric are

the inner forms and *experiences* of the same. The key here is to perceive
that there is a spiritual movement from the inner to the outer life,
from the invisible experience of God's Grace to the outer manifestations of this in one's awareness and practical living . . . and then back
from the outer to the inner.

When we understand the symbolic and analogical language of religion, we realize that it is, indeed, a *function of the level of consciousness
and being* of the person using it. Therefore, there is not *one* but *a great
many* interpretations for each word, image, symbol, or ritual, each
with its own implications and applications. For example, take the
symbol "Heaven" as used in the Lord's Prayer. The exoteric meanings of this symbol are: the "place of beatitude where God and the
Holy Ones dwell, and where we shall go after we die" (if we have led a
good life); or, more simply, the "space around the earth with the stars
and planets." The esoteric meaning of the same symbol (and the very
etymology of the Greek *Ouranos*) is what we call today the "superconscious"—a higher state of consciousness than the one we normally
function in, but which is *within our own nature* rather than *in the world*!
Thus it is that the notion of the exoteric (lower level, external, intellectual) aspects and the esoteric (higher level, internal, experiential)
aspects were, indeed, built into the fabric of every religion.

There is also the historical dimension; what is esoteric for one
generation can become exoteric for another generation, or it can
work the other way as well. In the above sense, what was "common
knowledge," say, to the early Christians may be considered today
esoteric, lying deep within the now exoteric framework of the
Christian Church. In that way the esoteric is also the "hidden." But,
overall, human evolution, the evolution of human consciousness,
does clearly move towards making *conscious* whatever was first *unconscious*, towards making *known* what was *unknown*, towards revealing
what is hidden.

Today, as we experience the massive quantitative and qualitative
transformations, external and internal, inherent in a paradigmatic shift
in human evolution and human consciousness, it becomes imperative, perhaps more than ever before, that awareness be focused on the
spiritual dynamic between the esoteric and the exoteric, that both be
revealed in the depth of their interplay. Part of this process is the
recovery of the hidden mysteries of Christianity, bringing them into
the light of day for a more general audience, not as spectators, but as
participants. Yet the vehicles for participation can be discovered as
already existing; rather it is the awareness, the depth of meaning, and
thus of our experience which will evolve. This in turn casts new light
on those traditional vehicles themselves, both in increased apprecia-
tion but also in giving direction for their future evolution.

The Mysteries of Jesus Christ were a central focus of the Christians in the early Church. There was at that time a living sense of the "hidden," the mystical, and what we would now call the esoteric. We can see how, down through the centuries, there was no time in which Christendom was left wholly devoid of mysteries, whether reflected in the traditions of emptiness or fullness, the apophatic or the katophatic, the imageless way or that of images. Individual Christian mystics may have emphasized one path over the other, whether that of negative theology or positive theology.

The pages in the history and traditions of Christian esotericism are graced with the names and works of such mystics as:

Julian of Norwich, *Showings*
Jacob Boehme, *The Way to Christ*
Gregory of Nyssa, *The Life of Moses*
Bonaventure, *The Soul's Journey into God, The Tree of Life, The Life of St. Francis*
William Law, *A Serious Call to a Devout and Holy Life, The Spirit of Love*
Johann Arndt, *True Christianity*
Origen, *An Exhortation to Martyrdom, Prayer and Selected Works*
Catherine of Genoa, *Purgation and Purgatory, The Spiritual Dialogue*
Teresa of Avila, *The Interior Castle*
Athanasius, *The Life of Antony, A Letter to Marcellinus*
Symeon the New Theologian, *The Discourses*
Hadewijch, *Visions and Poems*
George Herbert, *The Country Parson, The Temple*
John and Charles Wesley, *Sermons and Hymns*
Meister Eckhart, *The Essential Sermons, Commentaries, Treatises and Defense*
Francisco de Osuna, *The Third Spiritual Alphabet*
John Climacus, *The Ladder of Divine Ascent*
Francis and Clare, *Hymns, Prayers, and Letters*
Gregory Palamas, *The Triads*
Augustine of Hippo, *On the Trinity, On Prayer, The City of God*
Maximus Confessor, *The Trinity*
John Cassian, *Conferences*
Johannes Tauler, *Sermons*
John Ruysbroeck, *The Spiritual Espousals*
Angelus Silesius, *The Cherubinic Wanderer*
John of the Cross, *The Ascent of Mount Carmel, Spiritual Canticles, The Living Flame of Love*
Pseudo-Dionysius, *Mystical Theology, The Divine Names, The Celestial Hierarchies*
Bernard of Clairvaux, *On the Song of Songs, The Love of God, Sermons*

In the writings of the Early Fathers of the Christian Church, for example, St. Clement of Alexandria, Origen, and Justin Martyr, the esoteric and mystical aspects are apparent. St. Clement wrote: "It is requisite, therefore, to hide in a Mystery the wisdom spoken which the Son of God taught."[1] Origen, the best-known pupil of Clement, furthers this in saying there was, in the Gospels, "much doctrine difficult to be understood, not merely by the multitude, including a very profound explanation of the parables which Jesus delivered to 'those without' while reserving the exhibition of their full meaning for those who had passed beyond the stage of exoteric teaching."[2]

In the twelfth century, we find in the Church of Western Europe the holy torch of mystical learning passing from St. Bernard and St. Bonaventura, the Seraphic Doctor, to St. Elizabeth of Hungary, in whom it burned with sweetness and purity. Meister Eckhart (1260-1327) meanwhile proved to be a worthy inheritor of the Alexandrian Schools. For him, the Godhead is absolute Essence, unknowable not only by man but also by itself; though absolute indeterminateness, it is yet the potentiality of all things, coming to consciousness of itself as the triune God through all creation.

Eckhart, along with St. Thomas Aquinas (1225-1274) and John Tauler in the fourteenth century (instrumental in the founding of the Friends of God), drew upon the works of the Pseudo-Dionysius, who followed Plotinus, Iamblichus, and Proclus, who had in turn followed Plato and Pythagoras. One can see the linkage thus in the mystery traditions. Or, for example, another Friend was John Ruysbroeck, who in turn influenced the founding of the Brethren of the Common Lot (or Common Life), from which emerged Thomas à Kempis (1380-1471), the author of the classic *The Imitation of Christ*.

Less known perhaps today, living their lives in blessed obscurity at this critical juncture of the late fourteenth and early fifteenth centuries were Juliana of Norwich and the mysterious figure of Christian Rosenkreutz (d. 1484), the latter being a key figure in the Rosicrucian tradition.

In the next period of about two hundred years, we see the more intellectual side of mysticism develop, with Nicolas of Cusa, Giordano Bruno, and the much-maligned Paracelsus. Then, in the sixteenth century, appears the visionary cobbler Jacob Boehme and the glorious Spanish mystics St. Teresa of Avila and St. John of the Cross, both schooled in the Scholastics, reforming the Church from within with their burning flame of mystical inspiration and devotion.

The Reformation was not kind to mysticism; as Annie Besant puts it in her book *Esoteric Christianity*, "wherever its breath has passed the fair flowers of mysticism have withered as under the sirocco."[3] The Roman Church, while more often than not a torchbearer through centuries of the mystical tradition, had its exceptions. In England this was the time of Thomas More, Thomas Vaughan, and the Rosicrucian Robert Fludd. Somewhat later the Philadelphian Society was formed and William Law (1686–1761) became a figure of note.

The elusive esoteric figure of the Comte de St. Germain appeared at the end of the eighteenth century as did the Quakers, who emerged as a sect of the Friends. In France, Louis Claude de Saint Martin (1743–1803) continued the work of the Elect Priesthood, publishing *A Natural Table of the Correspondences Existing Between God, Man, and the Universe.* Another prominent name in the French Martinist movement is Maitre Philippe de Lyons (1849–1905), a master of divine magic and spiritual teacher of Dr. Philippe Encausse (Papus). Papus (1865–1916) was to become one of the greatest of French occultists, having also been influenced by the Qabalist Eliphas Levi and the logicism of Fabre d'Olivet and Saint-Yves d'Alveydre. It remains to mention Joseph Peladan (1858–1918) in this circle, who along with Papus, Sedir, and others formed the Martinist Order; Peladan later formed his own group, the "Rose-Croix."

In the 1870s the mysterious figure of Mme. Blavatsky appeared, who, along with Colonel Olcot, founded the Theosophical Society. It was her chosen successor, Annie Besant, together with Charles Leadbeater, who united the esotericism of theosophy with Christianity. In England, the Golden Dawn was on the horizon with its leading figures A.E. Waite and W.B. Yeats, while in Germany a branch of the Theosophical Society broke away under the seership of Rudolf Steiner to form the Anthroposophical Society.

A Goethean scholar and philosopher, Steiner (1861–1925) contributed a wealth of esoteric knowledge on the Christian Mysteries from his Initiate-level clairvoyance. A leading Russian student of his, Valentin Tomberg (1900–1973) was instrumental in later founding Christian Hermeticism, a wedding of hermeticism and Catholicism. Mention must be made of the Russian religious philosopher and poet Vladimir Soloviev (1853–1900), one of a group of Sophiologists which includes N. Berdyaev and Florensky; Soloviev was to influence the symbolist poets, Aleksandr Blok and A. Bely.

Among Catholic Christian esotericists in the nineteenth and twentieth centuries, there is as well a diversity of spiritual gifts, personalities, and earthly missions. They give witness in the world to Christ's incarnate and saving life, to a tree of life that in worldly terms is "upside down": its roots in heaven, its flowering right here on earth. The diversity spans John Henry Cardinal Newman, with his unique "personalist" sense of spiritual order and Baron Friedrich von Hugel, whose speculative mysticism bloomed in his classic work on the esoteric Catherine of Genoa. The span includes the Dominican trinitarian visionary Dom Marmion and the Carmelite philosopher and mystic, the Blessed Theresa Benedicta (Edith Stein). Further back in the nineteenth century, it embraces the Blessed Seer, Anne Catherine Emmerich, with her revelations of the life of Jesus Christ. The Jesuits have given us Pierre Teilhard de Chardin (the mystic of modern science), Bernard Lonergan (the mystic of modern philosophy), and Karl Rahner (the mystic of modern theology). Embracing the contemporary dialogue of world religions, we have the prophetic priest-monk Thomas Merton. Dorothy Day is another prophetic mystic with a spirituality in dialogue with contemporary politics, economics, and social thought.

In the reformed Christian tradition there are such souls as Dietrich Bonhoeffer, the martyr to fascism, and Albert Schweitzer, servant to Third World Africa. In nineteenth-century England, we cannot fail to note the great emergence of the esoteric life with the Oxford Movement, the Cambridge Platonists, along with Evelyn Underhill and others. The Pietistic tradition of Protestantism is reflected in the Shakers, and in Quakers Rufus Jones and Thomas Kelly.

In the Eastern Orthodox community the ancient wellsprings of Hesychasm or the *Prayer of the Heart* tradition spawns a mystical river, flowing across centuries. In the last two, we have the anonymous author of *The Way of the Pilgrim*, and the Starets of Optino, Sarov, and Valaam. The novelist Fyodor Dostoyevsky, Saint Serafim of Sarov, and Pavel Florensky are also giants of the contemporary esoteric world of Orthodoxy.

This is a brief indication of some of the representative figures in Christian esotericism, offered only in hopes that each reader will further explore the individual authors in depth.

If we accept that there is an evolution of consciousness, then there are individuals who are at different points along that rising gradient. If, too, religions are to speak to all humans, that is, to individuals at different stages of development, both in terms of intelligence and character, then there needs to be religious teaching suitable to each stage: what could reform the criminal is not necessarily what best helps the saint; what illumines the philosopher cannot be easily grasped by the uneducated. But all human beings need religion, all are evolving towards God; thus, religion needs to be as diversely graduated as evolution itself or else it cannot serve to "quicken human evolution."

Now, how do religions quicken human evolution? Perceiving a human being as a microcosm of the macrocosm—as a multidimensional and complex being—religions must reach, and have an impact upon, human beings in a holistic way and on various levels of consciousness and being. Specifically, they must touch and motivate the *mind*, or thinking, the *heart*, or feeling, and the *will*, or acting, if they are to become and remain alive, fulfill their purpose, and bring about spiritual transformation.

The difficult eventuality for religions is that they must do this for the complex strata of evolving humanity, in places of highly developed and diverse civilization as well as in those of the simplest polity; and then, within each culture, they must speak to the range of individual development, from the most spiritual to the least evolved. Each person must be reached and helped in the place where he or she is. Looking, then, at these facts concerning religion, considering its object and the nature and varying needs of the people to whom it is addressed, and recognizing the evolution of spiritual, intellectual, and moral faculties in humanity and the need of humans for such training as is suitable for them at the stage of evolution at which they have arrived, we are led to the absolute necessity of a varied and graduated religious teaching.

That this was true of the ancient religions is evidenced, for example, in the Mysteries of Egypt. Testimony of its esoteric aspects is found, for example, throughout Plato, in his references to the teachings of the "high priests" of Sais and Thebes. The Greek Mysteries, the Orphic, Bacchic, and later the Eleusinian, borrowing as well from the Mithraic tradition in Persia (and perhaps drawing from sources even further east), were incorporated in the exoteric work of Pindar, Sophocles, and Plutarch.

All the authentic Mysteries of the sacred traditions converge upon one central objective, which we find as well at the very heart of Christianity: *Communion and then Union with God, with the Source and Essence of our Being and of Reality, of all Life, Love, and Wisdom.* The culminating point of the Mysteries is achieved when the Initiate realizes the full loving union with God, who is then born and active in her, transforming her radically. As St. Catherine of Genoa, a well-known Christian mystic, writes, drawing from her own personally lived experience:

> He . . . draws it [the soul] and binds it to Himself with a fiery love that by itself could annihilate the immortal soul. In so acting, God so transforms the soul in Him that it knows nothing other than God; and He continues to draw it up into His fiery love until He restores it to that pure state from which it first issued. As it is being drawn upwards, the soul feels itself melting in the fire of that love of its sweet God, for He will not cease until He has brought the soul to its perfection. That is why the soul seeks to cast off any and all impediments so that it can be lifted up to God; and such impediments are the cause of the suffering of the souls in purgatory. Not that those souls dwell on their suffering; they dwell rather on the

resistance they feel in themselves against the will of God, against His intense and pure love bent on nothing but drawing them up to Him. And I see rays of lightning darting from that divine love to the creature, so intense and fiery as to annihilate not the body alone but, were it possible, the soul. These rays purify and then annihilate. The soul becomes like gold that becomes purer as it is fired, all dross being cast out. This is the effect of fire on material things; but in this purification, what is obliterated and cast out is not the soul, one with God, but the lesser self. Having come to the point of twenty-four carats, gold cannot be purified any further; and this is what happens to the soul in the fire of God's love.

All of its imperfections are cast out like dross. Once stripped of all its imperfections, the soul rests in God with no characteristics of its own, since its purification is the stripping away of the lower self in us. Our being is then God. Even if the soul were to remain in the fire, still it would not consider that a suffering; for those would be the flames of divine love, of eternal life such as the souls of the blessed enjoy. Though this fire can be experienced in this life, I do not believe that God allows such souls to remain long on earth, except to show His mighty works . . .

The last stage of love is that which comes about and does its work without man's doing. If man were to be aware of the many hidden flaws in him he would despair. These flaws are burned away in the last stage of love. God then shows that weakness to man, so that the soul might see the workings of God, of that flaming love. Things man considers perfect leave much to be desired in the eyes of God, for all the things of man that are perfect in appearance—what he seeks, feels, knows—contaminate him.

If we are to become perfect, the change must be brought about in us and without us; that is, the change is to be the work not of man but of God. This, the last stage of love, is the pure and intense love of God alone.[4]

The vision of the mystic acts in the world, is necessarily "actualized" into outer and exoteric form, into action in the world, as Evelyn Underhill aptly describes:

For [the mystics], the duty of creation is tightly bound up with the gift of love. In the passionate outflowing of the universe which offers itself under one of its many aspects to their adoration, that other-worldly fruition of beauty is always followed, balanced and completed, by a this-worldly impulse to creation; a desire to fix within the time-order, and share with other men, the vision by which they were possessed. Each one thus brings new aspects of beauty, new ways of seeing and hearing within the reach of the race, does something to amend the sorry universe of common sense, the more hideous universe of greed, and redeem his fellows from their old, slack servitude to a lower range of significances. It is in action, then, that these find their truest and safest point of insertion into the living, active world of Reality: in sharing and furthering its work of manifestation they know its secrets best. For them contemplation and action are not opposites, but two interdependent forms of a life that is one—a life that rushes out to a passionate communion with the true and beautiful, only that it may draw from this direct experience of Reality a new intensity wherewith to handle the world of things; and remake it, or at least some bit of it, "nearer to the Heart's desire."

Again, the great mystics tell us that the "vision of God in His own Light"—the direct contact of the soul's substance with the absolute—to which awful experience you drew as near as the quality of your spirit would permit in the third degree of contemplation, is the prelude not to a further revelation of the eternal order given to you, but to an utter change, a vivid life springing up within you, which they sometimes call the "transformative union" or "birth of the Son in the soul" . . . and makes of [the whole personality], not a "dreamy mystic" but an active and impassioned servant of the Eternal Wisdom. [5]

Looking at Christianity today, we can conclude that the experience of it would be immeasurably enriched if that knowledge which has remained hidden, and even lost, its mystical and occult teachings, could again take more the place their veracity merits, vested as they are with the authority of lived experience and of love. Nor need this be seen as a threat to the established exoteric order; on the contrary, in the words of Annie Besant: "If these teachings be regained, their influence will soon be seen in wider and deeper views of the truth; dogmas, which now seem like mere shells and fetters, shall again be seen to be partial presentments of fundamental realities." [6]

There is no doubt that Christianity began with the "Mysteries of Jesus Christ" and the "Mysteries of the Kingdom," as an esoteric and spiritual core. With the passage of time and with the conversion of large numbers of people, however, these went more and more underground, were buried, or obscured by the exoteric, external, and intellectual developments. It is important to note again that we find many direct and explicit statements made by Jesus Christ, the Apostles, and the Early Fathers pertaining to the esoteric or Mystery side of Christianity. From the Gospels, we have:

And when he was alone, they that were about him with the twelve asked of him the parable. And he said unto them, Unto you it is given to know the mystery of the kingdom of God, but not unto them that are without, all these things are done in parables . . . With many such parables spake he the word unto them, as they were able to hear it. But without a parable spake he not unto them; and when they were alone he expounded all things to his disciples. (Mark 4:10–11, 33–34)

And the disciples came, and said unto him, Why speakest thou unto them in parables? He answered and said unto them, Because it is given unto you to know the mysteries of the kingdom of heaven, but to them it is not given. (Matt. 13:10–11)

> And he said, Unto you it is given to know the mysteries of the kingdom
> of God: but to others in parables. (Luke 8:10)

Notice the words "when they were alone," and the phrase "them
that are without." So also from the Gospel of St. Matthew: "Jesus
sent the multitude away, and went into the house: and His disciples
came unto him" (13:36). These teachings given "in the house," the
inner meanings of his teachings, were to be handed on from teacher to
teacher.

Again, from the Gospel of St. John we have Jesus telling his Apostles, "I have yet many things to say unto you, but ye cannot bear
them now" (16:12). Perhaps they were spoken to them after his
death, when he visited with his disciples for a considerable period of
time, "speaking of the things pertaining to the kingdom of God"
(Acts 1:3). What has become of these priceless instructions? None
were publicly recorded, but are we to believe they were not valued,
that no attempt was made to preserve them and hand them down?

There were several names and images used to refer to the esoteric
Christian teachings and to the way of Initiation in these Mysteries.
Thus we have, for example, "The Kingdom," "The Kingdom of
God," "The Kingdom of Heaven," "the Narrow Path," "The
Straight Gate," "the Saved," "Life Eternal," "The Second Birth,"
"Life," "A Little One," "A Little Child," and others. Thus, "The
Little Child" was the name given to a candidate just initiated, in
whom spiritual consciousness was now born and who, therefore,
began to live in a completely different way, even though the external
aspects of his life and earthly conditions may not have changed. The
"Straight Gate" was the Path to spiritual Initiation, through which a
candidate entered the "Kingdom." And to be a member of the
"Kingdom," *poverty, chastity*, and *obedience* had to be embraced, but in
the esoteric meaning of these terms.

St. Paul very clearly and explicitly alludes to the hidden Wisdom,
or the esoteric side, of Christianity when he writes to the baptized
communicants of the Church in Corinth, full members, yet described
as "babes":

> I came to you bearing the divine testimony, not alluring you with human
> wisdom but with the power of the spirit . . . Truly we speak wisdom
> among them that are perfect, but it is no human wisdom. We speak of the
> wisdom of God in a mystery, even the hidden wisdom, which God
> ordained before the world began, and which none, even the princes of
> this world, know. The things of that wisdom are beyond men's thinking,
> but God hath revealed them unto us by His Spirit . . . the deep things of
> God, which the Holy Spirit teacheth . . . And I, brethren, could not
> speak unto you as unto spiritual, but as unto carnal, even unto babes in
> Christ . . . Ye were not able to bear it, neither yet now are ye able. For ye

are yet carnal . . . Let a man so account of us, as of the ministers of Christ, and stewards of the mysteries of God. (1 Cor. 2:4,6–8, 10; 3:1–3; 4:1)

St. Paul refers again and again to these Mysteries and in different ways. The central Mystery was the esoteric knowledge and experience of the "Inner Christ," the Divine Spark dwelling within each human being, which had to be "resurrected from its tomb." Evelyn Underhill further identifies it in the mystical life: it is that inward light found at the center of our being, which is at once one with, yet separate from the Uncreated Light, the ineffable Splendor of God.

That every human being is to learn and act upon this wisdom, not only saints and mystics, we can be assured. Once again from that great English student of mysticism, Evelyn Underhill:

> Man is free and holds the keys to hell as well as to heaven. Within the love-driven universe which you have learned to see a whole, you will therefore find egoism, rebellion, meanness, brutality, squalor: the work of separated selves whose energies are set athwart the stream. But every aspect of life, however falsely imagined, can still be "saved," turned to the purposes of Reality: for "all-things hath their being by the love of God." Its oppositions are no part of its realness; and therefore they can be overcome.
>
> To "Bring Eternity into Time," the "invisible into concrete expression"; to "be to the Eternal Goodness what his own hands is to a man"— these are the plainly expressed desires of all great mystics. One and all, they demand earnest and deliberate action, the insertion of the purified and ardent will into the world of things. The mystics are artists; and the stuff in which they work is most often human life . . .
>
> Then, that world of false imagination, senseless conflicts, and sham values, into which our children are now born, would be annihilated. The whole race, not merely a few of its noblest, most clear-sighted spirits, would be "in union with God"; and men, transfused by His light and heat, direct and willing agents of His Pure Activity, would achieve that completeness of life which the mystics dare call "deification." [7]

Thus no simple dialectical distinction can be made between the exoteric and the esoteric aspects of spirituality: For God and Christ *sought esoterically and perceived within oneself*, in one's highest state of consciousness and being, lead to this "earnest and deliberate action, the insertion of the purified and ardent will into the world of things," into the exoteric world. And within each individual life there is the inevitable drama between the exoteric and the esoteric, between being in history and yet having a transcendent being, beyond history.

In my own personal life, and in my intellectual and spiritual development, I experienced distinctions between the exoteric and esoteric aspects of religion which seemed fundamental. When I left Christianity as my basic point of reference and substituted Hinduism and Yoga, these distinctions were made explicit. Later, I was to led to the development of a "spiritual science" that would translate into modern, scientific terms, and to the esoteric aspects of religion and the ancient Mysteries, especially those of Christianity.

It seemed that the gist of these distinctions lay in conceiving of God, the Ultimate Reality, and Source and Essence of Life, Love, and Wisdom, as to be looked for *outside* (the exoteric approach) or *inside human nature* (the esoteric approach). But God is both personal and transpersonal, the Kingdom of Heaven is both within and without, inside and outside the human being. If we can find him *within ourselves*, as St. Paul, St. Augustine, and Angelus Silesius explicitly put it, we will find him in the world! Hence, the search can begin or end *within ourselves*, which is why *self-knowledge*, a knowledge of human nature and of human consciousness, and a spiritual science of man and of human consciousness are essential and, indeed inevitable.

In this integration of apparent opposites we are able to reconcile the universality of the One "religion" (because ultimately it is the integration and synthesis of science, art, and religion) with the many religions, that which emerges as unity out of diversity. This clearly points to the two central features of the new, emerging "face of religion"—that it must be fully *universal* and grounded in sound and "testable" *metaphysics*.

One of the stumbling blocks for the esoteric seeker in exoteric Christianity is to have the experience that its clergy are not always saints, sages, or seers, and that they may not know the Mysteries one's soul is longing for or wishing to integrate with the exoteric. Or, intellectually, their explanations of the Christian religion can feel less than satisfying, somehow not embracing the complex paradoxes and riddles of life. I can recall my own questions, for example: What would happen to those born before Christ or those who never came in contact with Christianity and yet whose leaders had reached a very high level of spirituality (love, wisdom, and creativity)? Why would an all-loving, powerful, and omniscient God send his Son to be martyred in this world for our "sins"? And how could another being take away my sins without destroying the notion of Divine Justice and of the perfect harmony of the universe, whereby every cause has an effect and every action has reactions? And were this possible, would it not destroy all authentic notions of responsibility? How could the same norms be applied to people who, obviously, were at very different stages of conscious moral and intellectual development and being, with very different needs? And I could go on listing many other such paradoxes which have, to others, seemed to be insoluble questions.

As we have seen, there is a concrete and specific example of the interplay between the exoteric and the esoteric: that of the ''House or Temple of God'' being an external building of wood and stone as well as being the internal Cross and Tree of Life within every human being. This conscious awareness can be extended to the teachings within that House. One can perceive the ''letter'' of the tradition, but with gathering light one can also perceive what lies within, the inner meanings, the mysteries veiled or hidden within the teachings of one's religion—then the ''letter'' is seen quite differently, that is, with a growing spiritual maturity. One can then experience being compelled from within rather than from without to live the ''letter'' of the sacred tradition.

The way of the Initiate in the Christian Mysteries, or the *Disciplina Arcani* as they are also called, proceeds by stages. Thus the candidate begins in becoming as a ''Little Child,'' then grows to achieve the ''measure of the fullness of Christ.'' In what does this consist? From Annie Besant we have one perspective:

> The Initiate approaching the Initiation that liberated from the cycle of rebirth, the cycle of generation, was called ''the suffering Christ''; he shared the sufferings of the Saviour of the world, as crucified mystically, ''made conformable to His death,'' and then attained the resurrection, the fellowship of the glorified Christ, and, after that, death had over him no power. This was ''the prize'' towards which the great Apostle was pressing, and he urged ''as many as be perfect,'' not the ordinary believer, thus also to strive . . . This resemblance of the Initiate to the Christ is, indeed, the very groundwork of the Greater Mysteries.[8]

The profound change here, from the Lesser to the Greater Mysteries, is found as well in that treasure of timeless spirituality, *The Imitation of Christ* by Thomas à Kempis. The final consummation of this process is the fusion, or atonement, of the Initiate with Christ—which completes and crowns his spiritual Initiation. In the beginning ''as many of you as have been baptized into Christ have put on Christ'' (Gal. 3:27). In this ''putting on of Christ,'' we are also ''babes in Christ'' and he is the Savior to whom we look for help, knowing him ''after the flesh.'' But when we have conquered our lower nature and are no longer ''carnal,'' then we are able to enter on a higher path, and to become ''Christified human beings.'' It was this which the Apostle had experienced and ardently wished for his followers: ''My little children, of whom I travail in birth again until Christ be formed *in you*'' (Gal. 4:19). St. Paul, elsewhere, says: ''I am crucified with Christ: nevertheless I live; yet not I, but Christ liveth in me'' (Gal. 2:20).

That the Apostolic Fathers knew these stages of Initiation and lived deeply in the Christian Mysteries is evident from their teachings and their letters. In this connection we can mention Polycarp, Bishop of Smyrna, and Barnabas, but let us quote from Ignatius, Bishop of Antioch, a disciple of St. John, who speaks (in his Epistles to the Ephesians and to the Trallians) of himself as

> not yet perfect in Jesus Christ. For I now begin to be a disciple, and I speak to you as my fellow-disciples . . . initiated into the mysteries of the Gospel with Paul, the holy, the martyred . . . Might I not write to you things more full of mystery? But I fear to do so, lest I should inflict injury upon you who are but babes . . . For even I, though I am bound (for Christ) and am able to understand heavenly things, the angelic orders, and the different sorts of angels and hosts, the distinction between powers and dominions, and the diversities between thrones and authorities, the mightiest of the aeons, and the preeminence of the cherubim and seraphim, the sublimity of the spirit, the Kingdom of the Lord, and above all the incomparable majesty of Almighty God—though I am acquainted with these things, yet I am not therefore by any means perfect, nor am I such a disciple as Paul or Peter.[9]

Purification was an essential in the preparation of the Initiate into the Mysteries of Christ, but this meant not only from all defilement but from what we can call lesser transgressions. The candidate had to be purified in heart and soul and, for a long time, conscious of no evil; to such a one then could the teachings be given, such as were given in private by Jesus to his genuine disciples. They alone might learn the knowledge of unseen worlds, enter this sacred domain where, in earlier times, angels had been the teachers of humanity directly. And it was a knowledge given not by words but by sight. Where today the goal of religion is often conceived as saintliness, in the early Mysteries this was only the beginning. The work could only begin with "saints," those pure in heart, mind, and soul, a work which led them to nothing less than the Beatific Vision.

This is what the rediscovery of the Mysteries of esoteric Christianity can aspire to today, continuing what has truly not been lost so much as eclipsed, and perhaps necessarily so, in the evolution of rational and analytic thought. As we now enter a new phase of human evolution, we can use what we have gained in thought and not only rejoice in the recovery of, say, the supreme truths of the Qabala, with its secrets of transcendental theology, but participate consciously and experientially in this rebirth of the Christian Mysteries.

With the recent dramatic events in Europe, the fall of the Berlin wall, the disintegration of Communist regimes in eastern Europe, we see Christ as Freedom working now in history. Christianity is and has remained a force of the people of all nations striving to incarnate that Freedom, individually and collectively, but what is the shape of its future? The present work, drawn from the life experience of its author, is offered in partial answer to this question. Here we can echo the thoughts of Dion Fortune when she writes:

> Christianity is very far from being a burnt-out cinder. Christianity must have a Gnosis as well as a Creed. The mystic who rises into the higher consciousness on the wings of love alone has much to give to the spiritual life of men . . . We need our Christian Mysteries—the deep teaching that cannot be given save after dedication and purification.[10]

Or, again from Annie Besant; after summarizing and highlighting her research and meditations in *Esoteric Christianity*, she concludes with the following statement:

> Will the Churches of today again take up the mystic teaching, the Lesser Mysteries, and so prepare their children for the re-establishment of the Greater Mysteries, again drawing down Angels as Teachers, and having as the Hierophant the Divine Master, Jesus? On the answer to that question depends the future of Christianity.[11]

The present work, drawn essentially from the *lived experience* of its author, is a partial answer to this question. It is because of the tremendous importance of showing the existence of an ''esoteric, inner, spiritual tradition'' in original Christianity, and in its *restoration and further developments today*, that I have focused, in such depth and detail, upon this question in the present chapter. For, if we are to make ''living and practical'' the esoteric aspects of Christianity—the central object of this work—these aspects must come from somewhere and must have been present at the beginning, as well as throughout, the history of Christianity!

CHAPTER FOUR

Sacred Language: Symbols, Images, and Archetypes

A major source of problems, misunderstandings, and controversies between the major "paths" into reality—religion, science, and philosophy—lies in the nature, function, and use of *language*. Within modern languages, for example, English, French, and Russian, we can see the evolution of three "sublanguages" which can be discerned as distinct from one another. These sub-languages are those of *everyday speech*, of *science*, and of *religion and poetry*. Let us have a closer look at each of them.

The language of *everyday speech* is made up of words as "units, instruments, or tools" designed to convey and elicit both thoughts and feelings, which, in semantics, are called *denotations* and *connotations*. Each word, moreover, can contain several denotations and connotations—which is what makes the language of everyday speech a little fuzzy and not very precise or objective. The language of *science*, on the other hand, is made up of concepts as units, instruments, or tools designed to convey and elicit only *denotations* and, ideally, only one denotation with an empirical point of reference. Finally, the language of *religion and poetry* is made up of *symbols, images*, and *archetypes*. Symbols are "units, instruments, and media" designed to convey and elicit thoughts, feelings, and intuitions, the core of the symbol being its ability to activate and focus the *intuition*.

Seen in this perspective, we can say that both the language of everyday speech and, even more so, the language of science are *descriptive* and *analytical* languages with very precise, well-defined, and specific denotations or meanings attached to them. These denotations and meanings are static and fixed in the sense that, for a given language, each person using a particular word or concept would attach the same denotation and meaning to it and this makes communication possible.

Not so for the language of religion and poetry. Here, we are dealing with a *symbolic* and *analogical* language with denotations, feelings, correspondences, and intuitions which are ever-changing, growing, and unfolding—which are "open to infinity." Hence, their meanings and intuitions are dynamic and absolutely not fixed, so that each person using the same symbol, image, or archetype might, in fact, get something very different from it. Paradoxes and contradictions can arise since one symbol or image might mean one thing on one plane of consciousness and the opposite on other planes. A specific example here would be the word *love*. On the physical plane, as sexual love, it denotes exclusivity, a focus on the two people who experience love on this level. On the level of humanity, as friendship, it is definitely inclusive and focused on the world. Nor do we exhaust the denotation of this word in just this respect of inclusivity and exclusivity, as testified to by the volumes on the subject written over the centuries. The point is that a word or symbol may contain within itself fundamentally opposing elements of meaning.

In Christian mysticism and spirituality, as well as in the classical tradition, sacred images, symbols, and archetypes were understood in terms of a "fourfold interpretation." Clergy, scholars, monks, and the laity were taught that without the "inspiration from the Holy Spirit" they would not be able to understand the Holy Scriptures and the deeper, more esoteric or spiritual meanings, implications, and applications of the basic prayers. Dante, too, is said to have applied this fourfold interpretation to his more important writings so that "those who have eyes will see, and those who have ears will hear." As Sandla Schneiders in *Christian Spirituality* puts it:

> The prayerful study of the Scriptures and the fathers . . . was known as the *Lectio Divina* and was governed by the method of the "fourfold interpretation" . . . to which the monastics devoted several hours each day. This method, which consisted in the theory of the four senses, which correspond better to Origen's actual exegetical practice than the three senses he propounded, dominated exegesis until the high Middle Ages . . .
>
> Thus, the literal sense refers to the events and realities of Jewish history. The other three are spiritual senses: the allegorical, which reveals the Christian or theological meaning of the text; the moral or tropological, which applies the test to the individual Christian practice; and the analogical, which points towards eschatological fulfillment. The classical example of fourfold interpretation is the understanding of Jerusalem as the Jewish city (literal), the church (allegorical), the soul (tropological), and the heavenly city (analogical).[1]

This author concludes the discussion of the fourfold interpretation by contrasting the ancients and moderns:

> It is not surprising that the ancient exegete saw it [the literal sense] as a door (albeit an important and usually indispensable one) to the true meaning of the text. Whereas the modern exegete, persuaded that the

true meaning of the text is determined by the author, would consider the literal meaning to be identical with the true meaning. For the ancients the spiritual sense was the true meaning of the text, the message God wanted to convey to the believer . . . [However, the] theory of the necessity of divine illumination for the proper understanding of the Scriptures was a constant in the tradition of spiritual exegesis.[2]

One can see that this fourfold method can be correlated with the four elements and the four basic levels of consciousness and being, which, in turn, are linked with C.G. Jung's four basic personality types. This is not to dispute what we have come in the last three decades to appreciate: that there are things which perhaps can be best expressed only in symbols and the language of symbolism, myth, and analogy; and that the profoundest truths and principles of the ancients were expressed in this language, rather than in descriptive or analytical language, for just this reason.

To return to our first point, it is confusion between these sublanguages which has given rise to conflict and misunderstanding between science and religion during the last five centuries, contributing much to a devaluation of religion in the modern world. The underlying reason for this is very simple: on the one hand, we have a progressive evolution of reason with a concomitant involution of emotion, imagination, instinct, and intuition in the Western world. Thus, symbols, images, and archetypes, the elements in the language of the nonrational and the suprarational were interpreted, more and more, in a descriptive and analytical way—that is, using the process by which the concepts of science are interpreted. Thus, in the historical sense, the original nature and meaning of symbols, images, and archetypes were lost and, in terms of modern cultural valuation, analogical and allegorical language was demoted.

With the development of modern psychology, particularly depth psychology, with the rediscovery and the slow exploration of the unconscious and then of the superconscious, with the anthropological and ethnological studies of alien and exotic peoples of the Far East, Africa, South America, and Polynesia, and with the resurfacing of the sacred traditions of mysticism, occultism, and magic, it was inevitable that the symbolic-analogical language would be looked at more critically and reexplored in its depths and potentialities. In the last three to four decades, a certain consensus concerning the nature, function, and use of symbols, images, and archetypes has been slowly emerging and can now be summarized:

1. They are the specific language and vehicles of the irrational or nonrational and suprarational—these being, of course, very different in their respective origins and nature—as opposed to that of the rational part of human nature, life, and the world.

2. They are the language and instruments of the unconscious and of the superconscious rather than of the conscious.

3. They are linked with the right part of the brain and the feminine principle rather than with the left part of the brain and the masculine principle.

4. They are connected with the night side of life rather than with the day side of life and with the lunar rather than with the solar principles.

5. In terms of the functions of the psyche, symbols, images, and archetypes deal with the intuition, the imagination, and the feelings rather than with thinking, sensations, and willing.

6. They use the *analogical-allegorical* method rather than the *descriptive-analytical* one. This means that they are *multidimensional*, having not one set of meanings, preestablished and socially standardized, but many sets of meanings and correspondences. In this regard, we see the consciousness of this multidimensionality emerging now, reflecting, analogically, and homologically, evolving human nature and culture. Thus, they are not static and closed but rather dynamic and open, with ever-new emergent levels that come to the foreground as new layers and states of consciousness are activated; they are based on the principle of *correspondence* and *homology*, derived from the classical assumption that all things in the universe are interrelated and that the microcosm (human nature) is a reflection of the macrocosm (the world).

This assumption can be found, in its essence, in the hermetic axiom "As Above so Below, as Below so Above." This axiom of the *Emerald Table* is said to contain the quintessence of Hermetic philosophy. In its English translation by Robert Steele and Dorothy Singer, the *Emerald Table* reads as follows:

1. True it is, without falsehood, certain and most true.

2. That which is above is like that which is below, and that which is below is like to that which is above, to accomplish the miracles of (the one thing).

3. And as all things were by contemplation (meditation) of (the) One, so all things arose from this one thing by a single act of adaptation.

4. The father thereof is the sun, the mother the moon; the wind carried it in its womb; the earth is the nurse thereof.

5. It is the father of all works of wonder (the *lema*) throughout the whole world.

6. The power thereof is perfect, if it be cast on the earth.

7. It will separate the element of earth from that of fire, the subtle from the gross, gently and with great sagacity.

8. It doth ascend from earth to heaven; again it doth descend to earth, and uniteth in itself the force from things superior and things inferior.

Thus thou wilt possess the glory of the brightness of the whole world, and
the obscurity will fly far from thee.

9. This thing is the strongest of all powers, the force of all forces, for it
overcometh every subtle thing and doth penetrate every solid substance.

10. Thus was this world created.

11. Hence there will be marvelous adaptations achieved, of which the
manner is this.

12. For this reason I am called Hermes Trismegistus, because I hold
three parts of the wisdom of the world.

13. That which I had to say about the operation of *sol* is completed.
(Translation from the Latin text *Tabula Smaragdina*, found in Proceedings
of the Royal Society of Medicine xxi, 1928, p. 42.)

Hence, while there are meanings and correspondences of a given
symbol, image, or archetype that are known and agreed upon, others
are purely personal and must be interpreted from within the context
of the occurrence and the level of consciousness and the personal
experiences of the person who is working with and using them.

7. Nor are they "ready-made," their meaning fully grasped at
once; they are like a mine which must be mined, a seed which must be
planted and allowed to grow to reveal its flowers and fruits. Symbols,
images, and archetypes also demand a good deal of personal work
(concentration, meditation, devotion, visualization, and contemplation) in order to come alive and incarnate in the life and being of the
person who uses them.

Their treasures and correspondences, richly veined, continue
growing and amplifying as human experience is acquired and as
consciousness is altered and expanded. Because they function as
doors of the unconscious, both higher and lower, and as channels to
connect the conscious with the unconscious and superconscious, they
open again and again with ever-new results and consequences.

8. They can be used to create a bridge, channel, or connection
between the field of consciousness and the unconscious (higher and
lower), between the personal and the transpersonal, the profane and
the sacred, so that the conscious and the known can expand and grow
into the unconscious and the unknown . . . at their own speed and
according to one's level of preparation.

9. Another interesting characteristic of symbols, images, and
archetypes is that they can both *unveil* and *veil*, reveal and hide, a
certain reality or truth, according to the level of consciousness and
readiness of the person who uses them; and, likewise, they can both
unite and synthesize different elements and levels or separate and
dissociate them. For this reason, symbols have always been the language of the sacred traditions and of the Mysteries, revealing their
inner truths to Initiates and hiding them from the profane: expressing

a fundamental truth or mystery on many different levels for different types of personality and of spiritual maturity.

10. While there are a great number of correspondences, associations, and meanings that may be derived from a specific symbol, image or archetype—when it is alive and active—there are essentially three basic dimensions to which they can be applied:

a. *The historical-literal level*: the meaning, implications, and applications, given to the symbol, image, or archetype by its historical connection and its literal denotation. This can seen as the "body," or embodiment of the symbol, image, archetype; it is a level of meaning which places it in the continuum of time, the order and sequence of historical events, which awaits further articulation and deciphering.

b. *The analogical-allegorical level*, applied to the microcosm, to human nature: Here the symbol, image, or archetype is applied to the human being, whether with regard to anatomy or physiology, or to some archetypal level of human experience. This can be seen as the "soul" of the symbol, which one can relate to one's own experience of self and life—this in contrast to what can be called its "spirit," which the "soul" experience of the symbol may or may not lead to.

c. *The analogical-ontological level*, applied to the macrocosm, to the world: Here the symbol, image, or archetype is applied to the world, to the outer universe, and to its anatomy, life, and evolution. These correlations naturally develop as one's experiences, perceptions, and conceptions of the world develop. What is involved is, again, the "soul" of the symbol, which again may or may not lead to its "spirit," which we identify as another major set of correspondences and homologies. The "spirit" of a symbol, image, or archetype is the specific energy, vibration, or material in the spirit of a human being by which this symbol, image, or archetype connects him with the Power and Energies of the Holy Spirit.

The line of progression in working with symbols, images, and archetypes is to go from the outer, exoteric, or historical-literal level to the analogical-allegorical level as applied to the microcosm, which is the work of the Lesser Mysteries, to the analogical-ontological level, which is the work of the Greater Mysteries.

11. All symbols, images, and archetypes can be seen then as having these threefold aspects. The "body" is its cultural and historical manifestation and embodiment—a letter, figure, sign, object, or gesture which stands for something or some things that can be discovered and experienced. The "soul" aspect is the many interpretations and sets of correspondences which can be linked with the symbol and discovered by working with it. The "spirit" aspect of the symbol is the *energy* and *life* with which it is connected; that is to say, it is the spiritual Power, Being, or Process with which it is connected. In

identifying oneself with this energy, one activates it in oneself. Caution must be exercised here, since in the Greater Mysteries the "discernment of spirits" becomes of utmost importance.

12. All symbols, images, and archetypes also have a *form*, a *color* or set of colors, and a *name*. To the form correspond focalization and concentration; to the color, various energies; and to the name, a particular consciousness. Thus in working with a specific aspect, facet, or process of one's self, of the world, or of life, one can invoke, then experience certain energies; finally, one can identify and evoke a certain level of consciousness, thereby altering and transforming the level one presently functions on.

13. Symbols, images, and archetypes are thus the psychospiritual means by which we focus our awareness, induce a certain state of consciousness or evoke a particular spiritual energy or presence; a means by which we recreate, within ourselves, a "facsimile," or representation of that which is without. They are the means by which a person can deliberately awaken and focus his thoughts, feelings, energies, and intuitions by an effort of the will to link his field of consciousness with something that stands outside, below, or above that field of consciousness, thus extending its range in ever-increasing syntheses. They are, therefore, the key regulators and main "switches" of human consciousness and of one's inner life. It is through them that all alterations, focusing, and expansion of human consciousness take place, for they are the regulators, accumulators, and transformers of human consciousness. They enable a person to connect himself (and his field of consciousness) temporarily and to identify with something *greater* and *larger* than he is and, thus, slowly to transcend himself and actualize his latent energies, faculties, and potentialities.

It is a well-known fact that the mind takes on the form of the object it beholds and that the vital energies of a human being will run along the lines traced and focused upon by the mind and will and "vivify" the areas or objects on which both are focused.

An example here is the experience of the symbols of Christmas and the archetypes associated with this Mystery of the Birth of Jesus Christ. On a historical-literal level, Christmas is the remembrance of the events which took place in Bethlehem nearly 2,000 years ago. On the level of correspondences and interpretations (the soul level of the associated symbols) in the microcosm, the Mystery can be experienced as an archetype of every human being's spiritual Initiation—not as a past event, but as either present or future. Christmas then can be seen to contain a process or a series of "core events" by which the Divine within is born to the conscious awareness of the human self, so that it may manifest the attributes of Divine Love and Wisdom, in one's field of consciousness and in the world. Thus in our

Christmas meditations, contemplations, songs, and rituals which make use of symbols and images, we are helping to bring about the realization of Christ born again in us; it is a creative process in which we actively engage.

How can a symbol speak to us reveal its mysteries? That is both a science and an art. It involves a certain body of knowledge which can be applied and certain practices which can be used and experienced in one's own being and life. The work with symbols, images, and archetypes uses three basic psychospiritual processes:

a. *Concentration*: This focuses our consciousness through the use of the will.

b. *Meditation*: This uncovers and unveils the deeper esoteric meanings and correspondences.

c. *Theurgy*: This "incarnates" the given symbol, image, or archetype, grounding it and realizing its spirit in our being and life.

These can be put into practice in a unified way. First, it is necessary to place oneself in the right relation to the powers of Light, so that the highest power to which one is aligned and which one is serving be clearly evoked. For Christians, this is the Triune God. That is one reason why every Catholic prayer, for example, opens "In the Name of the Father, the Son, and the Holy Spirit." This is not only the primary invocation, but also the dedication. Many Buddhist meditations begin with the dedication "To the Buddha, the Dharma, and the Sangha." Here one can offer too the results of one's work, that the fruits of one's efforts may benefit others, whether this is all humanity, the souls in Purgatory, or whomever one chooses. This consciously recognizes the spiritual law that it is in giving and in serving others that we receive.

Then, we concentrate our whole attention on the given symbol, image, or archetype to the exclusion of all else. In the process of *reflective meditation*, we gather and bring into consciousness all the information, associations, and experiences we have had that are connected with this symbol. In *receptive meditation* we empty our minds to experience new meanings, insights, and correspondences flowing into our field of consciousness from within and without. Finally, in *contemplative meditation* we experience an altered state of consciousness in which the essence and core of the symbol is revealed. Lastly, we can synthesize all the knowledge and information gathered so that this spiritual energy can incarnate in the world in an objective way.

Through the process of *creative meditation* and *theurgy*, we seek to become, to act out, and to incarnate what has been revealed to us through the foregoing processes. That is, we imagine that we are that which the symbol, image, or archetype has revealed to us; we act "as if" we were that which has been revealed. In so doing, we slowly begin to transform our attitudes and behavior in the everyday world so that they may conform with and live out of that which has been given to us via the symbol, image, or archetype.

Seen in this perspective and through this process, symbols, images, and archetypes are indeed, and function as, a *bridge* or *connection* between the known and the unknown, the conscious and the Deep Mind, actuality and potentiality. They are elements in a progressive developmental path or curriculum by which the many can become one, by which the profane can be linked with the sacred, and by which the supreme synthesis of finding Union with God can be realized—the true purpose and destiny of all human beings on earth. Thus are symbols, images, and archetypes indeed the language of the sacred traditions which claim that "by Names and Images are all Powers awakened and reawakened," as well as being the basic units through which the work in the inner worlds of consciousness can be carried out and accomplished. They are also fundamentally and radically different from the words of everyday speech and from the concepts of science and should not be confused with them or used as they are used. This is also why all sacred scriptures, clearly and explicitly, state that they cannot be interpreted in the normal way by the normal state of consciousness, and that to truly understand them one must be "guided and inspired by the Holy Spirit." This is also why I claim that they both reflect and develop our level of consciousness and state of being.

It is very important to understand that love is another fundamental means of cognition and a "language" in its own right. This thesis was developed and elaborated by such thinkers as Max Scheler, Blaise Pascal, Mother Teresa of Calcutta, and many saints and mystics. Thus did Pascal enunciate his famous motto "the heart has reasons that reason does not understand" and insist that one must distinguish between the *esprit de geométrie* and the *esprit de finesse* (the language of the heart). Today, the modern social sciences, sociology, humanistic psychology, and anthropology in particular, fully recognize that there are two fundamental ways of "knowing reality" which, though qualitatively different, complement each other:

Scientific knowledge, the human, mental, and "lower creative" form which entails an external and intellectual grasp of reality through rational thinking and experimentation.

Loving understanding, reached through contemplation or empathy, the spiritual and "higher creative" form which entails an internal and immediate grasp of reality through an emotional fusion and union with the object that is loved and contemplated.

In simple words, this means that we can grasp and understand reality through thinking and the objective study of reality as well as through love, empathy, and direct union with the object we contemplate and love. Nor is it a case of positing either as a permanent ideal means of cognition but rather in knowing both through reflection and love and through thinking and contemplation, in being a subject that studies an object and ceasing being a subject by becoming one with the object.

The sacred traditions have always admonished us to relate to and understand reality "in spirit and in truth"—that is, objectively and subjectively, through the mind and through the heart. Today, we have an empirical, analytical scientific knowledge which is multiply manifest, but which can bring many to inner confusion or a sense of the loss of all that is truly essential—somehow failing in a synthetic understanding of the relationship between the parts and the whole. This is why we are ready to move from analysis to synthesis, from the "knowledge of the head" to "thinking with the heart," which can bring us to the beating heart of reality, to the tabernacle of our being, the Inner Christ.

Evelyn Underhill, who made a lifelong study of mysticism, wrote of the results we might hope to achieve with this unified and unifying cognition:

> We know a thing only by uniting with it; by assimilating it; by an interpenetration of it and ourselves. It gives itself to us, just in so far as we give ourselves to it, and it is because our outflow towards things is usually so perfunctory and so languid, that our comprehension of things is so perfunctory and languid too. The great Sufi who said that "Pilgrimage to the place of the wise, is to escape the flame of separation" spoke the literal truth. Wisdom is the fruit of communion; ignorance the inevitable portion of those who "keep themselves to themselves," and stand apart, judging, analyzing the things which they have never truly known.
>
> Because he has surrendered himself to it, "united" with it, the patriot knows his country, the artist knows the subject of his art, the lover his beloved, the saint his God, in a manner which is inconceivable as well as unattainable by the looker-on.[3]

And she best can summarize all that has been attempted here in what we can hope to know in our work with the sacred language of tradition:

> We said, at the beginning of this discussion, that mysticism was the art of union with Reality: that it was, above all else a Science of Love. Hence, the condition to which it looks forward and towards, which the soul of the contemplative has been stretching out, is a condition of *being*, not of *seeing* . . . These . . . reveal to man a certain measure of Reality: not in order that he may gaze upon it, but in order that he may react to it, learn to live in, with, and for it; growing and stretching into more perfect harmony with the Eternal Order, until at last, like the blessed ones of Dante's vision, the clearness of his flame responds to the unspeakable radiance of the Enkindling Light.[4]

CHAPTER FIVE

The Seven Sacraments: Their Spiritual Nature and Dynamics

In the Eastern Orthodox, Roman Catholic, and Anglican traditions, there are seven Sacraments; in the Eastern Orthodox Church they are called Mysteries. The official, or exoteric, definition of the word *Sacrament* given by three Catholic traditions are:

Orthodox: A Sacrament is a holy act, through which grace, the saving power of God, works mysteriously upon man.

Roman Catholic: A Sacrament is an outward sign of an inward grace.

Anglican: A Sacrament is an outward and visible sign of an inward and spiritual grace given to us, ordained by Christ himself, as a means whereby we receive the same, and a pledge to assure us thereof.

Grace in the esoteric tradition is often equated with "Divine Light," the living energy and power of God. In this perspective, then, the Sacraments or Mysteries as the highest acts of worship are also a means to invoke, activate, and extend spiritual energies (the Divine Light) in our consciousness, Tree of Life, and Energy Bodies, or Auras. Simply stated, they are a means to call upon, extend and project light or spiritual energy. Not only are they part of the plan of each religion in leading its devotees on their upward path, but they are also a means by which the evolution of the world is ordered, which by the Initiate is seen in the repeated outpouring of floods of spiritual force. Thus, in participation with these Mysteries, we become what St. Paul calls "laborers together with God," that his will be done through us in the world.

We have spoken in earlier chapters of the dormant spiritual faculties within every human being and how these may be awakened and revitalized; this effort and preparation is realized when every aspect of life takes on a fullness and wonder, a wholeness. Thus, in the case of the services of the Church, we can see, as Charles Leadbeater, a Bishop of the Liberal Catholic Church, puts it, the result of the thoughts and feelings of devotion and love poured forth from the congregation, and the stupendous inflow of divine power which comes as a response to it. A thought or feeling is a definite and real thing and, in the finer matter of the subtle worlds, it shows itself in color and form. The seer is thus able to observe in detail how the services work.[2]

And, in so doing, we also make them more effective when, in a fuller and more conscious way, we play our part.

For the Eastern Orthodox, Roman Catholic, and Anglican Churches, there are seven Sacraments, or Mysteries, which are:

1. Baptism
2. Chrismation or Unction with Chrism
3. Penitence
4. Absolution
5. Communion
6. Holy Orders
7. Matrimony

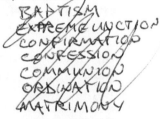

From the esoteric viewpoint, the seven Sacraments are correlated with the seven psychospiritual Centers that can be activated while we are incarnated on earth. They are also connected with the seven Initiations (the four Elemental and the three Spiritual), the seven Planes of Creation, the seven "Bodies" of human beings, and the seven Petitions of the Lord's Prayer.

Again, we shall have recourse to use certain esoteric terminology about which we should like to be clear. Along with the previous definitions given at the end of chapter 1, as well as in the Appendices, the following will also be helpful. We have already given some information on the auras, the energy fields or luminosities which surround the human bodies, and the energy bodies which we have mentioned as the etheric, astral, mental, and spiritual bodies. The latter three of these can be further subdivided into higher and lower and, thus, we get the seven energy bodies. Regarding the Planes of Creation, as we saw in chapter 3, the sacred traditions have taught that the spectrum of creation consists of different Planes, four when connected to the four elements (earth, physical; water, emotional; air, mental; and fire, spiritual), and seven when the three higher ones are subdivided into higher and lower. The physical plane is the plane of matter, the emotional plane that of emotional form and force, the mental plane that of mental form and force, and the spiritual plane that of spiritual form and force.

The psychospiritual Centers refer to the Centers of Light and Energy of the Eastern traditions and to the "Sephiroth" or "Roses" of the Western traditions. They are "centers" of energy and consciousness, visible to clairvoyant persons, which distribute and transform the basic life forces we receive from God and which can then radiate these into the universe.

Before looking at each Sacrament in depth and in detail, let us briefly gain an overview of each, looking at each in terms of the core of the exoteric aspect of each Sacrament, the body, or letter, of an exoteric tradition and then adding a few words which give something of the esoteric perspective. All quotations on the exoteric perspective throughout this chapter will be from the *Catechism of the Greek Orthodox Church: Studies in the Greek Church* by Archbishop Anthony Bashir.

1. *Baptism*: "In Baptism man is mysteriously born to a spiritual life." An esoteric perspective here is that, through Baptism, the neophyte reaches the "Foot of the Cross," or enters into the first stages of the Tree of Life, and activates the first psychospiritual Center, *Malkuth*, thus beginning the spiritual quest, the battle for self-knowledge and self-conquest, or the Great Work. Here, the neophyte begins to realize, first intellectually and then by personal experience, that there is more than a natural, physical body and life, and thus begins to seek the spiritual body and life by entering the Inner Temple, awakening and "climbing up" the Tree of Life.

2. *Chrismation or Confirmation*: "In Chrismation or Unction with Chrism, a person receives the grace of spiritual growth and strength." Here, the neophyte climbs from *Malkuth* to *Yesod*, where he receives the light and guidance to enter into higher worlds, which can be experienced within as that of the *imagination* and of the Astral Light, to do battle with the "devils" of negativity and separatism, that is, negative desires, emotions, and thoughts.

3. *Penitence*: "In Penitence he is healed of spiritual diseases, that is of sin." Here, the aspirant climbs from *Yesod* to *Hod*, where he learns how to conquer negative and wrong *thinking* and how to reframe and realign his thinking with the inspiration and guidance coming from *Tipphereth*, the Heart Center. Through fasting, suffering, and a new perspective, one's perception and conception are transformed.

4. *Absolution*: "Here man finds a medicine for his bodily and spiritual diseases." At this point, the aspirant goes from *Yesod* and *Hod* to *Netzach* and experiences *emotional purification* and transformation: learning how to cope with negative emotions, then to control them, and, finally, to transform them into positive emotions. Through suffering, forgiveness, and sacrifice ("making holy," or exchanging the lower for the higher) the emotions are changed, the aura is cleansed, and Netzach is unblocked. This leads to victory over one's unbridled emotional life, the emotional ups and downs that cause so much confusion, suffering, and illness in the world.

5. *Communion*: "Now man is spiritually fed." At this point, the aspirant climbs from *Netzach* to *Tipphereth*, where he learns how to

commune with the Divine Light and Fire, and with the Spiritual Self, and attunes his consciousness and will to that of the God within, the Divine Spark, thus becoming a genuine Initiate, or "Christ-Child."

6. *Holy Orders*: "Here man receives grace spiritually to regenerate, feed, and nurture others, by doctrine and Sacraments." Now the Initiate goes from *Tipphereth* to *Geburah* and, having completed the Lesser Mysteries, begins to work as an Adept of the Greater Mysteries to lead and guide others to the spiritual life and the realization of the Great Work. He becomes either an outer or an inner Priest.

7. *Matrimony*: "Man receives a grace sanctifying the married life, natural procreation, nurture of children." At this point the Adept goes from *Geburah* to *Chesed* to complete the Great Work to the extent that this can be done while incarnate on earth by the proper fusion or "marriage" of his Spirit (Life) with his Soul (Consciousness). From now on, it is the Divine Spark that rules the Soul (Christ who has become "Lord"), which rules the personality, which controls the body. Henceforth, it is the Consciousness, Love, and Will of God that manifest through the thoughts, feelings, desires, decisions, words, and deeds of the Adept.

In terms of the ministering of the Sacraments, it is not necessary that the priest be an Initiate of advanced level in order to validly administer any of the sacraments; he may even be of somewhat doubtful character, yet the power of Christ will still flow through him. As Charles Leadbeater, himself a priest in the Liberal Catholic Church, states:

> Christ works in His Church through those whom He has especially ordained and set apart for the work. When the bishop ordains, he lays his hands upon the head of the candidate and makes him a priest, but we must never forget that it is the Christ Himself who ordains, working through those who have been chosen to act for Him. It is always the Christ who administers every sacrament. The bishop or the priest may be a man of doubtful character and questionable morals yet still the power of Christ will flow through him. The unworthiness of the Priest does not interfere with the validity depended upon the character of the celebrant. A valid ordination alone is necessary for the validity of the sacrament.
>
> If a priest takes the full advantage of the mighty privileges which are conferred upon him at ordination; if he opens himself up to the full power and uses it always for the highest purposes, then indeed he has the most wonderful opportunities and is most blessed in his work. But even if the priest be careless, the sacrament is still valid. Even where the church building has been allowed to fall into decay, when services are irregularly conducted and are arranged for the convenience of the priest and not for the work in the parish; where the vestments, the altar and its vessels are of

the poorest description and badly maintained, the sacraments of Christ
are given to His people.

They might have been better administered, they might have been
surrounded with the reverence and the beauty with which those who
understand ever surround them, but at least the Life is there. That Life
lies ever behind His Church; even when men fail, the power of Christ
never fails.[3]

Evelyn Underhill, who has a good historical and intellectual grasp
as well as a personal and lived experience of the Christian Sacraments, states:

A symbol is a significant image, which helps the worshiping soul to
apprehend spiritual reality. A sacrament is a significant deed, a particular use of temporal things, which gives to them the value of eternal things
and thus incorporates and conveys spiritual reality. Hence sacraments
involve an incarnational philosophy; a belief that the Supernatural draws
near to man in and through the natural; . . . Generally speaking, however, it is true to say that from the point of view of cultures, symbols
represent and suggest, whilst sacraments work. Effective action is essential to them; and this action is from God to man, not from man to God.
The water cleanses, the bread and wine feed, the oil anoints, the imposition of consecrating hands conveys new character, the marriage act
unites; and all this in the interior and spiritual action cannot be achieved
by man. His part, as worshiper, consists in the preparation; the adoring
and confident reference to God, opening up a pathway for His grace. But
the essence of the sacramental action consists in the actual conveyance
of spiritual meaning and power by a material process . . . not only
God's meaning to the mind, but God Himself to the whole person of the
worshiper.

A valid sacrament, therefore, always leaves the situation different from
what it was before. By means of the natural needs and actions of men, it
effects a communication of the Wholly Other, over against men; and it is
a fundamental part of worship, because it is an acknowledgement of the
presence and priority of the Divine, and is directed towards the sanctification of life.[4]

Then, she continues:

Thus we may say in a general sense, that sacraments convey the
numinous, establish a relation between human and Divine, more precisely and more effectively than the most august of symbols; for their
contact with our life is more complete. This conveyance is achieved by
means of tokens; objects or actions set apart for special office, and therefore taking rank as effective instruments. These tokens constitute a
sacred currency which not only signifies but also conveys to those who
take it seriously the wealth for which it stands. Like any other coinage, it
may and often does become debased: yet still it is representative of spiritual gold. Moreover, the obvious inadequacy and arbitrary character of

the token over against the holy reality which comes by these humble channels to transform, refresh, and sanctify the life of men, once more reminds us of the freedom and priority of God's action; the homely plane on which human worship must be content to move.[5]

Finally, she concludes:

Thus sacramentalism emerging as a primary means of worship appropriate to the nature and situation of man, grows and deepens with our growth. It has something to give to the most naive of primitives; its possibilities have never been exhausted by the most supernaturalized of saints. For it reveals God, the Supernatural, ever at work seeking and finding us through the natural; the objects and actions of our temporal experience, as the effective means of our deepest and most transforming apprehensions of Eternity, and our most insistent invitations to worship coming to us where we are, and taking us as we are—creatures of soul and body, conditioned by time and space.

It is a very short-sight spirituality which ignores these patent facts; or tries to maintain an absolute contrast between matter and spirit, seen and unseen, nature and grace; and worship the Creator whilst disdaining the help of those things which He has made, and which are presupposed as the vehicles of the spiritual experiences of men. Since we are men and women and not angels, it is surely to be expected that God's prevenient action should reach us through and not in defiance of our humanity; penetrating, informing, and consecrating the life He has made for Himself, giving the invisible and eternal order through the visible and fleeting order to which our mental life is adjusted, and calling us to an intercourse consistent with our condition—in, and yet not wholly of the visible world. The ultimate aim of all expressive worship is the increase of Charity; the pure love of God, for Himself alone.[6]

The Sacraments, in other words, unite two basic realities: the physical and the spiritual, the visible and the invisible, form and force. They are the basic channels through which we can feed our soul, our higher consciousness, and activate and open up the psychospiritual Centers on the Tree of Life, to achieve union with God, and thus to do His Will on earth.

Participating in the Sacraments, particularly in the Eucharist, should always bring about a blood transfusion, an increase of Life which can bring about changes and effects an inner transformation on different levels, from the spiritual to the physical, and from the conscious to the as yet unconscious. They are thus inestimable treasures, filled with many potentialities . . . that await actualization and being brought to light. When we begin to understand the esoteric dimensions of the spiritual nature of the Sacraments, we move closer to that pure love of God, of himself alone. The tangible result in our everyday life is that we experience "life-forces" that vivify particular aspects of our consciousness and being, because these are associated with the different Sacraments; we know ourselves better and can express who we are, in the deepest sense, more fully.

BAPTISM

The Catechism

"Baptism is a Sacrament, in which a man who believes, having his body thrice plunged in water in the name of God the Father, the Son, and the Holy Ghost, dies to the carnal life of sin and is born again of the Holy Ghost to a life spiritual and holy. The essence of Baptism is a threefold immersion in water, in the name of the Father, the Son, and the Holy Ghost.

"What is required to be baptized? *Repentance* and *Faith.*

"Why before baptizing do we use *exorcism*? To drive away the Devil, who since Adam's fall has had access to men, and power over them, as his captives and slaves. Paul says that all men, without *grace*, walk according to the course of this world, according to the Prince of the air, the spirit that now worketh in the children of disobedience.

"The power of exorcism lies in the *name of Jesus Christ*, invoked with prayer and faith ('In My name shall they cast out devils').

"What force has the Sign of the Cross when made with faith and used in this or other occasions? This is another way of invoking Jesus Christ.

"What means the *white garment* which is put on after baptism? It symbolizes the purity of the soul, and of the Christian life.

"Why is a Cross given to the baptized person? As available expression and continual remembrance of Christ's command: 'If any man will come after Me, let him deny himself, and *take up his cross*, and follow Me.'

"What means the *procession* of the baptized round the font with a *light*? Spiritual *joy*, joined with spiritual *illumination*.

"Baptism is spiritual birth: a man is born but once; therefore he is also baptized but once.

"Is there a way to obtain pardon for our sins after Baptism? Yes, through *Penitence.*"

From the esoteric perspective, we begin with this excerpt from the work of Charles Leadbeater on the Sacrament of Baptism:

> We see from this that the Church meets the soul as soon as he comes into his new set of vehicles, and offers him welcome and assistance. What help can be given to a soul when he first comes into a new physical body?

Remember, we cannot reach the soul itself; we are dealing with vehicles on the physical plane. What the soul most needs is to bring that new set of vehicles into order, so that he can work through them. He comes laden with the results of his past lives, which means that he has within him seeds of *good qualities* and also seeds of *evil qualities*. Those seeds of evil have often been called original sin.[7]

The duty of the parents is clearly to stimulate the development of these good qualities, and this depends largely on the surroundings given to the child. If there is love, understanding, and gentleness in the home then these qualities are called forth from within the child; if there is anger and irritability (and there is sure to be at least some), then, likewise, these are developed in the child. Either way, the first influences are crucial. Leadbeater goes on to say how Baptism prepares the child to cope with the inevitable negative influence that he or she will meet in growing up:

The water used is magnetized with a special view to the effect of its vibrations upon the higher vehicles, so that all the germs of good qualities in the unformed astral and mental bodies of the child may thereby receive a strong stimulus, while at the same time the germs of evil may be isolated and deadened. The central idea is to take this early opportunity of fostering the growth of the good germs, in order that their development may precede that of the evil—in order that when at a later period the latter germs begin to bear their fruit, the good may already be so evolved that the control of the evil will be a comparatively easy matter.[8]

There is another aspect of the baptismal ceremony, namely that it is a consecration and a setting apart. This new set of vehicles, the energy bodies which in maturing can give rise to a true expression of the soul within, are thus consecrated to the Lord Jesus Christ and this is an act, therefore, of sacred magic. This, of course, must not be at all confused with the profane forms of magic, but is the "science of love," born of the union in love of Divine Will and human will.

Baptism is a "deed," as Evelyn Underhill calls all Sacraments, a major "turning point" in the life and evolution of an individual. For an adult, whether the remembrance of his or her baptism is a part of another ritual, perhaps the Mass, or the ceremony itself, it contains the realization that the purely material and mundane life cannot give full satisfaction and that the key to happiness, fulfillment, and the completion of our being and destiny, lies in developing and living a *spiritual life*, and in developing a spiritual consciousness. Baptism, therefore, is the major turning point between *involution* and *evolution*, wherein an individual now consciously aspires and works towards returning to the Source whence he came; and to accomplish this he must become aware of himself as a "Temple of God." It is also the activation of *Malkuth* and the beginning of the long climb, the spiritual journey, on the *Inner Cross of Light*, which is the Tree of Life.

This forms something of the meaning behind the words "dies to the carnal life of sin and is born again of the Holy Spirit to a life spiritual and holy." Until this point, Christ was "crucified" on the cross of matter, and the vehicles (the physical and astral bodies in particular) were in control of the personality of that particular person. With this turnabout, however, the Divine Spark, the Christ within, will slowly learn how to organize and acquire control over its physical, emotional, and mental vehicles, to enable the person to *act*, rather than *react*, to folllow his own inner conscience and intuition, rather than merely respond to external stimuli and internal subliminal drives. Thus it symbolizes and marks the beginning of the new spiritual life.

Water is the main agent of purification for the body, the emotions, and the mind, while the Name of the Trinity is the means to bring down the Divine Light, Fire, and Life to activate the personality which has been purified. The essential qualities that are, indeed, necessary to make the ceremony of Baptism become living and effective are *Repentance* and *Faith*: in other words, the strong inner desire to lead a more constructive and wholesome life, with the recognition that, hitherto, our life has not been very constructive or wholesome; and the belief that such a better and healthier life is *possible* by focusing all of our energies, thoughts, and feelings to work towards achieving this higher life.

Here *exorcism* points to the mental and emotional cleansing and transformation needed to be able to become open and receptive to the influx and power of the Light and thus to be freed from the power and control of the adversarial forces in and of the world. This psycho-spiritual transformation is necessary in order to become inner-directed and inner-guided and to be freed from merely *reacting* to the external and internal material, psychic, and sociocultural forces. For without the Divine Light and the "Spirit of God in us," we are, indeed, though unconsciously, *slaves* of this world and of biopsychic, psycho-social, and mental forces which control us and prevent us from being true children of God, doing our work, and accomplishing our duty on earth.

Obviously, the power of Exorcism, like that of any ritual, comes from the power of God in concert with the spiritual beings he directs to carry forth and administer this ritual, united with what resonates within us of these spiritual energies. Thus, in vibrating a Divine Name we awaken and activate the Life of the Divine Spark, which then projects its Light in extension into the personality. And this brings about the "alchemical" mental, emotional, and volitional *changes* implied in a genuine conversion or inner transformation of perspective, state of consciousness, and vibratory rate.

The Sign of the Cross is the simplest and most effective way to draw down and draw out from within the Divine Light to fill our field of consciousness, our whole Tree of Life, and our auras.

The white garment which is put on after baptism can be seen as the aura of the newly baptized neophyte which has been filled with spiritual Life and thus purified, and which he should strive to "wear" and to "preserve" at all times. A Cross is also given to the baptized neophyte, partly as a reminder that he has to activate, light up, and wear the Cross of Light within himself, to face all the tests and battles that life and his destiny will bring to him. It is also a reminder that he has to climb his own inner Cross of the Tree of Life by becoming more and more conscious, responsive, and aligned with the Divine Light reaching out to him from that inner Cross.

The procession of the baptized around the font with a light corresponds with the circulation of this Light within the aura. This circulation of the Light activates a particular psychospiritual Center —*Malkuth*. This is a prelude and a first step towards full Illumination, or the lighting up of the whole Tree of Life and the filling of the whole soul with the Light of God.

Finally, it is interesting to note that the Sacrament of Penitence, activating and cleansing *Hod*, will also reactivate and cleanse both *Malkuth* and *Yesod*, thus bringing about, each time, a "little inner Baptism," or a reenactment of what happened spiritually at Baptism.

Further information on the rite of Baptism is provided in the section of the Orthodox Catechism which describes the actual carrying out of this Sacrament. This also contains profound spiritual and esoteric significance.

The Exoteric Rite

"To perform the Sacrament of Baptism, the Priest puts on light-colored or *white* vestments, to express the joy of the Church at receiving a new member. Candles are lit around the edge of the font, the censer is swung, and the sponsors are given candles to hold. The lighted candles symbolize the spiritual illumination which is imparted through the Sacrament of Baptism, while the clouds of incense indicate the grace of the Holy Spirit through whose operation man's regeneration takes place in this Sacrament.

"The Order of Baptism consists of the consecration of the water, and anointing of the water and of the person baptized with consecrated oil, the immersion of the person into the water, the investing him with white garments, the circumambulation of the font, and the preparing of the lessons from Holy Scriptures . . .

"Having thus prepared the material for the Sacrament, the Priest now proceeds to prepare for it the person about to receive it. He anoints the brow, ears, breast, hands and feet with the consecrated oil, in token that, through Baptism, man, like unto a branch of the wold olive tree, is grafted unto the good olive tree, which is Christ."

An Esoteric Perspective

In the foregoing text explaining the basic steps and procedures used for the order of Baptism, we find many spiritual truths and treasures which complement and complete the first part of the exoteric text which we have already explored. Each Sacrament is embodied in an external physical process which awakens, initiates, and facilitates an inner spiritual process, connecting us and unifying us with the spiritual world. In each case, we have a ceremony in which the Light of the World is brought down and incarnated into the Tree of Life and field of consciousness of the neophyte—to awaken him or her spiritually and to reconnect him or her with the Source and Essence of Being.

The white garments of the priest and of the neophyte symbolize the human soul and aura which have been filled by the Divine Light and which have been illuminated, to the degree this ceremony betokens. The candles which are lit around the edge of the font again are seen as lighting up the psychospiritual Center to which the font corresponds, that is, *Malkuth*. The lighted candles represent the descent of the Light, bringing the expansion and transformation of consciousness; the clouds of incense prepare for the outpouring of the Holy Spirit, bringing a life and an energy more abundant. Thus, in this Sacrament, a double transformation takes place: an outpouring of Divine Light, transforming and expanding consciousness, and a down-pouring of Divine Life increasing vital energies and raising consciousness.

Here we see all the basic elements of a spiritual deed wrought both within and without: the purification of soul (and its aura) by water, the consecration of thought, feelings, and willing by fire, the lighting up and transformation of the aura, and the extension and circulation of Divine Light in the aura through the circumambulation, together with meditation seeds or thoughts from the Scriptures.

The anointing of the brow, ears, breast, hands, and feet with blessed oil are to focus and consecrate thinking, feeling, imagining, willing, speaking, and acting, which are the foundation of the newly beginning spiritual life. This is so that the candidate may, indeed, become a new being, with a new identity and new capacities, now capable of doing battle with the forces of evil so as to transform evil into good and become a true soldier of the Light in this world.

The Cross that is put on the neophyte's neck contains all the fullness which this most sacred symbol can evoke as the consciousness, love, and devotion of the neophyte grows in time. We can see it, too, as the Cross of Light which one will have to activate and "wear" on the higher bodies and in the auras as one cultivates and unfolds the spiritual life. The passage which is sung at this point clearly indicates the core of this Initiation—for an Initiation indeed it is: "Give unto me a shining robe, Thou that are invested with light as with a garment." It is the filling up of the aura and the Tree of Life of the candidate with spiritual Light. And the second chant, "As many as have been baptized into Christ, have put on Christ," clearly indicates that, from henceforth, it is the Divine Spark which should be one's true Self, and the integrating and unifying principle of one's psyche and behavior.

I do not remember my own baptism, since I was too young to understand consciously the deeper spiritual meaning of this beautiful ceremony. And yet, I am sure that it implanted deep seeds in the inner recesses of my consciousness. Since then, however, I have attended many Baptism ceremonies and even became the Godfather of the son of one of my friends. Each ceremony I attended was experienced in a unique way, successively growing with more meaning, depth, beauty, and feeling. Each ceremony, moreover, reactivated in my consciousness what I had experienced, unconsciously, as a child. I naturally identified with the baptized person and rededicated myself to the spiritual life, to becoming a child of Light. Each time I saw, felt, and experienced something new and unsuspected before as wonders, correspondences, and implications manifested to my consciousness while I was reliving this ancient Initiation.

I also became aware that the same principle applies to all the Sacraments—whether Baptism, Chrismation, Holy Orders, and Matrimony, which are, basically, undergone one time, or Penitence, Absolution, and Communion, which are experienced repeatedly. Each time we participate in a Sacrament, whether for ourselves or for others, something is reawakened, reactivated, vivified in our own consciousness. As we grow, expand our consciousness, raise our vibrations and energy levels, we will experience the same thing in a very different way. Later on, I also realized that, from the standpoint of the inner or higher worlds and of the inner or higher vision, each

Sacrament affects a given psychospiritual Center as well as the aura of
the one who receives it, in a very noticeable and specific way. Just as
we wear, in "color, shape, and sound" what we are, so do the Sacraments leave their indelible imprints in the inner and higher worlds,
visible to angels and the spiritually awakened.

CHRISMATION OR CONFIRMATION

The Exoteric Perspective

"Unction with Chrism is a Sacrament in which the baptized believer
is anointed with holy chrism on certain parts of the body in the name
of the Holy Spirit and receives the gifts of the Holy Spirit for growth
and strength in spiritual life. This Sacrament is mentioned in the
Holy Scriptures by the Apostle John: 'But ye have an unction from
the Holy One, and ye know all things. And the anointing which ye
have received of Him abideth in you, and ye need not that any man
teach you; but as the same anointing teacheth you all things, and is
truth, and is no lie; and even as it hath taught you, abide therein'
(1 John 2: 20, 27). In like manner the Apostle Paul says: 'Now He
which establishes us with you in Christ, and hath anointed us, is God:
Who have also sealed us, and given the earnest of the Spirit in our
hearts' (2 Cor. 1: 21, 22). This is where the words pronounced at the
Unction 'The seal of the gift of the Holy Spirit' are taken from.

"To impart to the baptized the gift of the Holy Spirit, the Apostles
used the imposition of hands. The successors of the Apostles, however, in place of this, introduced unction with chrism, drawn, it may
be, from their precedent of unction used in the Old Testament.

"The consecration of the holy Chrism is reserved to the heads of
the Hierarchy, as successor of the Apostles, who used the laying on of
their hands to communicate the gifts of the Holy Spirit.

"The anointing of the forehead is the sanctification of the mind, or
thoughts. The anointing of the chest is the sanctification of the heart,
or desires and emotions. The anointing of the eyes, ears, and lips is
the sanctification of the senses; and the anointing of the hands and
feet is the sanctification of one's life and deeds."

An Esoteric Perspective

While baptism deals mainly with *purification* (of desires, emotions,
thoughts, ideas, and decision) and activates *Malkuth* at the Foot of the
Cross to begin the long upward Path of the Cross, Chrismation

(Confirmation for the Roman Catholics) deals mainly with *consecration* and with *sanctification*, which is the next step after purification. On the Tree of Life, *Yesod* is the corresponding point which, now activated, enables the neophyte to receive the Light and Guidance to enter the inner and higher worlds of the imagination and of the mind. This is so one is better able to do battle with the adversarial forces, both as they are incarnate in the world and as "devils" within—negative thoughts, emotions, desires, and suggestions, along with depression, anger, frustration, self-deprecation, desire for revenge, and hardening of the heart. In other words, so one is better able to take up the whole range of the inner battle, the holy Jihad, that every aspirant child of the Light must face and engage, at different points, on the path of his evolution.

The holy Chrism is the vehicle for the gifts of the Holy Spirit (traditionally, these are Wisdom, Understanding, Counsel, Fortitude, Knowledge, Piety, and Fear of God), which are special vibrational energies, colors, and potencies of the Divine Light. These will affect and enliven the psychospiritual Centers and certain levels of consciousness of the neophyte. They also affect and condition the functions of the psyche in such a way that the candidate will now be able to acquire *conscious* control over his thoughts, emotions, and inner energies. Thereafter, the postulant will be able to put on the armor of Light of which St. Paul speaks.

Through the proper opening of *Yesod* and the activation of the imagination, there comes the possibility of inspirations and revelations which are now accessible to the postulant. This means that he or she can also now be guided from within by his or her Higher Self; hence, as the Scriptures say, "ye know all things," and "ye need not that any man teach you."

The anointing of various parts of the body also has symbolic and actual meanings and precise functions, namely:

—That of the forehead: the sanctification of thoughts, ideas, and the mind.

—That of the chest: the sanctification of the heart, emotions, and sentiments.

—That of the eyes, ears, and lips: the sanctification of the senses.

—That of the hands and feet: the sanctification of one's life and deeds.

All of these point, symbolically, at least in part, to the inner psychological work which must be accomplished by the postulant at this stage of his spiritual growth and development. Namely, to learn how to consciously direct and use his thinking, feeling, and willing, the use of his senses and of his imagination, and finally his behavior, actions, and life.

The Sacrament of Chrismation, or Confirmation, brings down the power of the Holy Spirit and its gifts: inspiration, understanding, strength, and energy upon both the soul and the personality, activating and opening up *Yesod*, the sexual psychospiritual Center. As such, it prepares the candidate for the trials and battles of life, in general, and for the inner warfare of self-conquest necessary for the aspirant to spiritual Initiation, in particular.

When it is conferred before puberty, it is designed to prepare and equip the young person for the battle of life by making it easier for the soul to reach and act through its vehicles; and it prepares the candidate for the trials and temptations of puberty, helping him to think, feel, decide, speak, and act for himself. Here, it is especially designed to help one achieve self-control and dominion over one's biopsychic drives (sex and aggression in particular), over one's newly awakened emotions and imagination, and, also, over thinking, to achieve true personal identity, integrity, and responsibility.

For the adult, this Sacrament represents a conscious confirmation of, and focus upon, his aspiration to live for God and to fight for the Light, for Good, and for Justice in this world. Moreover, it also actualizes his "linking" with the Church here on earth. Esoterically, we can see it functioning to strengthen the connection between the soul and its vehicles, the conscious and the superconscious, and between the human and the Spiritual Self. Thus with the increase of the individual's self-control, the mastery over the many forces of his personality and those in his or her environment, comes a greater receptivity to the Divine Light. Thus, as the Liberal Catholic Church puts it:——

> In this Sacrament of Confirmation the Church gives you both the opportunity to enroll yourselves in Christ's army . . .
>
> But before you enter His most holy service, take heed that you are such soldiers as He would have you be. Strong you must be as the lion, yet gentle as the lamb, ready to protect the weak, watchful ever to help where help is needed, to give reverence to those to whom it is due, and to show knightly courtesy to all. Never forget that God is Love, make it your constant care to spread love around wherever you go; so will you fan into a living flame the smoldering fire of love in the hearts of those in whom as yet the spark burns low. Remember that the Soldier of the Cross must utterly uproot from his heart the giant weed of selfishness, and must live not for himself but for the service of the world; for this commandment we have from Him, that he who loveth God loves his brother also. Remember that the power of God which you are now about to receive from my hand, will ever work within you for righteousness, inclining you to a noble and upright life. Strive therefore earnestly, that your thoughts, your words, and your deeds shall be such as befit a child of Christ and a Knight dedicated to His service.[9]

This Sacrament, therefore, prepares and strengthens the adult to undertake a mature life in the world while, at the same time, growing and unfolding spiritually—meeting successfully the various tests and temptations of life.

For the aspirant to spiritual Initiation, this Sacrament provides the psychological and spiritual foundation, as well as the social reinforcement and a community of like-minded persons, to undertake the long and arduous path of the upward climb on the Tree of Life and the Cross of Light—and it prepares him to face the many inner battles and ordeals which all true aspirants, of all ages, races, and religions must face.

While Baptism deals with the turning from the purely worldly and sensual life, with the opening and awakening of *Malkuth* and the purification of the personality, Chrismation deals more with the beginning of the inner life and its battles and tests, with the opening and awakening of *Yesod*, and with the sanctification of the personality to the service of the soul and of the Christ within. Here, the aspirant is guided and given the inspiration and strength to acquire the conscious self-control of his thoughts and to dedicate them to the service of Jesus Christ; to consciously develop mastery of his will, of his words, and of his deeds on the inner emotional dimension, rather than on the outer physical one.

Having learned how to protect his heart, his imagination, and his mind from evil thoughts, feelings, desires, and deeds, the aspirant is then ready to have his intuitive channel, the channel which connects the conscious with the superconscious, and the human with the spiritual self, open and activated. At this point, when he has really *lived* and *realized* this sacrament, he will find the source of all knowledge and guidance *within himself*, coming straight from the Christ within. This will emancipate him from all kinds of masters, teachers, experts, and gurus in the outer world, and it will help him achieve true integrity, authentic autonomy, and genuine responsibility—which are the earmarks of true maturity. But, for this lofty achievement to be realized, self-knowledge and self-mastery, the proper development and coordination of the personality (and of all the functions of the psyche) and its proper alignment with the Soul, must be first realized.

What is given in this sacrament, as well as in others, is not the finished product, for this can only be achieved by the *conscious and full cooperation* of the individual himself. It is the blueprint, the inspiration, and the necessary energies to achieve this work and to respond adequately to the many tests and trials of life and, in particular, of the underlying spiritual life. These are like seeds or possibilities which can be planted and properly nurtured . . . or also allowed to dry up and wither away, never truly actualized. According to one's level of consciousness and being, these seeds will be more or less developed, used, and actualized in the life and being of every aspirant. Today, however, when the forces of evolution and the major tests and ordeals of humanity are focusing, more and more, on the *inner emotional dimension*, rather than the outer physical one, the blueprints and possibilities offered by, and contained in, this Sacrament become ever more important and meaningful to the true seeker.

In conclusion let me quote the words of Leadbeater, who expresses deeply the inner process set in motion by this Sacrament:

> The power which the Bishop pours into the candidate is definitely and distinctly that of the Third Person of the Blessed Trinity, the Third Aspect of the Deity; but it comes in three waves, and it acts as the three levels upon the principles of the candidate, as in Baptism, there is first an opening of the force, which moves from below upwards; then there is a filling and a sealing process, which moves from above downwards.
>
> But we are dealing now with the soul, and not merely with his vehicles. At the words; "Receive the Holy Spirit," the Divine power rushes in through the soul or ego of the Bishop into that lower stratum of the soul of the candidate which we call the intelligence; at the signing of the Cross it pushes upwards into the next stage, the intuition of buddhi; and at the words; "I confirm thee with the chrism of salvation," it presses upwards into the spirit of atma . . . Some candidates are far more susceptible to the process of opening up than others; upon some the effect produced is enormous and lasting; in the case of others it is often but slight, because as yet that which has to be awakened is so little developed as to be barely capable of response.
>
> When the awakening has been achieved as far as it may be, comes the filling and the sealing. This is done, as ever, by the utterance of the great word of power, the Name of the Blessed Trinity. At the Name of the Father the highest principle is filled and sealed; at the Name of the Son the same is done to the intuitional principle, and at the Name of the Holy Spirit the work is finished by the action upon the higher intelligence (manas). As this further outpouring which I have called the filling takes place, the effect upon the spirit is reflected into the etheric double of the neophyte so far as his development allows; the impression upon the intuition is in the same way produced in the emotional vehicle; and what is done to the higher mind should similarly mirror itself in the lower. But all these reflections into the personality depend upon the extent to which it is able to express and reflect the soul behind it.
>
> The very intention of the Sacrament is to tighten the links all the way up—to bring about a closer connection between the soul and its vehicle the personality, but also between the soul and the spirit which it in turn expresses. This result is not merely temporary; the opening up of these connections makes a wider channel through which a constant flow can be kept going. Confirmation arms and equips a [person] for the battle of life, and makes it easier for the soul to act on and through its vehicles.[10]

I was confirmed in the Roman Catholic Church, when I was very young; then I was later chrismated in an Orthodox Church I had joined in New York. The ceremony was performed by my spiritual teacher after a long period of preparation and study in spirituality, including my "pilgrimage to the East." This ceremony was the true beginning of a new life form. It put into words and gave an objective form to many of my newly emerging needs and aspirations. It marked the true beginning of a new set of endeavors, which had begun a few years earlier, and this now put all the strings together. I felt, having completed my preparation, it was also my second birth. And, each time I later assisted at a confirmation, or chrismation ceremony, it reawakened what I had experienced at my own chrismation, but with new aspects and facets. It is also at this point that I consciously realized I belonged to the Mystical Body of Christ and the Communion of Saints—that subtle link and rapport that all spiritually growing and awakened persons have with each other, above and below, regardless of religion, race, or cultural background.

PENITENCE

The Exoteric Perspective

"What is penitence? Penitence is a Sacrament, in which he who confesses his sins is, on the outward declaration of pardon by the Priest, inwardly loosed from his sins by Jesus Christ Himself.

"What is the origin of this Sacrament? They who came to John the Baptist, who preached the baptism of repentance for the remission of sins, confessed their sins (Mark 1: 4–5). The Apostles were promised by Jesus Christ power to forgive sins, when He said: 'Whatsoever ye shall bind on earth, shall be bound in heaven; and whatsoever ye shall loose on earth, shall be loosened in heaven' (Matt. 18:18). After His resurrection He actually gave them this power, saying: 'Receive ye the Holy Spirit: whosoever sins ye remit, they are remitted unto them; and whosoever sins ye retain, they are retained' (John 20: 22–23).

"What is required of the Penitent? Contrition for his sins, with a full response of amendment of life, faith in Jesus Christ, and hope in His mercy. 'Godly sorrow brings repentance that leads to salvation and leaves no regret' (2 Cor. 7:10). 'But if the wicked turn from his wickedness, and do that which is lawful and right, he shall live thereby' (Ezek. 33:19). 'To Him, that is Jesus Christ, give all the prophets witness, that through His name whosoever believeth in Him shall receive remission of sins' (Acts 10:43).

"Are there certain preparations or aids to Penitence? Yes, such as fasting, prayer, and *epitimia*, and penance. What is *epitimia*? The word means *punishment*. Under this name, are prescribed to the penitent, according as may be requisite, diverse particular exercises of piety, and diverse abstinences or privations, serving to subdue sinful habits; for instance, fasting beyond what is prescribed for all, or for grievous sins suspension from the holy Communion for a given time."

An Esoteric Perspective

Penitence deals with the recognition that one has erred, made a mistake, or violated a physical, psychological, or spiritual law. It implies changing our attitude towards what we have done or failed to do, and, as such, it requires a mental, emotional, and volitional *change*. To do something (or fail to do something) and then to "repent" from having done (or not done) this thing by remaining in the same mental, emotional, and volitional framework does not work and is hypocrisy. In order for genuine penitence to be present and at work, a new *mental* perspective (which is linked with a new emotional and volitional viewpoint) is necessary. This new mental perspective must be a true *metanoia* (or transformation and expansion of our consciousness—specifically of our ways of thinking, feeling, and willing), and this transformation is the result of both human effort and spiritual grace. This is why, on the Tree of Life, it is *Hod* which is affected and activated by this Sacrament, corresponding as it does with the mind and with our mental outlook.

Here, because the Divine Light in its path of descent focuses upon and activates *Hod* in this transformation, we are given a new perspective that enables us to recognize in which ways we have transgressed and violated certain laws which bring, in their wake, certain outer and inner consequences. Likewise, to simply recognize that we have made a mistake or violated a certain law—from this new mental perspective and emotional attitude of contrition which follows—is not enough. The will must also be activated and brought into play, and we must make a firm commitment to correct our mistakes and not to commit them again. Penitence is thus the mental half of the forgiveness of sins; Absolution, which follows, is the latter half, involving *Netzach*, the emotional center.

Penitence is also the "male polarity," the human-effort side, of the psychospiritual process which opens up our Tree of Life, and our auras to the higher spiritual energies that come rushing down to transform and raise our consciousness. Properly understood and used, it opens up our etheric, astral, and mental bodies, as well as

Hod, *Netzach*, and *Tipphereth*, so that the Light may enter them and do its work of psychospiritual transformation.

The first fundamental insight into the inner, or esoteric, aspects of Penitence came to me when I was a child and still had my inner vision open. Then I used to observe what I now know to be human auras and the changes that would occur therein, in terms of color, luminosity, intensity, and field expansion or contraction, when someone did or said certain things. One thing that used to greatly puzzle me was why, when a person went to confession (in the Roman Catholic Church), the Light which would form around the priest (as he would say his prayers or carry out a ritual) would, sometimes, flow around the energy field of a person, leaving him unchanged, and, sometimes, flow inside them, changing them noticeably. Later on, when I began to study spirituality, I realized that this difference was due to Penitence. If a person would make an examination of conscience—really concentrate, meditate, and "feel deeply" about what he did or did not do—especially about the mistakes he made (by doing certain things he should not have done or not doing things he should have done), then this would set up "Energy and Light vortexes" which would open up his energy fields and some psychospiritual Centers, and thus enable the Light brought through by Absolution to enter him and change him.

Actually, it is impossible to live in the material world without committing sins and violating the Commandments—and the more we expand, deepen, and heighten our consciousness, the more we become aware and realize how many mistakes and transgressions we are committing on planes and dimensions that are more and more subtle. The key point there is not to fall prey to guilt and despair but to repent of our mistakes, as we become aware of them, and to make a firm commitment not to make the same mistakes again. Thus we must learn to forgive others—and to forgive ourselves—as God forgives us . . . which is seven times seventy times, as Jesus put it allegorically.

An exercise that can be of great use here is the *retrospection exercise* made at the end of each day, week, month, and year. Here, the candidate will review everything that was done or happened during the chosen period of time (a day, a week, a month, or a year) without passing any judgment at all, simply bringing back into awareness all the external events and the psychological perceptions, definitions, and reactions to them during the chosen period of time. Once this is done, then one should bring one's moral judgment into play, seeking to identify the areas where mistakes were made or where one could have done better. Finally, having identified these, one should make a firm commitment to rectify mistakes as soon as possible.

Let us also bear in mind the very perceptive insight and useful admonition Leadbeater gave concerning God's attitudes towards human mistakes:

> No one in his senses could suppose that God cherishes animosity against His people . . . On the contrary He is always waiting to help, just as the sun is always shining. The sun is not holding a grudge against us when a passing cloud shuts away his light and warmth. The sunlight is always there, and all we need to do is to wait for the passing of the cloud.
>
> The God who has hung our solar system in space, and has poured His life into it that we and His other creatures might come into being, superintends the progress of that tremendous Experiment with benevolent, paternal interest. He knows far more about us than we ourselves can know; He understands our strength and our weakness, and He could not more be angry with us than we can be angry with a flower in our garden. But He watches our growth, and puts various aids in our way; perhaps it pleases Him when we understand and take advantage of them, but even if we do not, the support of His helping hand is never far from us, else we should speedily cease to be.[11]

Penitence and contrition are, in fact, the preparation and the first half of Absolution and the "remission of sins" which follows organically and as an integral part of the same process—which is the reason why the Orthodox Church has no separate exoteric text for Absolution and links it with Penitence.

ABSOLUTION

An Esoteric Perspective

Since in the Orthodox Church the exoteric text is the same for Penitence and for Absolution, we shall continue with our esoteric exploration. Absolution follows Penitence, or contrition, in an organic fashion—as the second half of the same process. On the Tree of Life, Absolution affects *Netzach* by bringing it Divine Light, activating it and opening it up. This is where the actual emotional (and mental and volitional) release occurs and where a marked emotional (and mental and volitional) *change* takes place as our consciousness alters and expands, making us feel literally lighter, fuller, more ourselves, freer and happier than before.

The question of Penitence and Absolution raises the fundamental problem of Divine Justice and Divine Mercy: How can God be, at the same time, just and merciful? How can we make mistakes, violate laws, and then repent, receive Absolution, and not bear the consequences of what we have set in motion? This has been one of the most difficult and paradoxical problems in both theology and philosophy. To which the esoteric tradition, as I have described it, gives a very simple and even logical answer—without taking from the ultimate mystery of it!

As the Christian Scriptures (and many other sacred Scriptures) explicitly state: Absolution and the remission of sins are a reality and constitute one of the major contributions of the Church to its members. The central key here is to realize that *God's justice* operates on the *horizontal, objective plane*, while *God's mercy* operates on the *vertical, subjective plane*. Any mistake or sin that we commit, like anything we do, always has two basic sets of consequences: the first is in the world, where we inevitably will "reap what we have sowed," and where restitution is unavoidable and inexorable. The second is in our own psyche (or consciousness), where negative and wrong thoughts, especially feelings, desires, and emotions, immediately fill up the aura with negative energies and vibrations that clog up the psychospiritual Centers, affecting the ability of the spiritual Light to reach us and shine both within and without. Negative emotions, thoughts, and energies will, literally, have a threefold impact upon our consciousness, lowering it and diminishing it. Namely, they will:

a. *Confuse the mind* so that we are no longer able to think clearly and to distinguish what is good and what is bad for us—what we should and what we should not do. The mental confusion that ensues can be imagined by picturing what happens when we turn off the light in a room without windows and can no longer see anything, and so must grope in the darkness.

b. *Harden the heart and dry up our capacity to feel anything positive*, making us either insensitive or filled with negative feelings such as fear, guilt, insecurity, and despair. Here, it is the Heart Center which is clogged up and poisoned, whereby our capacity to love is blocked and atrophied, to be replaced by emotional explosions of anger, frustration, or fear. It is as if all life went out of the heart, so that normal emotions and feelings were replaced by a burning and unquenchable fire of frustration, anger, guilt, insecurity, and anxiety.

c. *Sap and deplete the energies of the will*, until one loses control over one's functions of the psyche—over one's thoughts, feelings, decisions, words, and deeds and, therefore, over one's life. Then, without will or self, one drifts through life, pushed here and there by emotional currents, a victim of circumstances, sinking deeper and deeper into lethargy and apathy, and into self-destructive behavior. A more sensitive person might even observe himself drifting downwards into self-destructive patterns and despair, but without being able to check this "descent into hell."

The common medical term which describes and summarizes what

this threefold impact upon our consciousness brings in its wake is *depression*. And depression is one of the most common and least understood epidemics of our time; medical science is helpless to resolve it because conventional science does not yet fully understand its true nature and dynamics, both of which have a large *spiritual* component.

What Penitence and Absolution do not eliminate are the consequences of our words and deeds upon others. If that could happen, it would destroy both Divine Justice and our sense of responsibility for what we do—the pattern of cause and effect between what we do and what we receive from life. Rather what they can help do, by bringing the Divine Light to *Hod* and *Netzach* respectively, is to alter our state of consciousness, to change our sense of perspective and our attitudes— our perception, definition, and reaction—especially towards external events. Together Penitence and Absolution transform and expand our consciousness by raising its vibratory rates, unclogging the psychospiritual Centers, and raising the Light and Energy level of our aura—which makes us *see and react* in a very different way to whatever happens to us in the external world. It is here that we find the old saying of the Roman poets "Things are not bad, it is *how we think about them*" coming true and being realized in our own consciousness and experience.

Thus if we do evil, if we cause suffering, if we violate cosmic laws, we will, always and inexorably, reap the consequences of what we, ourselves, have set in motion. Through the proper use of the Sacraments of Penitence and Absolution, however, we can always and at any time, no matter what we have done, change our consciousness and attitude. We can *experience* God's forgiveness and inpouring Grace and Light, which will, literally, *resurrect* our mental clarity, our emotional sensitivity and ability to feel deeply and positively, and the energies and control of our will. These, together, will immediately raise us out of our depression and enable us to perceive meaning and purpose in all that happens to us, no matter how bad things seem to be. These will also enable us to perceive the loving and protecting "hand of God" behind us and with us even in the very worst situations. And, since it is not what is done to us but rather how we perceive, define, and react to what happens to us that is a really essential factor, Penitence and Absolution make a tremendous difference in our lives. They can give us a new sense of identity and direction, new courage and hope, and a fuller sense of the *joie de vivre*.

At this point we can say that Penitence and Absolution in no way contradict God's Justice, violate natural or spiritual laws, nor can they in any way demoralize a human being by disrupting the cause and effect relationship of words, deeds, and human relationships. Rather, they crown and fulfill them by adding God's Mercy and by making possible a channel through which Divine Light can flow into our hearts, minds, and wills on all levels of our being and consciousness. This will restore inwardly the disrupted harmony and alignment of the parts to the Whole. For when God is with us ("Emmanuel"), when the soul is filled with Light and Grace, and when the living and conscious communion with the Divine is preserved in our consciousness, then we can indeed walk through the "valley of death and damnation" without fear of losing our inner peace and serenity. It is then, and only then, that we can truly say: "*Nihil Humanum Alienum a me Puto*—nothing that is human is alien or foreign to me." This means perceiving meaning and purpose, and the hand of God together with his Love and Protection, *in all human experiences*, with no exception—which is the true sign of wisdom and spiritual maturity.

In these two Sacraments, moreover, we can find one aspect of the *Panacea*, the "universal medicine" which official science has not yet found and does not even believe exists. This universal medicine can soothe and relieve much human suffering and many ailments, the greatest of which is *depression*, the true modern epidemic for which there is neither effective remedy nor even an adequate understanding of its nature, causes, and dynamics. For these, as we have said, are not only physical, psychological, and social, but also *spiritual*. The implications of this are that the remedy for this ailment of our times must be psychological, social, moral, *and* spiritual, and not simply a pill or a good word!

At the practical level, the fundamental question is: How do we achieve Penitence and how can we receive Absolution? What are their psychospiritual dynamics? These are explained in the Rite of Confession and its operation. The Eastern Orthodox Church and the Roman Catholic Church link the two Sacraments of Penitence and Absolution in the Rite of Confession. Here is the exoteric side of the Orthodox Rite of Confession:

"When a Christian falls into sin after Baptism, he separates himself from Church and forfeits the right to partake of holy Communion. But there remains to him the possibility of cleansing himself again from sins and being saved; for Jesus Christ gave to His disciples the power of remitting the sins of those who repented and of again joining them to His Church. This power of the Apostles transmitted to their successors, the Bishops, and these again empowered the Priests to hear the repentant confessions of the faithful and to remit their sins in the name of Jesus Christ, if they judged that their repentance was sincere and strong. This remission of sins is given in the Sacrament of Penitence and Absolution which is, therefore, called a 'second

Baptism' and the office in which it is performed is called the 'Rite of Confession.'

"Here the Christian who confesses his sins before the entire Church or her representative, and sues for pardon, receives absolution from the Priest, and at the same moment is invisibly absolved by Christ Himself. Hence the rite of Confession consists of three acts: prayers for the remission of sins; confession of sins before the Priest (or Christ Himself); and absolution from sins in the name of Jesus Christ. After hearing the preliminary prayers, the penitent, standing before the Icon of the Savior, confesses his sins to the Priest, concealing nothing, making no excuses for his transgressions, and then asks for pardon and absolution. After confession, he kneels and bows his head. The Priest then prays that the Lord may forgive the penitent's sins and join him to His Holy Church, covers his head with the Stole in token that he, the Priest, through the grace of God, has the power to remit sins in the Name of Jesus Christ, blesses him, and utters the words of absolution: 'Our Lord and God, Jesus Christ, by His grace and the bountifulness of His loving kindness, forgives thee, N., all thy transgressions; and I, an unworthy Priest, by His power which is given unto me, forgive thee and absolve thee from all sins, in the name of the Father, and of the Son and of the Holy Spirit, Amen.' With these words the grace of the Holy Spirit descends into the soul of the penitent and cleanses it of sins, so that he, by the grace of God, goes from the presence of the Priest a pure and holy man."

Because he only receives absolution of sins who, repenting of them, profoundly regrets having committed them and firmly determines to abstain from them in the future, such repentance necessitates a period of preparation. During this time the Christian lays aside all worldly preoccupations and devotes himself to *fasting, prayer,* and *meditation on his soul,* and to better do all this, seeks *solitude* and keeps away from all amusements and distracting things. The length of time of preparation depends on how long a time is needed in altering, deepening, and heightening one's state of consciousness and in opening one's Heart Center to God's Grace.

The Rite of Confession, on the esoteric, inner side, connects and brings about Penitence and Absolution, by requiring a *human effort* and a *downpouring* of Grace, or Divine Light. The human effort can be seen as representing the male and the psychological aspect of this process, while the downpouring of Divine Light represents the female and the spiritual aspect of the same process. Here, the priest is the *external channel* and the visible representative of the Divine Spark, the Christ within who helps to *facilitate* both Penitence and Absolution. When a human being grows in Faith and in spiritual awareness, and when he knows how to do it, he can also bring about the same process without the external help of the Priest.

The purpose of human effort is to open up the doors of one's Soul and of the psychospiritual Centers to the inrush of the Divine Light and the spiritual Energies. It consists, specifically, in altering, deepening, and heightening one's state of consciousness and opening one's Heart Center to God's Grace, which can then *pour into* and activate, cleanse and unclog, *Hod* and *Netzach*, thus affecting *Tipphereth*—which, in turn, brings about a true *metanoia* or mental, emotional, and volitional transformation. The downpouring of Grace consists, essentially, in the invocation, activation, and extension of the Divine Light—which we now become aware of and perceive—into our soul and psyche and, particularly, into the appropriate psychospiritual Centers that are to be affected and activated. By way of his *Ordination*, the priest is an *unconscious* channel and transformer for the Divine Light. But every human being, after he undergoes Initiation, can become a *conscious* channel for the Divine Light. The most important factor to invoke, activate and extend the Divine Light is FAITH.

From the esoteric viewpoint, Penitence and Absolution, as carried out by the Rite of Confession, involve three major elements. These the Orthodox Church calls "prayers for the remission of sins, or preparation," "confession of sins or Penitence," and "Absolution, or the remission of sins itself."

a. *Preparation and prayers for the remission of sins*: This first phase in the psychospiritual aspects of this process is not as simple as may appear at first sight. For it involves an actual alternation and expansion of one's consciousness. This is to be able to look at one's life, words and deeds, from a different and higher perspective than one did before. The traditional steps and factors which are involved here are:

—*Seek solitude*, either in the external way (from people and activities) or in the internal way (freeing the mind, the heart, and the will from all worldly concerns), or in both ways if this is possible.

—*Practice fasting* on the physical level (abstain from bad food, activities, and human relationships that are stress-inducing), on the emotional level (abstain from negative emotions and desires), on the mental level (abstain from negative thoughts, ideas, and anxiety-producing subjects), and on the spiritual level (refrain from doing the will of the human self and from feeding your ego, accepting, unconditionally and with joy, God's Will).

—*Pray regularly* to deepen the relationship we have with God, that in our seeking we can find and be given what is necessary to know him and love him and do his Will in our lives. We know from Christ's instruction on prayer in the Gospel of St. Luke (11: 5–8) that we must persist, keep knocking on that door until He is roused to answer even our most inopportune request for the "three loaves." But once received these bring to the penitent healing, transformation, and resurrection on many levels.

    —*Meditate* on the course of your life, daily events, what you are and what you want to become; on the nature of your soul and of your destiny, and on what God asks of you at this point in your life.

    b. *Confession of sins or Penitence*: This second major phase can get under way only after a major alteration of consciousness and a new perspective have been achieved, and when the penitent feels that the Divine Light and his inspiration are working within him. The opening of the Heart Center and the experience of deep and genuine *contrition* for having lost one's higher state of consciousness and one's harmony with the spiritual Self (and, consequently, one's inner peace and serenity) are particularly important at this point. Then, and only then, can one "confess his sins," either externally to the Priest or internally to the Christ within, by going through a systematic *examination of conscience*—from the standpoint of the *new perspective and higher state of consciousness*—carefully analyzing and evaluating what one has done and has not done since he either lost his higher state of consciousness and harmony with God or last went through such an exercise. To simply review what one has done, or not done, mechanically complying with the Church's expectations of what is right and what is wrong, without a *transformation of consciousness* and a genuine *contrition* bringing with it the firm resolve to "live a more holy life," will not open the doors of the soul and of the Heart Center to the downpouring of Divine Light in the final phase of Absolution.

    c. *Absolution and the remission of sins*: This is the final and culminating phase of this whole process, wherein God's Grace, or the Divine Light, now really *manifests* and answers the "call from below" of the penitent, healing, transforming, and resurrecting him on many levels. This will affect, in particular, his mental, emotional, and volitional processes. It will, literally, transform his state of consciousness and inner being, which will enable him to see all the external events and happenings in a *new light* and as part of God's Plan—as being integrated in the human destiny one has come here to realize.

    At this point, the penitent will either stand or kneel before the Priest, before an Icon of the Savior, or before a mental image of the Savior, confessing his sins, verbalizing his sins, guilt, insecurities, and fears, as well as his hopes, aspirations, and ideals, and asking for Absolution. The priest will then direct him to fulfill some task or discipline, which may demand a sacrifice or which otherwise can facilitate the transformation in process particularly for that individual. This is the traditional penance, which corresponds to the vow (giving one's word to do this or that, or not to do this or that) that the aspirant to the Mysteries knows will bring down the blessing and help of the spiritual forces. This is because if one wishes to receive, one must give, and because "Heaven must be paid" with its own coin, just as an earthly physician must be paid for his help and services. Moreover, this *penance* or *vow* strengthens and recharges the will, compels one to improve his life on the human-psychological level. In ascribing a penance, or taking a vow, the wisdom of the spiritual father and his knowledge of his spiritual son is very important, as is the aspirant's level of maturity and judgment in choosing the appropriate vow. For, once taken, the vow *must be carried out* or one will find oneself even worse off than before, having forfeited one's honor and integrity.

The priest then prays for the penitent, having put his stole over his head, symbolizing the transmission of Light and Energy, the "Pillar of Light" going from the Head to the Heart Center, and from God to man. Finally, the priest will vibrate the words of absolution which actually bring down the Power of the Holy Spirit into the soul and psyche of the penitent. In esoteric terms, we can say the Holy Spirit then flows down the internal Tree of Life, and in so doing affects and enlivens *Hod* and *Netzach*. This has a cleansing effect, unclogs them, and activates them so that they can again receive and transmit the spiritual energies in the psyche and aura of the penitent in an unbroken and undistorted way.

When this happens, the Holy Spirit has vivified the penitent, and he is "baptized" again; his aura and Tree of Life are purified and cleansed, and the connection between the human and the spiritual worlds can be experienced anew. At that moment, the penitent is pure and holy within and without, but with the consequences of his previous words and acts, and the lessons and tests of his life before his eyes, now seen in light of this transformation. This state of being is the part of the kingdom of Heaven we are admonished to seek above all else, in which we see all things in their right place and position. It is what has also been called a "state of Grace," enabling us to pass all the tests and trials of life, and to learn the lessons of the earthly pilgrimage. Then the tests and trials of life are made easy and light.

A final passage in the exoteric text of Penitence that has profound esoteric meanings is: "Whatsoever ye shall loose on earth shall be loosed in heaven" (Matt. 18:18). This passage applies not only to sacred privileges bestowed upon the Priesthood by Christ himself, but also to what the soul of each human being accomplishes or fails to accomplish during his earthly pilgrimage. For spiritual regeneration, self-realization, and its ultimate end in the conscious Communion and Union with God is to be accomplished during out earthly pilgrimage. This is one of the reasons why we do come back many times, that is, until we can accomplish our destiny and realize God's Plan for each one of us individually and for humanity collectively.

Thus, Initiation, Sainthood, self-knowledge, and self-mastery must be realized and achieved here on earth, in the incarnate state, and not in any of the discarnate states. Moreover, the "Church" of which the exoteric text speaks is not, esoterically speaking, solely the Orthodox Church, the Roman Catholic Church, or the neighborhood Temple or Church one belongs to. It is *also* the Inner Church, which can be found and entered only through an expanded state of consciousness that links us directly with Christ and with His Servants —other Initiates who have also attained this state of consciousness and of personal alignment with the Divine within and without. Lastly, it is not bishops or priests, as some may believe, who themselves remit sins and grant Absolution but, always and only, the Christ within . . . who may well work through different channels, both conscious and unconscious. The priest or bishop, however, can greatly facilitate the human and spiritual work involved in the process of Penitence and Absolution, especially if he himself has attained spiritual consciousness and is a holy and wise person!

Once more, I have found several deep insights in and share similar experience and conclusions with what Leadbeater discovered and described:

> Let us accept, then, the definition of sin or transgression as any thought, word or act which is not in harmony with God's Will for man—that is, evolution. Instead of progression it is transgression, not a movement forward with the evolutionary force, but across the line of its flow. That divine Will acts as a steady pressure upward and onward, and actually does produce in higher matter (even down to the etheric level) a sort of tension which can be described in words only as a tendency towards movement in a definite direction—the flowing of the spiritual stream. When a man's thoughts, words and actions are good, he lays himself more fully open to this influence; he is permeated by it and carried along by it.
>
> When he does or thinks evil, he wrenches himself away from the direction of this spiritual current, and thereby sets a definite strain in etheric, astral, and mental matter, so that he is no longer in harmony with nature, no longer a helping but a hindering force, a snag in the river of life. This strain, or cross-twist, almost entirely arrests his progress of the time, and renders it impossible for him to profit by all the impulses of good influence which are constantly rushing along the current of the stream of which we have spoken. Before he can do any real good for himself or anyone else, he must straighten out that distortion, and come into harmony with nature, and so be once more fully amenable to good influence, and be able to take advantage of the many and valuable aids which are so lavishly provided for him.

The various vehicles of man [his "energy bodies"] are not really separated in space, for the finer types of matter always interpenetrate the grosser. But looked at from below they give the impression of being one above the other, and also of being joined by innumerable fine wires or lines of fire. Every action which works against evolution puts an unequal strain on these—twists and entangles them. When a man goes badly wrong in any way the confusion becomes such that communication between the higher and lower bodies is seriously impeded; he is no longer his real self, and only the lower side of his character is able to manifest itself fully.

It must be clearly understood that in the long, slow course of evolution the natural forces are perfectly capable of righting his unfortunate condition of affairs. The steady pressure of the current will presently wear away the obstacles, but a period of many months or even years may elapse before the readjustment is fully effected, though earnest effort on the man's own part will somewhat shorten this period. But even then there is a certain tendency for the distortion to reassert itself.

It is therefore obviously to the man's interest that he should discover some more rapid method of regaining uniformity. Such a method the Church provides, for the power of straightening out this tangle in higher matter is one of those especially conferred upon a Priest at ordination . . .

But the Priest cannot perform this wonderful miracle of healing alone; he needs the co-operation of his patient. No one can force a man into harmony if he is persistently striving for disharmony; it is only "if we confess our sins" that "He is faithful and just to forgive our sins and cleanse us from all unrighteousness." It is requisite that the candidate be anxious to rise above the imperfections of nature, and to live the higher life . . . There is no doubt that the divine force which flows through the Priest when he pronounces the absolution does rush through that man's higher vehicles, combs the entanglement, and straightens the twisted lines until he is once more in perfect harmony with God's Will . . .

It must be clearly understood that the effect of absolution is strictly limited to the correction of the distortion above described. It reopens certain channels which have been to a large extent closed by evil thought or action; but it in no way counteracts the physical consequence of that action, nor does it obviate the necessity of restitution where wrong has been done . . .

The Sacrament puts man right with God; but it does not relieve him from the responsibility for his acts, nor in any way affect their physical consequence. It is a spiritual process, a loosening from the bondage of sin, a process of at-one-ment with the Higher Self, a restoration of the inner harmony of being which is disturbed by wrong-doing, so that the man can make a fresh effort towards righteousness, fortified by the uninterrupted flow of the divine power within. A man cannot escape the consequences of his misdeeds, though he can neutralize them by sowing fresh causes of a righteous kind.[12]

At this point in my life, I participate in the sacraments of Penitence and Absolution often. First and foremost, this is before going to

Communion or before engaging in advanced ritual or spiritual work. It is also when I get depressed, "lose myself," become confused or unhappy—realizing that the normal condition of a human being is that of being oneself, filled with life, anticipating the opportunities that present themselves, with joy and gratitude.

I learned firsthand through an interesting experience the importance of these sacraments and the role they can play in our lives. One day, I became aware that one of my business associates had "royally ripped me off"! As this realization dawned on me and the evidence became overwhelming, I became, in turn, very angry, depressed, and mad at myself for having let myself be taken. At that time, however, I had important things to do and realized that I could not afford to be mad, sad, or guilty because this would add insult to injury and harm me further, in the here and now, in terms of not doing what I was supposed to do. So, I used some techniques I had learned to redirect my attention to what I was doing and to let go of this unfortunate situation. But, I did not process it or resolve it; I merely shoved it into my unconscious and promptly forgot it.

A couple of days later, I was doing some deep spiritual work; at the appropriate time I began invoking the Divine Light and Fire, first to manifest it in my Head Center. As the Light and Fire began to fill my internal Tree of Life and its psychospiritual Center in my solar plexus, the image of the person who had "ripped me off" was formulated in my field of consciousness. At that point I felt an incredible anger surge through my being and flood my consciousness! Never, in my entire life, had I experienced anger in such an intense and powerful way. Had the person been there, I do not know what I would have done to him. But, fortunately, he was not there, and I discharged my anger by smashing the furniture of the room I was in . . . which also cost me a pretty penny. But, I learned a profound human and spiritual lesson that was well worth the money I lost and the trouble caused by the experience. Now I understood, *experientially*, the true meaning and function of Penitence and Absolution and the very harsh saying of St. Paul, "He who eats and drinks unworthily of the Body and Blood of the Lord, eats and drinks damnation"—which had long been an unresolved puzzle for me. The spiritual energies (the Light and Fire which engender Life) will vivify whatever they come in contact with, good or evil. Thus, before invoking them, it is most important to purify and reconsecrate oneself, for if any negative emotions, thoughts, complexes, and unfinished business remain, emotionally charged in the unconscious, they too will be vivified and intensified, greatly increasing their power and effects—for ourselves and for others, for which we are also responsible. This is why it was said in the Mystery Schools, "Unpurified and unconsecrated thou canst not approach the Holy Powers."

THE EUCHARIST OR COMMUNION

Of all the Sacraments, Communion, or the Eucharist, is unquestionably the central and most important, literally and figuratively the raised Chalice around which the other Sacraments array themselves. Each Sacrament is, ultimately, a Mystery for in each we experience the evolutionary meeting place between heaven and earth, matter and spirit, human effort and divine grace. Each has an organic connection and a sequence with the others, but Communion is the true center or core to which they all point. Why? Because in conscious Communion man and God, the finite and the Infinite, meet and merge. Here, when we can deeply experience and live this Sacrament in full consciousness, we are reconnected with the very Source and Essence of all that is—Life, Love, Wisdom, Reality—including our own being, our true Self. There are many sources to support this realization, but three, in particular I believe, best represent the others. First, let me quote a contemporary contemplative:

> Usually our discussion of the spiritual-psychological journey is in terms of consciousness and its developmental milestones—transcendence of the ego, transformation, realization of the true Self or Unitive state, and so on. This approach is largely ecumenical because these stages of consciousness are common to everyone regardless of religious tradition, culture or background. Within each tradition, however, there is a distinctive way of travel not generally shared by others and thus, for the Catholic, the distinctive path of realization and revelation is the Eucharist. Not only is the Eucharist central to the belief and practice of the church but the fountainhead of its mystical, contemplative dimension—the alpha and omega of the ultimate reflection of Christ . . . The Eucharist embraces all dimensions of Christ and offers a dimension of His Godhead not accessible from a purely historical perspective. Then too, the Eucharistic Christ offers a profound dimension of contemplative experience and insight wherein the unfolding revelation of Christ is equally an unfolding of ourselves, our own human mystery and destiny.
>
> One of the first things I became aware of, however, was that for some time after communion there was a "difference"—or that some difference had been made—but that as the day got under way this difference imperceptibly wore off or faded away. Initially, it was impossible to put my finger on this subtle change or explain it in any way, but through sheer repetition of the experience I one day discovered its true nature—the difference was as simple as silence . . .
>
> My interpretation was that the Eucharist was imperceptibly drawing me into its own silent state, for I realized that the living Christ was wordless, formless, motionless—silence itself, and that it was asking me to make the match or to become as silent as it was silent.

Thus the silence seemed to be two things at once, on the one side it was the silence itself, and on the other it was myself—or my self increasingly being silenced. This experiential phenomenon of the Eucharist—silence —became the singular consistent phenomenon of my journey . . .

Gradually it dawned on me that this journey was not only a gradual revelation of God, but equally a revelation of myself, or aspects of myself I never knew I had prior to the divine silence. Like two sides of a coin the Eucharist was revealing two things at once: on the one side, myself; on the other side, Itself; and so too, the silence was two things at once, the positive and the negative of self. Thus the ever deepening path of the Eucharist was a path of self-knowledge and divine-knowledge wrapped into one. Initially, I had not planned on this somehow; I had the notion that the self would quietly be phased out . . . whereas I learned (so long as the journey is in progress) the divine is only revealed in proportion as self-knowing is revealed. Thus through the journey the true nature of self is revealed along with the true nature of the divine. Even at the definitive end of the journey, what is ultimately revealed is the true nature of the divine as well as the true nature of the self . . .

After this it dawned on me what it really meant to "follow" Christ; it meant to follow his most profound experiences of God, His own spiritual journey and not merely the externals of His life—limited as they are to historical circumstances and mentality. Thus everything He said and did came out of His interior experiential life with God which was the source of His external public life—His words, insights, and behaviors. What He wished for us was that we too discover the inner source and from this same source work out our own historical life—manifest the source in whatever circumstances we might find ourselves.[13]

Geoffrey Hodson, from his own clairvoyant perceptions, explains:

The Celebration of the holy Eucharist is a ceremonial and sacramental method of awakening, quickening, and releasing the powers of Divinity in every form of life. Properly performed and producing its ideal results, it evokes the powers of the Blessed Trinity hidden deeply in every form within its sphere of influence, in the priests, the servers, the incarnate and discarnate congregation, the holy angels, and the nature spirits, in the material buildings and the furniture, and even in the natural surroundings outside the church.

From a purely human point of view the Mass might be regarded as a method of meditation, by means of which the worshiper passes progressively into more and more intimate union with the God within himself, and with the second or Wisdom Aspect of the Divine Trinity which is the Son. This process reaches its culmination in the reception of the Blessed Sacrament when, in His most divine Love, the Lord Christ, made manifest in the Host, becomes one with the communicant . . .

Great floods of power and blessing are also liberated upon the world every time the Mass is performed. Every being who is touched by them is blessed, and experiences an awakening of the consciousness of the Divine within . . .

In the normal individual the power of the highest spiritual principle, that of the divine will in man, very rarely, if ever, reaches the personality. The reason for this is that the Christ-consciousness or divine love in man is not sufficiently awakened and developed at this period of human evolution to convey that power (whence, the "esoteric" root of "human sins" or "Mistakes"). In the services of the church, and especially at Holy Communion, however, our Lord in His tender love and care for mankind draws so near to, and unifies Himself so closely with, His people, that He Himself becomes the Christ principle actively awake in them. By this "at-one-ment" He provides them with a vicarious contact with those highest spiritual worlds which are normally beyond their reach. This hastens the time when the Christ-child shall be born in the human heart and makes immediately possible a descent of power and blessing from the very highest and most divine aspects of human nature . . .

If we examine these results (of partaking of the Eucharist) from the human and angelic point of view, we find that their most direct effect is to arouse the spiritual Self in each one into increased self-conscious activity and life . . .

Few men, at the present stage of evolution, are very wide awake at the spiritual levels of consciousness. The Mass helps us to stir in our egoic dreams and to begin to express down here the lofty powers enshrined in the "shining Augoeides" of man. The ultimate purpose of this wonderful help which the Lord has Himself designed for us is that we, ourselves, should reach that state of "the measure of the stature of the fullness of Christ," and no longer need outward aids. Then we shall follow His most glorious example and in our turn become Saviors of men.[14]

To conclude, let us see what another remarkable clairvoyant, Charles Leadbeater, writes concerning the Eucharist:

The Eucharist, as we know it, is not altogether new. It was celebrated in some older religions but has now reached a more perfect form. It was found in Mithraism. Bread and wine and salt were used, but the form of their rite is somewhat vague. There is a secret ceremony in the Egyptian Mysteries in which consecrated bread—a sort of cake—was given, but never to the general public; only to a very small and especially prepared group something like a Masonic Lodge. As soon as a man partook of this sacrament, the others bowed to him, saying "Thou are Osiris."

Our present scheme calls for a church in every village so that many points of radiation are found to be spread over the country. It is a beautiful thing to realize that people are taking part in this great work although they may not fully understand what they are doing . . .

It [the Mass] is undoubtedly a very great help and stimulus for those of us who partake in it, and especially if we communicate. Just as it is a spiritual sun shining forth from the altar and pouring its rays upon us, so we may be spiritual suns for the rest of the day to those among whom we go. We bear the Christ along with us when we have thus received Him into ourselves; we radiate His special influence, and so we are doing His work among our fellow creatures.

It is the greatest of all works that we can do for our fellow men. Here we join together to pour forth our love and devotion to Christ, and in return comes the response. If we send up our prayer, there comes down the flood of grace from on high and so, by joining in this act, we are calling down from heaven a special outpouring of spiritual force and blessing. That which is returned to us is far greater than that which we give, and yet it is in proportion to it . . . For to every one there comes a tenfold, a thirtyfold, a hundredfold return; according to the strength of devotion which he himself puts into it is the amount of the response which comes to him. So a greater congregation is a greater hope to the world than a smaller. But, most assuredly, few or many, the help is always poured out not only upon us but upon the whole neighborhood and the city in which we live.

This is the chief reason why we should join in this most holy ceremony, in order that there may be more of this great spiritual outpouring to flow over our surroundings, to help and strengthen every person in them who is capable of responding . . .

The Host does not change physically. The physical wafer remains a physical wafer composed of flour and water even after the Consecration. But it is just as truly a *vehicle of Christ,* just as truly ensouled by Him and filled by His mighty power *as the body He wore in Palestine.* It has not changed its physical character; it is still the same on the physical plane, but what *lies behind or "stands behind" it on the higher planes has been changed.*

The Christ Himself now "stands behind it" instead of the type of higher matter which normally does. The original substance has gone but the accidents remain the same . . .

If you examine the meaning of the original Latin word you will find that the "substance" is not the outside form at all, but *the reality within.* That which stands underneath or behind physical appearance is the real substance. Behind every physical object is what is called its counterpart; there is astral matter and mental matter; there is matter of higher planes running right up to the Logos Himself. All this lies behind the wafer, the piece of unleavened bread. What is done at the moment of the consecration is not to change the physical bread but to substitute for the life behind it a *ray of the Life of Christ Himself.* And so the Christ is truly there upon His altar manifesting Himself in an earthly form, not of flesh but of bread. So also with the chalice. There is also His Life manifesting itself, but the outer form of wine is unchanged even though the substance within has been put aside in order that He may pour Himself down to the physical plane for the helping and the strengthening of His children.[15]

Having set forth the thoughts of some writers who share my own views and experiences regarding the Eucharist, let us now continue, though not as before in first explicating an exoteric view and then an esoteric one, because truly we come here to the Communion of the two, where all that promotes division or seeks to divide does indeed "rend His garments." Thus, we proceed here, as the Divine Light will guide us, by seeking the wholeness of vision so demanded by the subject itself, gathering together what the exoteric tradition and the esoteric can offer to that end. Let us start with what is given from the Orthodox catechism:

"What is Communion? It is a Sacrament in which the believer, under the forms of bread and wine, partakes of the very Body and Blood of Christ for the healing of soul and of body, for the remission of sins, and for Life everlasting. How was this Sacrament instituted? Jesus Christ immediately before His passion consecrated it for the first time, exhibiting in it an anticipation and lively image of His sufferings for our salvation; and after having administered it to the

Apostles, He gave them at the same time a commandment ever after to perpetuate this Sacrament. This Sacrament forms the chief and most essential part of the Divine Liturgy. The Divine Liturgy, in which the Elements are consecrated, must always take place in a Temple on the *antimense* which must have been consecrated by a Bishop. Why is the table on which the Sacrament of Communion consecrated called the *throne*? Because on it Jesus Christ, as King, is mystically present. What is the general order of the Liturgy? First, the Elements are prepared for the Sacrament; secondly, the faithful are prepared for the Sacrament, and thirdly, the Sacrament itself is consecrated.

"What is the name for that part of the liturgy in which the Elements are prepared for the Sacrament? *Proskomide*. What is the meaning of the word *Proskomide*? Offertory. Why is this name given to the first part of the liturgy? From the custom of the primitive Christians to offer in the Church bread and wine for the celebration of the Sacrament. On the same account this bread is called *prosphora*, which means *oblation*. In what consists the Offertory? In this, that which the mention of the prophecies and types, and partly also because of the events themselves, relating to the birth and suffering of Jesus Christ, a portion is taken from the prosphora for use in the Sacrament, and likewise a portion of wine mixed with water is poured off into the holy chalice, while the Celebrant makes commemoration of the whole Church, honors the glorified Saints, prays for the living and the departed, especially for the ruling powers, and for those who, of their own faith and zeal, have brought prosphorae, or oblations.

"The bread should be leavened, pure, wheaten bread. What is meant when it is said that the bread or loaf which is strictly to be used for the Communion is only *one*? It signifies, as the Apostle explains, that we, being many, are *one* bread, and *one body*; for we are all partakers of that *one bread* (1 Cor. 10:17). Why is the bread, when prepared for Communion, called the *lamb*? Because it is the figure of Jesus Christ suffering, as was in the Old Testament the *Paschal Lamb*. What is the Paschal Lamb? The Lamb which the Israelites, by God's command, killed and ate in memory of their deliverance from destruction in Egypt. Why is the wine for the Sacrament of Communion mixed with water? Because the whole of this celebration is ordered so as to figure forth the suffering of Christ; and when He suffered, there flowed from His pierced side blood and water.

"What name has that part of the Liturgy in which the faithful are prepared for the Sacrament? The ancients called it the *Liturgy of the Catechumens*; because, besides baptized communicants, the catechumens also, who are prepared for Baptism, and the penitents, who are not admitted to Communion, may be present at it. With what does this part of the Liturgy begin? With the Blessing, or glorification of the kingdom of the most Holy Trinity. In what consists this part of the Liturgy? In prayers, singing, and reading from the books of the Apostles, and from the Gospel. How does it end? With the order given to the catechumens to go out and leave the Church. What is the name for that part of the liturgy, in which the Sacrament itself is celebrated and consecrated? *The Liturgy of the Faithful*; because the faithful only, that is the baptized, have their right to be present at this Service. What is the essential act in this part of the Liturgy? The utterance of the words which Jesus Christ spake instituting the Sacrament: 'Take, eat, this is My Body; Drink ye all of it, for this is My Blood, of the New Testament' (Matt. 26:26–28). After this the Invocation of the Holy Spirit and the blessing of the Gifts, that is, the bread and the wine, which have been offered. Why is this so essential? Because at the moment of this act, the bread and wine are changed, or transubstantiated, into the very *Body of Christ*, and into the very *Blood of Christ*.

"What does the word *transubstantiation* mean? In the exposition of the faith by the Eastern Patriarchs, it is said that the word *transubstantiation* is not to be taken to define the manner in which the bread and wine are changed into the Body and Blood of the Lord; for this none can understand but God; but only this much is signified, that the bread truly, really, and substantially becomes the very Body of the Lord, and the wine the very Blood of the Lord. What should we remember at that time in the Liturgy when they make the Procession with the Gifts from the table of preparation to the altar? Jesus Christ going to suffer voluntarily, as a victim to the slaughter, while more than 12 legions of Angels were ready around to guard Him as their King. What should we remember at that moment of the consecration of the Sacrament, and while the clergy are communicating within the altar? The mystical supper of Jesus Christ Himself with His Apostles, His suffering, death, and burial. What is set forth after this, by the drawing back of the veil, the opening of the royal doors, and the appearance of the Holy Gifts? The appearance of Jesus Christ Himself after His resurrection. What is figured by the last showing of the Holy Gifts to the people, after which they are hidden from view? The ascension of Jesus Christ into heaven. Will the use of the Sacrament of Holy Communion ever continue in the true Church of Christ? Yes, it will until His second coming. According to the words of the Apostle Paul: 'For as oft as ye eat this bread, and drink this cup, ye do show forth the Lord's death, till He come' (1 Cor. 11:26)."

There can be no attempt at what for other subjects may be called "completeness" when we are speaking of this most profound of

Mysteries, for we are faced again and again with the inadequacy of human expression and the limits of human understanding. For we indeed here seek to approach the very Throne of God, as we have heard described above, before which the highest seraphim tremble with a holy fear, and veil their faces through respect. What can be attempted here is to cast our net in gathering further thoughts from both the exoteric and esoteric traditions as I have experienced and lived them.

Communion is the greatest and most important of all Sacraments and Mysteries. It is the center or core towards which all the other Sacraments are leading and in which they culminate. It is also the deepest and most intense of all human experiences, the ultimate goal and experience towards which all genuine religions and yogas are working—the communion of man with God leading to the union of God with man. Thus, consciously or unconsciously, directly or indirectly, all genuine self-actualization and self-realization disciplines, ultimately, aim at communion, at the Communion of man with God and thus man with his true Self, with the Ultimate Reality, with the Essence of Consciousness, Love, and Life.

As Evelyn Underhill beautifully puts in her own words, but quoting St. Augustine as well:

> The experience of the Presence and the reception of the Heavenly Food—which together constitute the primitive Christian mystery—represent the loving movement of God towards His creatures. The historical memorial commemorates the way in which that act of Divine Charity was accomplished; the Incarnation and its costs. In his graceful adoration and his oblation, man makes his small acknowledgement of the prevenient self-giving of the Holy; and unites his response on the one hand with the worship of the whole created order, on the other with that perfect sacrifice of Calvary where the *divine and human love meet*.
>
> For throughout the whole action, the seen and the unseen, the sensible and the spiritual, the historical and the eternal interpenetrate. The Oblation is ours and yet it is His. In the words of the Sanctus we unite our adoration, our abasement, and our self-offering with the young Isaiah standing awestruck in the Temple, and with the angels who stand forever in the Uncreated Light. In the act of communion, as St. Augustine so forcibly reminded his flock, we who are part of Christ's Mystical Body, receive our share in the Body's life. "If then you are the Body of Christ, and His members, then that which is on the altar, is the mystery of ourselves. Receive the mystery of ourselves.". . .
>
> [If] Christianity be indeed the disclosure of the eternal God to men, it follows that the Eucharistic principle—the free offering and consecration of the natural life, that it may become the sensible vehicle of the divine Life—must radiate beyond its ritual expression; gradually penetrating and transforming all of the actions of humanity . . .

The Christian hope of the future is that this, the true meaning and message of the Incarnation, will come to be more deeply understood: and the demand on man's worshiping love and total self-offering, will receive a more complete response—a response stretching upward in awestruck contemplation to share that adoring vision of the Principle which is "the inheritance of the saints in light," and downwards and outwards in loving action, to embrace and so transform the whole world . . . For it will be recognized as the ritual sign of our deepest relation with Reality, and so of the mysterious splendor of our situation and our call: the successive life of man freely offered in oblation, and the abiding life of God in Christ received, not for our own sakes, but in order to achieve that transfiguration of the whole universe, that shining forth of the splendor of the Holy, in which the aim of worship shall be fulfilled.[16]

From an esoteric viewpoint, a development of awareness or the evolution of consciousness is pointed out in all things spiritual; thus, with respect to Communion a progression of conscious awareness can be seen where, in the initial stages, there may be found the case of a Christian going to Communion routinely, but experiencing very little (by his or her own estimation), and not being conscious of any noticeable change. The other end of the spectrum is no less than the achievement of the Holy Grail, the conscious Communion of the participant with Christ Himself—experienced within as the Divine Spark. Between these two poles stands a long continuum of growing awareness, personal awakening, and enlivened participation which leads deeply within to more truly experience the "without," indeed to recognize, ultimately, their inseparability.

The Body of Christ and the Blood of Christ are subjects which arouse in the aspirant the most profound feelings of devotion and love, increasingly so as his or her path in the Mysteries evolves. The Seer or Initiate has prepared himself or herself in the ways of Initiation to see with new eyes, hear with new ears, feel with a pure heart, and live deeply into each part of the Mass. Thus, in the Chalice of the Holy Blood can be perceived Spiritual Love, the cup of our salvation, offered to us once again in Communion. It is apprehended as well as the Divine Fire. In the Bread and in the Body of Christ is Spiritual Consciousness, all that was and is given to us by our loving God that we may come in time to know Him. And this is apprehended as the Divine Light. These together engender Spiritual Life and Spiritual Will, aligning and integrating human will with the Will of God. This, moreover, is also the culminating experience of all valid Mysteries and Initiations: to consciously commune with the Divine and to become transformed by the Divine.

The Orthodox Church explicitly states that Communion has three basic functions: to help with the healing of soul and of body, to bring about the remission of sins, and to help one achieve, by degrees, Life everlasting.

a. *To bring about the healing of soul and of body*: One of the greatest gifts of the Eucharist is, indeed, in bringing about the full healing of the mind and of the body. Here we experience the *Panacea* contained within the cup of the Holy Grail which is effected by the inflow of the Divine Light energizing and integrating all the cells and organs through which it manifests. From the loftiest of spiritual planes, it flows down to us, first through the mental plane, bringing a new perspective and a cognitive transformation which enables us to see, clearly and distinctly, and to understand things which, before, were confused or misapprehended. From the Mental Plane, it then flows throughout the Emotional Plane where it transforms our emotions from negative into positive, reactivating the Heart Center. Finally, from the Emotional Plane it flows to and fills the Physical Plane, having first enlivened and clarified the Etheric, bringing additional energy and life so that the body can harness its own inner resources to bring about physical healing. In this way can Communion be experienced as the most powerful, effective, and comprehensive of medicines, the universal medicine of the ancients and the New Medicine of the New Covenant.

b. *The remission of sins*: Most diseases and problems are the inevitable results of causes which we have ourselves set in motion, and for which we are responsible; hence, nothing ever happens by chance, hazard, or bad luck. The remission of sins, in this context, involves dealing not only with the removal of *symptoms* in the body and psyche, but with the removal of the *cause* of the disease or problem—which always implies a *change in consciousness* (attitude) *and deeds* (behavior). With the inestimable gift of the Eucharist we are given a means of illumination, the possibility of insight and true understanding as to the *why*, the cause, meaning, and purpose of various events. This can bring a whole and permanent healing. This illuminating insight allows us to pull the sword of truth out of the *Philosopher's Stone*.

c. *The achievement of Life everlasting*: After the healing of soul and body, after the insight and illumination that comes with the true remission of sins, the final and highest experience of Communion is achieved; this as with all the preparatory stages proceeds in most cases by degrees of awareness. Spiritually speaking, Life everlasting is simply *conscious immortality*, or our becoming aware that we are spiritual, immortal beings, true Sons and Daughters of God! This is the epiphany of the eternal now; it is "Thy kingdom come" in the present moment; and it is experiencing ourselves as transcendent beings in nature, as spiritual beings, first and foremost, who may, through grace and striving, in time, realize the timeless merit of taking our place before the Throne of God and, with the heavenly choirs, raising our voices in everlasting praise and grateful love.

We are told in Genesis that with the Fall man went from immortality, sinlessness, and happiness to mortality, sinfulness, and suffering. To achieve Life eternal, or consciousness of the eternal Life we regain through the life, death, and resurrection of the New Adam, Jesus Christ, is the final goal and destiny of humanity, as it is that of all human and spiritual training and growth—once union with God has been realized. To partake of the Body and Blood of Jesus Christ in Communion is to take within us His Life which is eternal. Moreover, we can experience how the identification of Himself with life, "I am the way, the truth, and the life," extends itself throughout all time, past, present, and future; these are linked in time through the fulcrum that is the Sacrifice of Golgotha, central in history as the Eucharist is central to all the Mysteries; when death is overcome on the Cross, He who is the "Gate" opens, pouring forth Blood and Water to renew and redeem the earth on which they fall and all who stand or ever shall upon it; beyond death, in His Resurrection, this Gate now open reveals Itself as Eternal Life.

Partaking of Communion increasingly opens us to the manifold mysteries which no human tongue can speak, but which can be "tasted." The Blood and Water poured out upon the earth did once and for all change the earth; that bread we taste today is constituted differently out of the different earth from which it grows. The wine is new wine, grown in new earth, and this newness now exists inexhaustibly, rising up and overflowing the Holy Grail as the *Elixir Vitae*, the Fountain of Eternal Youth.

The Sacrament of the Eucharist was instituted by Jesus Christ during the Last Supper and is, as we have seen, intimately connected with His Passion. Yet it never did not exist, and witness to this is in the ancient Mysteries, as shown, for example, by Melchisedech, who comes with Bread and Wine. With the Sacrifice of Golgotha and the transformation and redemption of the earth, it became the Universal Sacrament, available not only to a "chosen people," in all senses of this word, both exoterical (historical) and within esoteric streams (those who had been prepared and guided in very strict and specialized ways), but now available also to all humanity.

Let us return to the general order or sequence of the liturgy in the Orthodox Church and its three basic parts: the preparation of the Elements, the preparation of the faithful, and the consecration of the Eucharist. From the spiritual viewpoint, Communion does indeed involve a threefold preparation: that of the Elements, which must be prepared and consecrated to bring the Divine Light and Fire *down upon them* so it can flow through them; that of the Priest or the channel that is used for the consecration; and, finally, that of the faithful, who must alter their consciousness, heighten their sensitivity and receptivity, and open their activated psychospiritual Centers to the Divine Light and Fire that they will receive through Communion itself. In this fashion, the exoteric and the esoteric aspects complement and complete each other.

a. *The preparation of the Elements culminating in their consecration*: The Elements, the bread, wine, and water, are the focal points through which the spiritual energies, the Divine Light and Fire, are mediated in the physical world. They are thus prepared in accordance with ancient custom. The first part of the liturgy, which is dedicated to this preparation, is called *Proskomide* or Offertory. Here, the prophecies and the events relating to the birth and suffering of Jesus Christ are spoken by the Officiant. If we bear in mind the ancient esoteric axiom "By Names and Images are all Powers awakened and reawakened," we can better understand the role of this first part of the Liturgy, wherein the Priest and the faithful are being slowly prepared and spiritually "purified and awakened."

A portion of the prosphora, or bread, and some of the wine and water are then put into the chalice while the Celebrant commemorates the Church, honors the Saints, prays for the living and the dead, for those who occupy positions of power in the nation, and for those who have asked to be remembered at this Eucharist. Here, a sympathetic and telepathic link and connection is forged between the Elements and various members of the Universal Church so that "in Christ" those who will partake of Communion can be linked, in a spiritual way, with many other persons. Remember what He said: "Where I am, there are My servants also." Here, the Communion of Saints is being reenacted and opened to all who would enter in.

When prepared for Communion, the bread is called the *lamb*, identifying Jesus Christ with the *Paschal Lamb* of the Israelites which was killed and eaten in memory of their deliverance from destruction in Egypt. The esoteric meaning of the word *Lamb* is "one who submits completely to the Divine Will without rebellion or holding back." This is, in fact, what Jesus Christ did with his sufferings and death on the Cross. This is what happens analogically when the consecrated bread becomes completely impregnated with and a channel for the Divine Light.

Why is the wine for Communion mixed with water? When the Body of Jesus was pierced with a spear and the Precious Blood and Water flowed forth, this Blood consecrated the earth, renewed it and transformed it as the planet of Love. It was also manifesting the way in which this evolution proceeds, which has been, is, and will be through suffering or a great love. Water as an element in the Mysteries is the vehicle for purification, and is especially connected with the Emotional Plane; it is also a natural element. The wine is connected with all man has made of himself, not of course without the help of God; rather than a natural element, it is the product of evolution, and in that it contains the forces of the ego, the human "I" and self-consciousness. Water is the channel for the emotional or astral forces, while wine is the channel for the spiritual forces. The water that is turned to wine at Cana, at the beginning of the ministry of Jesus Christ, thus recreates the evolutionary miracle of Creation and Evolution of human consciousness by Divine Consciousness and signifies a new step in that evolution. At the end of his ministry, in his most perfect Passion, the wine becomes the Blood of Life, uniting for all time in Communion both human and Divine Consciousness by an act of supreme Love. Thus, in the mixing of the water and the wine, we can experience the Mysteries of the Alpha and the Omega, the unity of dualities inherent in evolution, the beginning and the end of Creation incarnate in the present and Presence of Jesus Christ.

b. *The preparation of the faithful and of the Priest or Officiant*: This is the part of the Liturgy which the ancients called the *Liturgy of the Catechumens*. This part begins with the blessing and glorification of the Kingdom of the Holy Trinity which moves us from the twofoldness of the water and wine, the Alpha and the Omega, to the threefoldness of the Father, Son, and Holy Spirit. In this we are reminded of the Cross of Light within us and the Centers of our being which lie on it, the Head, the Heart, and the Shoulder Centers, through which Divine Grace and Light can flow, suffusing our auras and consciousness. The Liturgy of the Catechumens ends with the order given to the Catechumens to leave the Temple, which again signifies the stages of Initiation, that one can consciously be readied and prepared, and this on the different planes of consciousness, the etheric, astral, and mental levels, in the reception of Communion. Such preparation, whether exoteric or esoteric, aims at insuring that this Sacrament is approached as a conscious experience. This occurred naturally when Christianity was still more a Path of Spiritual Initiation than a religion in which *direct personal and conscious experience* is substituted by *doctrinal and ritual conformity*, and a mere mental acceptance and automatic repetition of sacred formulas and "dogmas".

In this part of the Liturgy, prayers are said together with the reading of the books of the Old Testament, the Apostles, and of the Gospel, and the singing of songs. These prayers, readings, and songs all begin this process of preliminary training and work; here Christ is working as the Word, the Logos. "In the beginning was the Word," as St. John's Gospel opens. And this Word brings Light into the darkness, so we can feel how, out of the "darkness" of our normal consciousness, something begins to light up within us. In fact, this is exactly what happens in the next part of the Liturgy, which is the true core. "To make Gold one must have Gold" says an old alchemical proverb, and here the Light lit within us, however this is represented (as one's Tree of Life, as the Cross) and on whatever levels of consciousness it manifests within, calls to Light. Light calls to Light. The conscious experience of the descent of the Light is normally dependent upon having done some preliminary work to make the full process possible.

c. *The Liturgy of the Faithful*: This is the heart and culmination of the whole, around which all prayers, rites, and ceremonies revolve. The Elements (the bread and wine) and the Priest and Faithful have been prepared. That is, the elements have been blessed and the priest and the Faithful have purified and have transformed their consciousness, lit now from within by the descent of the Light which works to open all the centers of awareness for the theurgic work that will now begin.

At the heart of this part of the Liturgy, we find the Institution with the following words of Jesus who said: "Take eat, this is my body which is broken for you, for the remission of sins," and, "Drink ye all of it, for this is my blood of the New Testament, which is shed for you, for the remission of sins." The Priest then says: "In remembrance therefore of this command of our Saviour and of all those things which He did for us: the Cross, the Tomb, the Resurrection of the third day, His sitting on Thy right hand and of His second and glorious coming again, we offer unto Thee, on behalf of all and for all." Then comes the Consecration itself when the Priest says: "And we ask and pray and beseech Thee to send down Thy Holy Spirit upon us and upon these gifts here presented . . . and make this the precious Body of Thy Christ. And make that which is in this cup the precious Blood of Thy Christ. Transmuting them by Thy Holy Spirit. Amen. Amen. Amen. So that they may be to those that receive them for the purification of the soul, the remission of transgressions, and the fulfillment of the Kingdom of Heaven, and for our boldness to approach Thee." And he concludes: "And again we offer this reasonable service for those who have departed this life before us in the faith; for our ancestors, fathers, patriarchs, prophets, apostles, preachers, evangelists, martyrs, confessors, and for every righteous soul. Furthermore, we offer unto Thee this reasonable service on behalf of the whole world, for the Holy, Catholic, and Apostolic Church, and especially for our most holy, pure, and glorified Lady, and Birth-Giver, the ever-blessed Mary."

The above is the the traditional and theurgic means by which the bread and wine are transubstantiated into the Body and Blood of Christ. That is, chemically and to physical vision, they still remain bread and wine but now, by the above institution and words, they

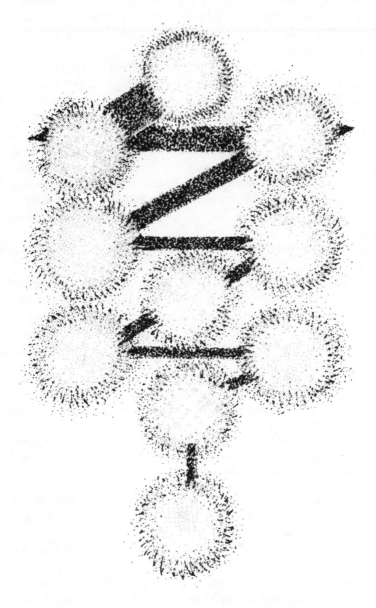

Figure 5.1 The Flashing Sword
(Melita Denning & Osborne Phillips, *The Sword and the Serpent*. Llewellyn Publications, 1975.)

have become the *vehicles* for the *Divine Light* and the *Divine Fire* in the same manner that copper wires become the vehicles for electricity which flows along them in a corona of electrons. The spiritual energies, which Mystics apprehend as and call "Light" and "Fire," flow into the bread and wine through the psyche of the Officiant and, more specifically, through his own *Tree of Life* which has been *consciously* (for the Initiate) or *unconsciously* (for the uninitiated Priest) activated by the words of the ritual described above.

What can be experienced here on the level of supersensible perception is that, in the macrocosm, the Divine Light and Fire flow from the Godhead, the Christ, through the Nine Celestial Hierarchies, or Order of Angels, to the Priest, who acts as the Tenth Hierarchy, the focal point in the world of matter for those spiritual energies that will transform the bread and wine into the Body and Blood of Christ. In the microcosm, on the other hand, these Energies flow from *Kether* to *Malkuth* (see Figure 5.1), taking the Path of the Flashing Sword, going through the hands of the Officiant into the bread and wine to transmute them into the Body and Blood of the Savior.

The Eucharistic Mysteries center on this transformation which the Adept seeks not to explain but to behold more truly within and without, in its fullness and divine splendor, and to enter into more worthily and more completely. The Body and Blood of the Savior are to be *experienced*, in deepening and intensifying degrees, related to one's state of consciousness. But as a lover is not so moved to analyze the nature of love, but to surrender to the beloved, so too can we experience this movement as described by Evelyn Underhill:

> So the individual worshiper who gives himself without reserve to the total movement of the Eucharist finds himself caught into, and made part of a spiritual drama in which the deepest impulses and needs of his spiritual life are represented and satisfied; a drama that brings together, and exhibits in their fullness under sacramental tokens, the life-giving love of God for man and the life-surrendered love of man for God.[17]

Or as St. Teresa of Avila put it succinctly: "The aim and end of human life is Union with God, it is the transformation of our being and its divinization."[18]

Thus, by partaking consciously of the consecrated Bread and Wine, we do actually, but temporarily, become one with Christ. It is no longer "I," my human self, that thinks, feels, wills, and lives but CHRIST IN ME. Naturally, from the time we first begin to experience Communion consciously, to give ourselves without reserve to it, to allow the profound response and resonance within our inner being to the bread and wine we are eating, until the time when we shall achieve Union with God, there are innumerable growing and unfolding personal experiences that one can live through in "going to Communion."

As is often the case, it is easier to speak of the effect than the cause, in this case, of the impact and consequences which going to Communion can have upon our consciousness and being and in our lives. A threefold transformation and expansion of our consciousness can be experienced: First, our vital energies, those life forces within us that make us glad to be alive and eager to live and work and create, are enlivened and reinvigorated. Then, a feeling of warmth, fullness, and expansion envelops our Heart Center and area, with our feelings and emotions greatly intensified with love, our love of God and his for us, wanting to push out, such is the sense of pressure of this expansion. Tears may come, as well they might at so many stages in the unfolding of these Mysteries of Our Most Tender Lord. Finally, to our minds is given the gift of new life as well, our thoughts clarified, our perspective changed, putting all into its proper perspective and giving every faculty, talent, and endeavor of our being its proper measure and right relation to the others and to the whole.

And in and behind all of this is the presence of our Beloved God who has reached out his hand to us with the cup of his Love and said: "Drink!" And having drunk, we are his and he is in us. From his hand was offered the bread of Life, and, having eaten, we know him and what in us is now him. This is the self's experience of the Spiritual Self. Evelyn Underhill views that Self, or what we have before called the Divine Spark, in the following way:

> That invulnerable spark of vivid life, that "inward light" which [they] find at their own centers when they seek for it, is for them an earnest of the Uncreated Light, the ineffable splendor of God, dwelling at, and energizing within the heart of things: for this Spark is at once one with, yet separate from the Universal Soul . . .
>
> Only the real, say the mystics, can know Reality, for we "behold that which we are," the universe we see is conditioned by the character of the mind that sees. This is no mere glimpse of Eternal Life, but *complete possession of it* must apply to every aspect of your being, the rich totality of character, all the "forces of the soul," not to some thin and isolated "spiritual sense" alone.[19]

When this occurs, even to a very slight extent or for a brief moment at the conscious level, we experience something that we shall never forget: We realize where we come from and where we are going, why we are here on earth and what we are to accomplish in our daily living. We know, experientially, that GOD IS LOVE; in all the love that exists in the world, in all that we love, he is there as that love. And in this love, which began and binds and redeems the world, he is with us, working his plan with us, never abandoning us. We know, too, in knowing him, who we are, and acquire a deepening sense of our own identity. For who we are is not collapsed into the Absolute but further differentiated as unique and individual. We realize that redemption (this gift of harmonious reintegration with the whole) can be extended to every aspect of human life, a work both joyously and sorrowfully complete and joyously and sorrowfully ongoing. Finally, we know now where to find him, where to find God and how to have access to him, *at the conscious level*, whenever we need his Love, his Inspiration, and his Life and Strength.

I have often had the experience when going to Mass and to Communion that C.W. Leadbeater describes so well in *The Hidden Side of Things*. This taught me many things but, in particular, two major lessons: First, it showed me the impact of the Eucharist not only upon him who receives it, but also upon the *surrounding area* and upon the *whole world*. It revealed to me some aspects of its double impact, at the *subjective* and at the *objective* levels. Second, it manifested to me something about what I call the *unconditional* (female?) and *conditional* (male?) impact of the energies of the Eucharist and about the difference between being and not being ready, prepared and open. Finally, it also explained part of the paradox that, for some, going to Communion is the most intense, important, and life-giving experience, while for others it is just a religious duty with no consciousness-impact and transformation. Leadbeater's passage was so moving and revealing to me, putting in words what I had seen, felt, and realized, that I will quote it extensively because I suspect more and more people will have the same experience and will thus be in the same situation I was.

> My attention was first called to this [the impact of the Eucharist] by watching the effect produced by the celebration of the Mass in a Roman Catholic Church in a little village in Sicily. Those who know that most beautiful of islands will understand that one does not meet with the Roman Catholic Church there in its most intellectual form, and neither the priest nor the people could be described as especially highly developed; yet the quite ordinary celebration of the Mass was a magnificent display of the application of occult force.
>
> At the moment of consecration the Host glowed with the most dazzling brightness; it became in fact a veritable sun to the eyes of the clairvoyant, and as the priest lifted it above the heads of the people I notice that two distinct varieties of spiritual force poured forth from it, which might perhaps be taken as roughly corresponding to the light of the sun and the streamers of his corona. The first rayed out impartially in all directions upon all the people in the church; indeed it penetrated the walls of the church as though they were not there, and influenced a considerable section of the surrounding country.
>
> This force was of the nature of a strong stimulus and its action was

strongest of all in the intuitional world, though it was also exceedingly powerful in the three higher subdivisions of the mental world. Its activity was marked in the first, second, and third subdivisions of the astral also, but this was a reflection of the mental, or perhaps an effect produced by the sympathetic vibration. Its effect upon the people who came within the range of its influence was proportionate to their development. In a very few cases (where there was some light intuitional development) it acted as a powerful stimulant, doubling or trebling for a time the amount of activity in those intuitional bodies and the radiance which they were capable of emitting. But for as much as in most people the intuitional matter was as yet almost entirely dormant, its chief effect was produced upon the causal bodies of the inhabitants.

Most of them, again, were awake and partially responsive only as far as the matter of the third subdivision of the mental world was concerned, and therefore they missed much of the advantage that they might have gained if the higher parts of their causal bodies had been in full activity. But at any rate every ego within reach, without exception, received a distinct impetus and a distinct benefit from that act of consecration, little though he knew or recked of what was being done. The astral vibrations also, though much fainter, produced a far-reaching effect, for at least the astral bodies of the Sicilians are usually thoroughly well-developed so that it is not difficult to stir their emotions. Many people far away from the church, walking along the village street or pursuing their various avocations upon the lonely hillsides, felt for a moment a thrill of affection or devotion, as this great wave of spiritual peace and strength passed over the country-side, though assuredly they never dreamt of connecting it with the mass which was being celebrated in their little cathedral.

It at once becomes evident that we are here in the presence of a grand and far-reaching scheme. Clearly one of the great objects, perhaps the principal object, of the daily celebration of the Mass is that every one within reach of it shall receive at least once a day one of these electric shocks which are so well calculated to promote any growth of which he is capable. Such an outpouring of force brings to each person whatever he has made himself capable of receiving; but even quite undeveloped and ignorant people cannot but be somewhat the better for the passing touch of a noble emotion, while for the few more advanced it means a spiritual uplifting the value of which it would be difficult to exaggerate.

I said that there was a second effect, which I compared to the streamers of the sun's corona. The light which I have just described poured forth impartially upon all, the just and the unjust, the believers and the scoffers. But this second force was called into activity only in response to a strong feeling of devotion on the part of the individual. At the elevation of the Host all members of the congregation duly prostrated themselves— some apparently as a mere matter of habit, but some also with a strong upwelling of deep devotional feeling.

The effect as seen by clairvoyant sight was most striking and profoundly impressive, for to each of these latter there darted from the uplifted Host a ray of fire, which set the higher part of the astral body of the recipient glowing with the most intense ecstasy. Through the astral body, by reason of its close relation with it, the intuitional vehicle was also strongly affected; and although in none of these peasants could it be said to be in any way awakened, its growth within its shell was unquestionably distinctly stimulated, and its capability of instinctively influencing the astral was enhanced. For while the awakened intuition can consciously mold and direct the astral, there is a great storehouse of force in even the most undeveloped intuitional vehicle, and this shines out upon and through the astral body, even though it be unconsciously and automatically.

I was naturally intensely interested in this phenomenon, and I made it a point of attending various functions at different churches in order to learn whether what I had seen on this occasion was invariable, or, if it varied, when and in what conditions. I found that at every celebration the same results were produced, and the two forces which I tried to describe were always in evidence—the first apparently without any appreciable variation, but the display of the second depending upon the number of really "devotional people" who formed part of the congregation.

The elevation of the Host immediately after its consecration was not the only occasion upon which this display of force took place. When the benediction was given with the Blessed Sacrament exactly the same thing happened. On several occasions I followed the procession of the Host through the streets, and every time that a halt was made at some half-ruined church and the benediction was given from its steps, precisely the same double phenomenon was produced. I observed that the reserved Host upon the altar of the church was all day long steadily pouring forth the former of the two influences, though not so strongly as at the moment of elevation or benediction. One might say that the light glowed upon the altar without casting, but came forth as a sun at those moments of special effort. The action of the second force, the second ray of light, could also be evoked from the reserved sacrament upon the altar, apparently any time, though it seemed to me somewhat less vivid than the outpouring immediately after the consecration.

Everything connected with the Host—the tabernacle, the monstrance, the altar itself, the priest's vestments, the insulating humeral veil, the chalice and pattern—all were strongly charged with this tremendous magnetism, and all were radiating it forth, each in its degree.

A third effect is that which is produced upon the communicant. He who receives into his body a part of that dazzling center, from which flow the light and fire, becomes himself for the time a similar center, and radiates power in his turn. The tremendous waves of force which he has thus drawn into the closest possible association with himself cannot but seriously influence his higher bodies. For the time these waves raise his vibrations into harmony with themselves, thus producing a feeling of intense exaltation. This, however, is a considerable strain upon his various vehicles, which naturally tend gradually to fall back again to their normal rates. For a long time the indescribably vivid higher influence struggles against this tendency to slow down, but the dead weight of the comparatively enormous mass to man's own ordinary undulations acts as a drag upon even its tremendous energy, and gradually brings it and themselves down to the common level. But undoubtedly every such experience draws the man just an infinitesimal fraction higher than he was before. He has been for a few moments or even for a few hours in indirect contact with the forces of a world far higher than any that he himself can otherwise touch.[20]

The Orthodox Tradition, in accordance with the teachings of esoteric spiritual tradition, teaches that the best way to prepare for Communion is to do the following: To examine one's conscience and meditate; to purify and cleanse one's auras and consciousness from negative thoughts, feelings, desires, words, and deeds (by raising its vibrations and bringing the Light of God as a cleaning and healing agent); to seek penance or true remission of sins; and to pray and fast. Let us briefly examine each of these four steps in the light of esoteric teachings.

Fasting, here, can mean to abstain from feeding the ego, the human self, on any level of the personality, not just to refrain from eating physical food. Thus one can fast by not eating food; but one can also fast by not feeding, receiving and giving certain emotions, thoughts or ideas, and even intuitions and inspirations. Spiritually speaking, fasting is very closely connected with the desert experience, with *solitude*, wherein one is deprived of human interaction, external stimuli, and the normal supports of one's daily life. At the highest or spiritual level, fasting also involves being temporarily cut off from the Divine Light, from the inner conscious link with the Divine Spark, and from one's attunement with Christ. Finally, fasting is also connected with "dying" and being "reborn," or growing from one level of consciousness, existence and vibration to another higher level. Only one who is truly hungry can experience the food of Communion.

Fasting and prayer are closely linked with one another in all the major spiritual traditions. The reason for this is that fasting greatly enhances one's ability to pray—the receptivity one has to prayer and the intensity one can pour into it. Conversely, it is also prayer that makes certain kinds of fasting really possible and which greatly helps one to practice any type of fasting, including physically not eating.

Briefly put, prayer is the reaching out of the soul for God, the dialogue of the human with the divine; how the response is felt in our lives is as varied as the individuals involved; also, within their relationship to God there are changes over time in the unique way he works in each life. What food is to our biological organism, what human relationships are to our psyche (the "I" only becomes an "I" through a "Thou"), such is prayer to our spiritual consciousness—

the essential nourishment which keeps it alive and growing! Prayer is, most importantly, our response to God's gifts, to his Love, his Wisdom, his Mercy, all that we experience of him—it is how we praise, how we give thanksgiving. And this we can do in the converging and focusing of our will, thoughts, feelings, and imagination, which, when they function with perfect synchronicity, can open the doors through which we can offer to God what is right to give Him; and then too can the Divine Light pour into our souls and personalities—into our consciousness to purify and prepare it for conscious Communion with Christ.

To purify and cleanse one's auras and soul from negative thoughts, feelings, desires, words, and deeds, two concomitant operations and factors are necessary: a human or psychological factor and a spiritual factor. The first consists in examining one's daily life in terms of one's deeds, words, desires, feelings, thoughts, and aspirations: in terms of becoming aware and evaluating what one has done, and what one has failed to do, over a certain period of time which could range from a day to a year. It involves becoming aware and evaluating what one has done and how one has responded psychologically to what life and destiny have brought. Finally, it also consists in making plans and being determined to correct the wrongs one has done and to improve and seek anew to do what has not been done or achieved at the highest level of our capacity. The spiritual preparation is not at all separate, but focuses more on how God sees us, feeling our way forward to what he wants us to be, reaching out for the insight that prayer alone can bring. We are then guided in how best to deepen our act of contrition, and whether to seek Absolution, the traditional preparatory Sacrament for Communion.

From the foregoing, it is now clear what value ensues from the conscious preparation and partaking of the Holy Eucharist. A warning is also in order for one who earnestly prepares in all the ways we have suggested, who opens himself across the spectrum of his entire being and consciousness to this profound experience. It is a spiritual law that those to whom spiritual gifts are given are also given more responsibility; and this entails tests, trials, or temptations. If the gifts are not wisely used, then one can be placed in a worse state than before. All conscious spiritual development should proceed with caution, where one has recourse to a spiritual director or master or teacher who has the experience and the wisdom to act as a guide through the inevitable difficulties and chimeras that arise. With the opening and activation of many higher levels of consciousness possible, through developed powers of concentration, devotion, meditation, and visualization, it can also be an attractive force for all that which seeks to retard evolution. It is also the case that should there be any negative thoughts, emotions, and passions (anger, self-pity, jealousy, lust) which have not been purified and transmuted, then, when one experiences the inrush of higher spiritual energies, these untransmuted negativities can be energized and intensified, wreaking havoc in the life and personality of the seeker. This is magnified at the more advanced stages of spiritual development where one takes the responsibility for guiding others.

Given this word of traditional caution, let us return to what the fruits are of the Eucharist. Basically, they are four: Christ Himself, fusing his Consciousness, Will, and Life with ours, temporarily, manifests in and through us—and this to the degree which he ordains and for which we have been prepared. In this is a profound and holistic healing or harmonization both within our entire being and with respect to all that is without—our relationships to others, to the world, and to the spiritual realities that interpenetrate all existence. In particular, we feel ourselves members of a congregation of spirits, as spiritual beings ourselves, in the Communion of Saints. And we can experience, again if only at first for a brief time, our true nature, which becomes more and more uniquely differentiated. Finally, we are given the transcendent experience, perhaps only for a moment, of Life in the Presence of Eternal God, or Life Eternal.

While the Orthodox Church makes it mandatory for the faithful to partake of Communion at least once a year and suggests that we go to Communion four times a year or even once every month, it has been my experience that going to Communion once a week is a healthy rhythm. The seven-day cycle of the week has profound roots and many esoteric correspondences, and is a spiritual octave reflected in nature, in the human being, and in the world, and thus, not surprisingly, in the Christian Church. Thus it is on the day of the Sun that we are rightly joined to the Spiritual Sun, with Saturday, the day of Saturn, being a natural day to prepare and "clean our karma." By Wednesday or Friday, in my experience of this weekly rhythm at least, one begins to sense the need for renewal as the longing grows for all that is given in Communion.

We are reminded by the Orthodox Catechism that, during the procession with the Gospel, we should focus our attention upon and visualize Jesus Christ himself appearing to us to teach us his Mysteries. This is something which is *experienced* when one has achieved, by dint of one's long efforts and the grace of God, spiritual consciousness. When the procession with the holy Gifts is made, all that has been meditated and contemplated upon regarding the Most Perfect Sacrifice of Our Lord does come before the heart and mind, welling up out of our soul, and responded to with our spirit, as now the living memorial of that Deed is enacted in solemnity before us.

During consecration, we can see with our spiritual eyes the High Priest once again as Christ did at the Last Supper offer the Life-giving Chalice of his Holy Blood, the bread of his Body, prophetically and for all time, transforming and informing the ritual of the Old Testament in instituting the New Covenant. In the consecration, we see, too, what is to follow the Last Supper as its fulfillment in the Crucifixion, Suffering, Death, and Burial of the Lamb "who taketh away the sins of the world." When the royal doors are opened and the Priest appears with the holy Gifts, we can now visualize before us the appearance of Jesus Christ after his Resurrection. Finally, the last showing of the holy Gifts to the people before they are hidden from view calls to mind Christ's last acts while on earth and then his Ascension into heaven, which should be reflected upon and visualized as fully and vividly as possible.

All who dare to speak of this most sublime of all Sacraments, this the most intense and uplifting of all human experiences, are thereby humbled in feeling their own inadequacy and the paucity of their own words. Error and limitation are incumbent to human existence, and never is the first more likely nor the second more obvious than in speaking of this Mystery. Thus does the author, having failed Truth, implore Mercy! As will all rightly prepared and rightly guided aspirants in the Christian Mysteries, for the living correspondences and implications of Communion are vouchsafed to the direct personal experience of each—as the "crossed keys" of esoteric and exoteric wisdom. But this preparation, this stage-by-stage initiation, is nothing less than arduous and can be harrowing, as Evelyn Underhill would have us bear in mind:

> True and complete self-knowledge, indeed, is the privilege of the strongest alone. Few can bear to contemplate themselves face to face; for the vision is strange and terrible, and brings awe and contrition in its wake. He is converted, in the deepest and most drastic sense; is forced to take up a new attitude towards himself and all other things. Likely enough, if you really knew yourself—saw your own dim character, perpetually at the mercy of its environment; your true motives, stripped for inspection and measured against eternal values; your unacknowledged self-indulgences; your irrational loves and hates—you would be compelled to remodel your whole existence, and become for the first time a practical man.[21]

It was when I was recovering from a motorcycle accident, practicing faithfully my spiritual exercises and going to Communion regularly, that I first began to experience the inner dimensions of the Holy Eucharist. At first, I merely felt more energy flowing throughout myself. Then I felt lighter as though I had lost some weight. What then appeared to be happening was that my entire consciousness was coming alive in a way I had not experienced before. I seemed better able to understand my situation, perceiving it in a new light. New ideas appeared; I felt incredible love and joy. My creative energies and the ability to, at last, "be as I am" came together all at once. And I was able then to finally understand the language of St. John of the Cross when he says:

> The bride knows that now her will's desire is detached from all things and attached to her God in most intimate love; that the sensory part of the soul, with all its strength, faculties, and appetites, is in harmony with the spirit, and its rebelliousness brought into subjection; that the devil is now conquered and far withdrawn as a result of her varied and prolonged spiritual activity and combat; that her soul is now united and transformed with an abundance of heavenly riches and gifts; and that consequently she is well prepared, disposed, and strong, leaning on her beloved, coming up from the desert of death, flowing with delights, to the glorious throne of her Bridegroom . . .
>
> The Bride sets all this perfection and preparedness before her Beloved. The Son of God, with the desire that He transfer her from the spiritual marriage, to which He desired to bring her in the Church Militant, to the glorious marriage of the Triumphant.[22]

And, again from this Spanish saint of whom Thomas Merton says, "of all saints he is perhaps the greatest poet as well as the greatest contemplative":

> There are many kinds of awakening that God affects in the soul, so many that we would never finish explaining them all. Yet this awakening of the Son of God, which the soul wishes to refer to here, is one of the most elevated and most beneficial. For this awakening is a movement of the Word in the substance of the soul containing such grandeur, dominion, and glory, and intimate sweetness that it seems to the soul that all the balsams and fragrant spices and flowers of the world are commingled, and stirred and shaken so as to yield their sweet odor, and that all the kingdoms and dominions of the world and all the powers and virtues of heaven are moved; and not only this, but it also seems that all the virtues and substances and perfection and graces of every created thing glow and make the same movement all at once.[23]

Evelyn Underhill also caught the heart of this process and realization:

> This realization—sometimes felt under the symbols of personality, sometimes under those of an impersonal but life-giving force, Light, Energy, or Heat—is the ruling character of the third phase of contemplation, and the reward of that meek passivity, that "busy idleness" as the mystics call it, which you have been striving to attain.
>
> To use St. Teresa's well-known image, you have been watering the garden of your spirit by hand; a poor and laborious method, yet one in which there is a definite relation between effort and result. But now the watering can is taken from you, and you must depend upon the rain;

more generous, more fruitful, than anything which your own efforts could manage but, in its incalculable visitations, utterly beyond your control. Here all one can say is this: that if you acquiesce in the heroic demands which the spiritual life now makes upon you, if you let yourself go, eradicate the last traces of self-interest even of the most spiritual kind—then, you have established conditions under which the forces of the spiritual world can work on you, heightening your susceptibilities, deepening and purifying your attention, so that you are able to taste and feel more and more of the inexhaustible riches of Reality.[24]

These experiences will literally open the doors to a new world, a world lived in as a creature in perfect conformity with it. In this strengthening and maturing of our personality, in which these "last traces of self-interest, even of the most spiritual kind" are eradicated, the effort is no longer at all on what is to be gained, that God is to come to serve us and our awakening. All is now guided in service to his Will out of our freely governed choice, the last trace of rebelliousness, that first evil, not only brought into subjection but itself seeking redemption—and this as we now take upon our shoulders the sufferings of others, bearing his Cross.

This is as much as can be said in human words concerning the most sublime of all Sacraments and the most intense and uplifting of all human experiences: *conscious Communion with the Living God.* The deeper Mysteries, the living correspondences and implications, of Communion can only be discovered and revealed through *direct personal experience*—which is the true key to all esoteric mysteries and arcana.

HOLY ORDERS

The Orthodox Catechism

"What are Holy Orders? Holy Orders are a Sacrament, in which the Holy Spirit, by the laying on of the bishop's hands, ordains them that be rightly chosen to minister Sacraments, and to feed the flock of Christ. As the Scriptures put it: 'Let a man so account of us, as of the minister of Christ, and stewards of the Mysteries of God' (1 Cor. 4:1). And: 'Take heed therefore unto yourselves, and to all the flock over which the Holy Spirit hath made you overseers, to feed the church of God, which He hath purchased with His own Blood' (Acts 20:28). What is to feed the Church? To instruct the people in faith, piety, and good works. What are the necessary and higher degrees of Holy Order? Three: those of Bishop, Priest, and Deacon. The Deacon serves at the Sacraments; the Priest hallows Sacraments in dependence on the Bishop; the Bishop not only hallows the Sacraments himself, but has power also to impart to others, by the laying on of his hands, the gift and grace to hallow them. Of the Episcopal power, the Apostle Paul thus writes to Titus: 'For this cause left I thee in Crete, that thou shouldest set in order the things that are wanting, and ordain elders in every city' (Tit. 1:5).''

And the Catechism continues: "The Sacrament of Holy Orders is that in which one who has been canonically selected and ordained by a Bishop receives the grace of the Holy Spirit and is instructed to perform the Sacraments and to tend the flock of Christ, i.e. to govern a Christian Church. As the grace of the Holy Spirit is imparted in this Sacrament through the imposition of the prelate's hands, the act of performing the Sacrament is named *Cheirotony*, the 'stretching out' or 'laying on of hands'. The rite is the same for all grades of Priesthood—that of Bishop, Priest, or Deacon—differing only in that it is performed at different moments of the Liturgy. And it consists essentially of the following acts: presentation of the person selected for Holy Orders, circumambulation of the altar, the prayer of consecration, the laying on of hands, and the vesting with the sacred vestments.''

Esoteric Considerations

Again, the division of esoteric and exoteric is given here only insofar as it reflects more the historically separate lines or streams of development, which were by no means exclusive—that is, certainly Saints can be regarded as Initiates, and there were Christian mystics both within and outside the Church. There are esoteric traditions, for example, Rosicrucianism, just as there are exoteric traditions, for example, that of the Orthodox Church, though when the primary elements of discourse are things spiritual, there are bound to be, as there are, many overlaps—different languages used to describe the same thing. It is fundamentally, of course, the same spiritual Reality which underlies and informs both streams. And just as there are levels of initiation to which we have referred often, there are also exoteric levels, as we see especially in regards to Holy Orders—indeed, the word *order* implies them—structure and organization being inherent in nature and the human experience.

The differences lies with regard to the outer nature of the exoteric traditions, which take their places publicly in the world, and the esoteric orders which have tended to work behind the scenes. This is coupled with the notion that esoteric knowledge has been the preserve of the few, those trained in the disciplines who can both further and safeguard knowledge which a general public is not, as an objective fact, ready for. The perception all along in the esoteric traditions has been that if certain hermetic, alchemical, or esoteric secrets were to be misused then the consequences could be grave, which is perhaps one of the reasons why the exoteric tradition was chary of their inclusion in a greater public sphere of accessibility in the first case. However, in time, the exoteric tradition could no longer so easily recover for itself substantively what it had excised, perhaps for functional reasons, even in assimilating this through its own mystical tradition. Likewise, the esoteric traditions, which often had to suffer at the hands of certain zealous exotericists, reacted by "throwing out the baby with the bath water," alienating themselves from what continued to develop and grow within *exoteric* spirituality. In our time, the impetus in esoteric work has been that the "secrets of the past" are now to be made more and more public, befitting the stage of evolution which humanity now enters. As more esotericists enter, reenter, or rediscover exoteric religion, the Church is sure to feel the need to reexamine its own roots and relationships to this esoteric mystery wisdom.

The exoteric text to this Sacrament, or Mystery, which plays a central part and fulfills an essential role in the Western spiritual tradition, can be further unveiled in its basic nature and functions by certain esoteric insights. As we continue with the correspondences with the Qabalistic Tree of Life for each of the Sacraments, here we can identify Holy Orders with *Geburah*, which in the human body is connected with the Right Shoulder Center. This Center is further related to Severity or Strength and, as opposed to *Chesed*, Mercy, which is related to the principle of expanding life, Energy, and Enthusiasm, this Center corresponds to the principle of contracting life, Order, and Discipline (see Appendix B).

As mentioned above, there is a direct homology and correspondence between the Mysteries and Initiation system of esoteric spiritual schools and the Holy Orders of the Catholic Christian traditions. Both contain seven fundamental degrees. The number seven is replete with esoteric and exoteric significance—there being seven notes in the musical scale, seven planets, seven days of the week, seven "ages" of man, seven Deadly Sins, seven Gifts of the Holy Spirit, just to begin with. Plato in the *Timeaus* teaches that from the number seven was generated the Soul of the World, *Anima Mundana*, Adam Kadmon.

In these seven degrees there are four minor ones associated with the Lesser Mysteries and the development of the human personality and three major ones, connected with the Greater Mysteries and harmonization with the individuality or the soul. Whereas in the esoteric tradition, initiation must proceed on a conscious, experiential plane, the exoteric seven degrees of the Priesthood (as seen from within the esoteric) are connected with the spiritual world on the superconscious or supersensible plane; thus degrees are achieved by *Ordination*, rather than through personal merit or achievement. This is another way of saying that Christ calls to his own, that each soul called to Holy Orders comes by the Will and Grace of God; it is not an achievement, nor reward which can be earned. Yet, there is an esoteric Priesthood as well, in the sense that disciples of Christ Jesus can achieve through their conscious efforts and with his Grace and Will, increasing responsibility and service to the wider sense of *ecclesia*, or Church. In both, it is a vocation, the highest vocation to which one can be called. A Priest in this wider spiritual sense, embracing both traditions, is a Priest both in the world of action, through acts, gestures, words, deeds, and in the world of being— through what one is, as a vehicle or channel (though this is a much overused word in the New Age) for Divine Grace and manifold spiritual energies.

In the esoteric tradition, to be an authentic Priest is to fulfill the following seven essentials within one's vocation:

1. To act as a Priest not because of duty or circumstances but out of deep personal commitment, love, and interest—for one's own sake and for the sake of Jesus Christ, without regard to worldly attachments.

2. To serve more by what one is, by personal example, than by what one preaches or says. One can feel here how the Blessed Virgin who is the Mother of the Eternal and High Priest does inspire devotion in this regard—and vocations!

3. To seek to live and embody, in one's being and life, that which one wishes to teach and exemplify, so as to understand it by personal experience and to convey it to others through genuine, though subtle, authority.

4. To bear in mind that a Priest should be the easiest person in whom to confide, and to offer help and hope when all other human relations prove to be in vain or impossible.

5. To balance severity and mercy; to always pray before evaluating or seeking to discern someone else's actions or state of being.

6. To know that an authentic calling as that which Christ ordains is what makes a real Priest, not Ordination alone, as important as that is. This calling is experienced as a heightened capacity to love and a desire to help others unfold so that they may realize their highest possible spiritual potential.

7. To cultivate an attitude of reverence for all life and to have a passion for excellence in all one does.

By his calling, training, and Ordination, a Priest becomes a vehicle by which Christ can manifest in this world, reaching and affecting others. In all that he does, the various spiritual forces and energies emanating from the Lord can work with him and through him, guiding and directing his steps, his gestures, his words, and his thoughts. During Ordination, by the prayers, by the laying on of hands, and by the Hand of God, centers within the higher bodies of the Priest are activated so that Grace may flow through him and be released in the world. Irrespective of his personal achievements and qualifications (whether he is saint, sinner, genius, or idiot, a creative or uncreative person), his aura and psyche, one can say "body and soul," have now become a channel for Divine Light.

Of course, one can become an increasingly better vehicle for the spiritual energies and the Power of the Holy Spirit, and, in order to serve others more effectively, the lifelong aspiration and training of the Priest is to become ever more conscious of his office, his duties, his powers, and his opportunities . . . so as to realize them. In this, he should endeavor to make the prayers he says and the rituals he enacts become ALIVE, awakening higher energies and states of consciousness in himself and in others, that these prayers and rituals will reveal their mysteries to him progressively—or perhaps all at once, who is to say! Then is he able to see their impact in the inner worlds with his unfolding spiritual vision.

The central function of a Priest is to act as a channel or vehicle for the Light, Fire, and Life of the Divine Spark and of the Holy Spirit in order that they may be extended and manifested in human consciousness and in the world. It is to *bless man and the world* as a channel of the Spirit that now acts through him. Various kinds of prayers and rituals, the Sacraments, and the very Eucharist are, in fact, all forms of blessing (that is, of conveying, transforming, manifesting, and projecting Light in this world). The true Priest alternately strives to learn how to perform this act of blessing in God's Name as fully and as consciously as possible and to surrender to the Ineffable that he may be worthy, through devotion and purity of heart, to do God's will.

The Ordination of a Priest opens up and activates the psychospiritual Center located around the right shoulder, through which spiritual Light, Fire, and Life (God's Spirit) can enter and fill his own psyche and Tree of Life. From there, they can streak forth and be released as he projects them, through his *right hand*, upon others and into the world. This Light or spiritual Power is, in fact, one of the most precious and powerful energies that exist: it is *spiritual gold*, which is of priceless value as it is the very essence and fountainhead of all other energies. It is the very substance of Life, Consciousness, and Love. Depression, anxiety, fear, and a whole host of negative emotions, thoughts, and states of consciousness result, in fact, from a depletion, blockage, and diminution of this Energy and Light in one's psyche and consciousness.

A Priest is thus, literally, a consciousness expander, a life giver, a joy bringer, and a transformer of evil into good, by the Spirit of God acting through him. To act as a transformer and radiator of such spiritual Energy and Light is the function of the Priest par excellence. When he is, himself, suffused and charged with this Energy and Light, wherever he goes, whomever he meets, he will bring with him, extend, and radiate a little bit of the same Energy and Light, and a lot of hope, joy, encouragement, and revitalization. In other words, he will bring in this capacity that "Life more abundant" which Jesus Christ promised to us.

From the standpoint of esoteric spiritual tradition, Ordination as a Sacrament brings with it a blueprint for, acts upon, and demands the progressive training of the psyche to make it a fit, clear, coordinated, and effective Temple for the Living God. This is the homologue to the "building of the Temple of Solomon" and the "development of Christ's Church," and is what is working behind attempts at self-actualization and self-realization as we see this manifesting in so many ways today. As we have mentioned earlier, this Sacrament is directly related to the ancient mystery tradition and, in the major Catholic traditions, it parallels exactly the four minor "Elemental Initiations" and the three major "Spiritual Initiations." Quoting the basic doctrinal position of the Liberal Catholic Church, which has deep esoteric roots and integrates the "clairvoyant viewpoint" in its teachings and practices, we have the following:

> Holy Orders is the Sacrament by which, in their various degrees, ministers of the church receive power and authority to perform sacred duties. Our Lord works through human agency, and to the end that those who are chosen for this sacred ministry as Bishops, Priests, or deacons shall become readier channels for His grace, He has ordained that they shall be linked closely with him by this holy rite, and shall thereby be empowered to administer His Sacraments from the hand of Christ Himself, and that the Priest is but an instrument in that hand.[25]

In the Catholic Christian Tradition (Roman, Orthodox, Liberal), just like in the esoteric mystery schools and spiritual fraternities, we see that Holy Orders are subdivided into two basic groups: the Minor Orders, paralleling the Lesser Mysteries, and the Major Orders, paralleling the Greater Mysteries. Holy Orders are genuine forms of Initiation. Unfortunately, today, neither the Roman Catholic nor the Orthodox Churches pays a great deal of attention or gives much importance to the Minor Orders, perhaps because the esoteric dimension has been eclipsed, as we described before, a dimension which can deepen understanding throughout the community about the real nature and functions of these Orders.

The Minor Orders, in esoteric tradition, consist of one preliminary step, that of the Neophyte, Aspirant, or Cleric, and of four Minor Orders proper, that of Doorkeeper, Exorcist, Reader, and Subdeacon, or Acolyte. These correspond to the Lesser Mysteries, which focus their attention and training upon the microcosm, personal preparation and training leading to the achievement of a certain degree of self-knowledge, self-mastery, and self-integration, and which are preparatory to the Greater Mysteries, which focus their attention and work upon the world. As such, the Minor Orders correspond to the Neophyte's degree and the four Elemental Initiations, each of which is linked with the opening and activation of one of the four lower psychospiritual Centers.

The Neophyte, Cleric, or Aspirant degree does not yet bring one to actively enter the Tree of Life and begin the long ascent thereon on the Cross of Light. But it prepares the Aspirant for a possible entry on the Tree of Life and for religious and spiritual service. In essence, persons in this probationary degree were instructed and tested to see whether they were ready to leave the purely worldly life and devote themselves, giving time, attention, energy, and work to the needs of the Church, forgoing worldly ambitions and personal interest. The ideal of this grade is to seek a better life by undergoing the personal training to become a fellow-worker with God and by cooperating in his Plan for perfecting both human nature and the world. For, in order to incarnate this ideal and realize it, one must necessarily acquire self-knowledge, self-mastery, and self-integration, and must unfold new powers.

The Order of the Doorkeeper now leads one to enter the Tree of Life and to activate, purify, and consecrate *Malkuth*, the Feet Center. Here, the central lesson and achievement (at the conscious level, of course) is to learn how to master and express oneself consciously in the physical or material world. This is, basically, the first Elemental Initiation, the Earth Initiation, where the Aspirant learns how to know, control, and express his consciousness through his physical body. Here personal hygiene, the laws of holistic health, and the proper use of the physical body play an important role. In the deeper, spiritual sense, Initiation at this level might involve the "breaking of the body" through a physical illness, to teach one the importance of the body and the laws of physical health. Then, one might recover one's physical health through both material and spiritual help, which will teach one that there are higher laws and energies than those which are presently known and how to properly work with the physical and the spiritual energies and dimensions of one's being.

The Order of the Exorcist, which follows that of the Doorkeeper, leads one from *Malkuth* to *Yesod*, the sexual Center, where the central lesson and major achievement (at the conscious level) is to learn how to control, develop, and express both the imagination and the power of the will. This is in order to confront and conquer evil both in oneself and in the world, and to help others recognize and overcome evil in themselves. It is also linked with the knowledge and control of the etheric body, which follows that of the physical body. Since ancient times, the duty of Exorcists was to "cast out devils"; today, we could also say it involves learning how to say yes and how to say no to oneself and to others, that is, knowing and developing the power of one's will and imagination, learning how to recognize and to deal with negative images, emotions, and thoughts to avoid becoming "possessed" or controlled by them.

As to the origin of evil in the evolution of consciousness, suffice it here to say that what we observe as the realities of pain and sufferings, temptation and sin, are necessary if we, as truly free beings, are to be presented with the possibilities of choices, in order to develop further our worthiness to share in Life Eternal. We know Jesus Christ was able to "cast out the unclean spirits," that he overcame the temptations in the desert, and that through his Death and Resurrection these cosmic forces and personal forces were brought under subjection (1 Cor. 6:3; 1 Pet. 3:22; 2 Pet. 2:10–11), with the final victory to be fully realized only through his glory in the final revelation at the end of the Age. The battle within of these forces, the Higher Self against the lower self, a true Jihad, is for control of the personality, which, in turn, governs our behavior. Moreover, it is not a question of "killing" or destroying evil but, rather, of recognizing it, in order to reequilibrate it and transmute it into the good by harnessing its energies: one can say, of ultimately redeeming it. This begins with a proper knowledge of the nature of imagination.

In a deeper, spiritual sense, Initiation at this level may involve the "breaking of the will," whereby one experiences being helpless and unable to cope with negative circumstances or forces, thus becoming a victim of circumstances; or it might involve becoming obsessed, controlled, or invaded by the creatures of one's own imagination or of the lower psychic planes which have found entrance to our consciousness through the misuse of our own creative imagination. It is here, therefore, that an essential discernment of good and evil takes place and that we must learn to guard the doors and powers of our own creative imagination and will. It is here also that we find the doors or gateway from the physical to the spiritual worlds, a door that must not be opened unless one is duly purified—especially with regard to the erotic energies of lust and possessiveness—consecrated, and has a specific task to accomplish.

The Order of the Reader leads one from *Yesod* to *Hod* (this corresponds to the Right Hip Center) where the central lesson and major achievement (at the conscious level) is to learn how to control, develop, and express the powers of the mind which must be, henceforth, devoted to the service of God. Without the knowledge, mastery, and integration of *thinking* and concentration, service to God and for others would remain, even with the best intentions, unconscious and relatively ineffective; seen in this light, the right relationship to thinking is the fundamental foundation of the three following Major Orders. It is also here that we find the true home of the Devil (the lower, unregenerated human self which is cut off from the spiritual Self). This means that the inner battle for the control of the personality and of one's actions in the world must be fought on a very important dimension—that of the lower mind. Thinking is also linked with the knowledge and control of the *mental body*, which is closely connected with the astral or emotional body, which follows, in polarity, that of the etheric body. In order to become a teacher and to influence for good the minds of others, one must first know and have mastered the powers of one's own mind. In a deeper spiritual sense, Initiation at this level might involve the "breaking of the mind," the loss of one's sanity, or the distruction of one's basic philosophy of life, basic values, and guiding reference points. One might, literally, become *mindless* (or paralyzed at the level of the mind) for a certain period of time. Through prayer, patience, humility, and right guidance, one can then rediscover and reactivate one's mind to connect it, this time with the higher mind that reflects the higher worlds and God's Mind. Thinking is also involved with the right relationship to the Word, with assimilating and meditating upon the "lore of tradition," and with being able with one's vehicle of speech to either bring forth or, as may be needed, veil the Truth. Through developed thinking, meditation, contemplation, and prayer, this becomes the expanded capacity to "read" on all levels, social, psychological, and spiritual as well as to be, as the prophets were, the vehicle of God's Prophetic Word.

The Order of the Subdeacon or Acolyte leads one from *Hod* to *Netzach*, the Left Hip Center, where the central lesson and major achievement (at the conscious level) is to learn how to purify, control, and express one's emotions and feelings, which must also be aligned and dedicated to God's service. Here it is the knowledge, mastery, and integration of the emotions and of the power of devotion—of the astral body—which is crucial. One must be well acquainted with and able to direct and transform one's emotions and passions before the Light of the soul may truly flow and express itself through the personality. The control of one's emotions and passions thus play a most important role for, without their proper purification, consecration, and utilization, they would generally rule the personality and cut off the harmony and proper alignment with the soul and the Divine Spark. Herein, can be found the keys that will open the doors of the Heart at the next and higher level, that will energize and dynamize the personality, drawing one to what is noble, beautiful, and true. This is way in ancient times, subdeacons in the Orthodox Church were given the keys to the Church (representing the keys to one's inner consciousness and heart) and instructed to ring the bells of the Church to call the faithful to worship. In a deeper spiritual sense, Initiation at this level might involve becoming the slave of all kinds of passions and emotions, losing one's emotional equilibrium, and falling prey to powerful, compelling, opposite emotions, which we would call today the emotional roller coaster or the manic-depressive syndrome. Again, with "emotional fasting" and purification, with prayer and consecration, and with proper guidance and nourishment of the emotional side of one's being, one might in time reacquire the lost control and integration of one's emotions, connect them with the higher emotions, and activate one's astral body, Center, and faculties to then be able to enter and explore consciously the astral world.

Taken as a whole, the four Minor Orders deal with Four Elemental Initiations and the Tau Cross on the Tree of Life. They involve the necessary *personal self-knowledge, self-mastery, and self-integration*, leading to what we call today *self-actualization*, to truly qualify one for the Greater Mysteries—work on the macrocosm and the world. Without this necessary self-preparation and training, all the work that we could do for God and for others would remain, even with the best intentions of which we are capable, *unconscious* and *ineffective*. Seen in this light, the Minor Orders are the fundamental foundation for the three following Major Orders to be lived and exercised at a conscious and effective level. It is thus truly a pity that they have been put into the background, glossed over, and rapidly integrated with the Major Orders. But, this probably had to be, and fulfilled a purpose, until the present day when we are again rediscovering the ancient Mysteries, aspiring to genuine spiritual Initiation, expanding our consciousness, sensibilities, and expectations—and demanding a great deal more from our clergy, if they are to continue fulfilling a distinctive and important role in our communities. One of my core theses is, precisely, that the Catholic traditions have preserved, down the centuries, to the very end of the twentieth century, integrated fragments of the Holy Wisdom and of the spiritual Mysteries . . . to be rediscovered, reinterpreted, and *lived again* as a *direct personal experience*.

In the Catholic traditions, the Major Orders are three: Deacon,

Priest, and Bishop. Just as the four Minor Orders correspond to the four Elemental Initiations of the Lesser Mysteries, focusing upon the microcosm and the activation of the four lower psychospiritual Centers, so the three Major Orders correspond to the three Spiritual Initiations of the Greater Mysteries, focusing upon the macrocosm and the activation of the three higher psychospiritual Centers (the Heart and Right and Left Shoulders). As with the previous ones, they are still initiations which release Divine Light and Power at the super-conscious and not at the conscious level. But while the four lower Orders focus their attention upon *self-preparation* and training—upon the personality of the candidate—the three higher Orders focus their attention upon the *world*. Their basic function is to prepare spiritual channels for the Light, Fire, and Life of Christ to be released in the world and awakened in the personalities and souls of human beings. In esoteric tradition, the Major Orders, like the Minor ones, also prepare one to bring these Energies and the Divine Light on the conscious level, and this within the context of personal spiritual initiation; this will become clearer as we continue. What now comes into play, in the Major Orders, is what we might call the evolutionary status of the individual, his level of conscious development, and his personal efforts, as these are, of course, spiritually informed and guided by the Beloved. Naturally, the Major Orders, like the Minor ones, can also prepare conscious channels so that one can bring these Energies and the Divine Light at the *conscious level* by undergoing a personal *Spiritual Initiation* (becoming a Sage, a Saint, and a true Master). This depends first on God's direct Gifts and upon the evolutionary status, level of consciousness, and personal efforts of the candidates.

For all practical purposes, the Deacon is an apprentice Priest. He does not yet have the power to consecrate the Eucharist, to bless the people, and to forgive their sins. Only the Priest is able to do these things. And, if he eventually becomes a Bishop, he will then have the power to ordain other Priests and thus carry on the apostolic succession, to administer the rite of Chrismation, and to consecrate a Church. The entire clergy structure and system exist for the benefit of the world in the service of God, acting as channels for God's grace. Unfortunately, it can and has happened that Bishops and Priests succumb to the temptation to seek power for themselves and for the branch of the Church to which they belong. This is one reason the faithful are urged in the course of the liturgy of the Mass to pray for priests and all clergy so that this energy of inspiration will rise to God and descend to his servants in the Church. Any official of the Church who entangles himself in politics thereby betrays his spiritual heritage and departs from the path which our Lord has marked for him—for his Kingdom is *not of this world* and his throne is the *heart of man*!

The Grace of God, the Divine Light, and Spiritual Energies, are poured incessantly upon the world, in many ways and at many levels. It is one of the most fundamental purposes of every religion to provide its members and the world at large with channels for this outpouring, and to prepare them to fully receive. It is clearly the Will of God that human beings evolve, actualize their potentialities, and learn to see and understand him better and to comprehend his plan better, that they might have the opportunity and privilege to cooperate in this wondrous scheme of Creation. To grasp and understand how they can achieve this, we need more knowledge of the "anatomy and physiology of the higher worlds," the laws under which these operate and how we can work with these laws. This is the time of history when the Great Synthesis can come about, when esotericists can enter or reenter more fully the Sacramental life and exotericists can appreciate what has been preserved for all within the esoteric streams. What is most urgently needed are the teachings of the Spiritual Tradition, backed up by *personal observation and experience.*

On every plane of being, God pours forth his Light, Fire, and Life; and, naturally, it is on the higher planes that his outpouring of Divine Life is given more fully and with fewer restrictions. The Divine Life flows forth with much greater fullness on the spiritual plane than it does on the mental, emotional or physical plane. Under normal conditions, each of these waves of Light, Fire, and Life spreads and remains on its own plane and does not pass down to the plane below without major qualitative transformations. But, there are exceptions to every rule, including this rule. Repeated experiments and qualified observations reveal that this downward flow can happen when a special channel is prepared—and this can only be achieved from below through the efforts of human beings. As Leadbeater writes:

When a man's thought or feeling is selfish, the energy which it produces moves in a closed curve, and thus inevitably returns and expends itself upon its own level; but when the thought or feeling is absolutely unselfish, its energy rushes forth in an open curve, and thus does not return in the ordinary sense, but pierces through into the plane above, because only in the higher condition, with its additional dimension, can it find room for its expansion. But, in thus breaking through, such a thought or feeling may be said to hold a door of size equivalent to its own diameter, and thus furnishes the requisite channel through which the divine force appropriate to the higher plane can pour itself into the lower with marvelous result, not only for the thinker but for others. An infinite flood of the higher type of force is always ready and waiting to pour through the first pipe that may be opened. The result of such a descent of the divine life is not only a great strengthening and uplifting of the maker of the channel, but also the radiation all about him of a most powerful and benevolent influence. This effect has often been described as an answer to prayer, and has been attributed by the ignorant to what they call a special interposition of providence, instead of the unerring action of the great and immutable divine law. [26]

Saints and Angels have a power of devotion far superior to our own. There have been, in fact, saints in all religions who have been flooding the world with spiritual power so that a great reservoir of this energy has been formed which is available for helping humanity under certain conditions. Many men and women of spiritual inclinations who practice prayer, especially those in contemplative orders, devote themselves to this work and we, too, may participate in this privilege when we have the proper knowledge and motivation. These thoughts and feelings *literally* open the door of heaven, bring down benedictions and blessing which swell that reservoir and stand ready to be used for helping the evolution and growth of mankind. Thus it is within the power of every one of us, even the weakest, poorest, and least educated, to contribute to the welfare of the world. As Leadbeater perceptively writes,

> The arrangement made by the Christ with regard to His new religion was that a kind of special compartment of that reservoir should be reserved for its use, and that a set of officials should be empowered by the use of certain special ceremonies, certain words and signs of power, to draw upon it for the spiritual benefit of their people.
>
> The scheme adopted for passing on the power is what is called *ordination*, and thus we see at once the real meaning of the doctrine of apostolic succession, about which there has been so much argument . . .
>
> It is by this Sacrament of Holy Orders that a man is endowed with power to draw for certain definite purposes upon the reservoir of which I have written. The three stages of Deacon, Priest, and Bishop present three degrees of this power, and at the same time three degrees of connection with our Lord. Each ordination confers its own special powers, and as the ordained rises from one rank in the Church to the other he draws nearer and nearer to his great Master the Christ. He comes more and more closely into touch, and he controls more and more of the mighty reservoir. In that reservoir itself there are different levels and different degrees of power. [27]

Ordination, in the Catholic traditions, rests upon two basic factors: First, we have the Gift of the Holy Spirit which is what connects the ordained person with the reservoir of spiritual Light. Then comes the personal link with Christ himself and with the Divine Spark. It is the first that actually enables a Priest to bless people, to give the absolution for one's sins, and, finally, to consecrate the Host. As Leadbeater further explains:

This is the irreducible minimum of power [the Gift of the Holy Spirit], which is equally possessed by all properly ordained Priests and is quite independent of their acquirements in other directions—their spiritual or devotional development, for example, or their comprehension of the mechanism of the Sacraments which they administer—just as one may be a rapid and accurate telegraphist, even though he does not know what electricity is, and though his moral character is not above reproach.

Many people think this strange, because they have not grasped the nature of the Priest's relation to the Sacrament. If the Host were a talisman into which he had to put his personal magnetism, obviously the nature of that magnetism would be all-important. There is, however, here no question of magnetization, but of the due performance of a certain ceremony, in which the character of the performer has nothing to do with the matter. If the faithful had to institute an exhaustive enquiry into the private character of a Priest before they could feel certain of the validity of the Sacraments received from his hands, an element of intolerable uncertainty would be introduced, which would practically render this wondrously-conceived device of Christ for the helping of His people ineffective. He has not planned His gracious gift so ineptly as that. To compare great things to small, to attend a celebration of the Holy Eucharist is like going to a bank to draw out a sum of money in gold; the teller's hand may be clean or dirty; but we obtain the gold all the same in either case. It is obviously better for all points of view that the Priest should be a man of noble character and deep devotion, and should thoroughly understand, so far as mortal man may, the stupendous mystery which he administers; but whether all this be so or not, the key which unlocks a certain door has been placed in his hands, and it is the opening of the door which chiefly concerns us . . .

First, only those Priests who have been duly ordained, and have the apostolic succession, can produce this effect at all . . . Secondly, neither the character of the Priest, nor his knowledge or ignorance as to what he is really doing, affects the results in any way whatever . . .

I think that we can see a very good reason why precisely this arrangement has been made. Some plan was needed which should put a splendid outpouring of force within the reach of every one simultaneously in thousands of churches all over the world. Perhaps it might be possible for a man of most exceptional power and holiness to call down through the strength of his devotion an amount of higher force commensurate with that obtained through the rites which I have described. But men of such exceptional power are always excessively rare, and it could never at any time of the world's history have been possible to find enough of them simultaneously to fill even one thousandth part of the places where they are needed. But here is a plan whose arrangement is to a certain extent mechanical; it is ordained that a certain act when duly performed shall be the recognized method to bring down the force; and this can be done with comparatively little training by anyone upon whom the power is conferred. A strong man is needed to pump up water, but any child can turn on a tap. It needs a strong man to make a door and to hang it in its place, but when it is once on its hinges any child can open it . . .

It must not for a moment be understood as saying that the devotion and earnestness, the knowledge and the good character of the officiant makes no difference. They make a great difference; but they do not affect the power to draw from that particular reservoir. When the Priest is earnest and devoted, his whole feeling radiates out upon his people and call forth similar feelings in such of them as are capable of expressing them. Also his devotion calls down its inevitable response, and the down-pouring of the force thus evoked benefits his congregations as well as himself; so that Priest who throws his heart and soul into the work which he does may be said to bring a double blessing upon his people, though the second class of influence can scarcely be considered as being of the same order of magnitude as the first. The second outpouring, which is drawn down by devotion itself, is of course to be found just as often outside the Church as within it. [28]

In this world, the Priest is, therefore, a vehicle or channel for the Christ (in the macrocosm) and for the Divine Spark (in the micro-cosm) to manifest and express their energies (Light, Fire, and Life). It is interesting to note that, in English speaking countries, a Priest is also called a Parson and *parson* means the person who represents Christ. The etymologies speak clearly: *person* comes from *persona* (*per* = through and *sona* = sound, or the "vehicle for the word"), which was also used to describe the mask that a Roman actor wore, through which came the sound of his voice. Hence, the role of a Parson, or Priest, is to reactivate and vivify the connection between the human and the Divine.

The Ordering of a Deacon: The Exoteric Orthodox Ritual

"As the Deacon does not perform the Sacrament of the Eucharist, his ordination takes place after the consecration of the Holy Gifts. Two Subdeacons conduct the Deacon-elect from the middle of the church before the Bishop, who is seated on a throne at the left of the altar, and the deacons utter the words: 'Bid ye and ye, and thou, Right Rever-end Master.' The first 'bid' is addressed to the people, the second to the clergy, and the third to the Bishop. This reminds us that in ancient times the people and the clergy as well as the Bishop took part in the election of persons to be ordained.

"The Deacon-elect bows himself to the ground before the Bishop and receives his blessing. Then the deacons lead him twice around the altar in token that he vows to devote himself forever to the service of the church. He kisses the corners of the altar in token of reverence for God, and after each circumambulation bows himself to the ground before the Bishop and kisses his hand. All through this ceremony are sung the following sacred hymns: 'O ye holy martyrs, who valiantly contended and received the crown, pray to the Lord that our souls may be saved.' And: 'Rejoice O Isaiah! The Virgin is with child and bringeth forth a son, Emmanuel, God and Man, the Orient is his name.'

"Then the Bishop rising from his throne covers the candidate's head with the end of his Omophorion, blesses him, lays his hand upon his head, and speaks the prayer of ordination: 'The Divine Grace, which ever healeth what is infirm and supplieth what is wanting, passing through my hand, ordereth this most pious Sub-deacon for Deacon; let us therefore pray for him, that the grace of the All-holy Spirit may come on him.' During the prayer of ordination the recipient of the Sacrament receives the Grace of the Holy Spirit which orders him for a sacred ministry.

"After the laying on of hands, the Bishop delivers to the newly ordained deacon the vestments and signs of his office: the Orarion, the maniples, and the fan, uttering the Greek word 'Axios' [worthy] which is repeated by the choir in the name of the people and the clergy. Having received the fan, the newly ordained Deacon takes his stand at the left side of the altar and fans the Holy Gifts, calling to mind as he does so that he must minister at the altar of God with the same reverence with which the Holy Angels minister to God himself."

An Esoteric Perspective

Now the Aspirant Priest passes from the Lower Mysteries to the Higher Mysteries, from work on the personality (the various degrees of self-knowledge, self-mastery, and self-integration, achieved by the four Elemental Initiations) to work for the world, and from the personality to the soul. It is important to remember, however, that when someone truly works on self-actualization and personal growth, he or she also works for the world (as one becomes more conscious, knowledgeable, loving, capable, responsible) just as one who truly works for the world is working on his own development and perfection (since every objective action in the world has a subjective reaction in the psyche and on the person). Hence, the two are really two sides of the same coin.

The ordination of the Deacon focuses upon and opens up *Tiphereth*, the Heart Center, activates the intuition, or higher mind, and establishes a channel between the personality and the soul. Naturally, it is still an *unconscious* Initiation, which parallels the conscious one obtained through personal preparation, training, and achievement and through the downpouring of the Energies of the Divine Spark.

The Deacon must serve both at the altar of the Church (in the macrocosm, consciously) and at the altar of his heart (in the microcosm, superconsciously). He must learn to offer himself as a "living sacrifice" to God and to represent and embody the heart Initiation. It is the great lesson of love that he must learn, and, in so doing, he exemplifies the love of God for man, of the greater for the lesser. Herein is also enshrined the passage from "soft" to "tough" love— from satisfying the wishes of a person to doing what is truly best for that person. And it is through that love and the heart Initiation that the Deacon will learn and exemplify that the Light which dwells in the heart can be awakened and how to become conscious of that Light. This is the process that will quicken and activate the spiritual faculties of the Deacon and those of the congregation.

Finally, he must also render physically visible the invisible realities. In the visible physical altar and sanctuary of the Church, he stands as the invisible Heart Center and inner sanctuary, so that from the outer and visible, people might be lead, by degrees, to the inner and invisible realities. It is the Gift of the Holy Spirit, conferred to him by the Bishop, which activates his Heart Center and makes him, in fact, a Deacon.

As a postscript here, we should mention that there is evidence that in the Early Church there were woman deaconesses, with the relevant scriptural texts being Romans 16:1 and 1 Timothy 3:8–13. In the Roman Catholic Church these were abolished in the sixth century, in the Orthodox Catholic Church in the eleventh century. Before the Second Vatican Council, the office of the deaconate had been a temporary ministry required for ordination to priesthood; now it has been restored as a "proper and permanent rank of the hierarchy." As the role of women today in the Church is one which is receiving a great deal of discussion, we may, one day, see the further restoration of the role of the deaconesses.

Dion Fortune gives us an insight into spiritual realization and the opening of the spiritual senses that are of particular significance for the work of deacons:

> There is a technique of consciousness to be employed in spiritual realisation. We cannot apply to it the same methods that would enable us to solve a philosophical problem. We cannot arrive by reasoning at an understanding of *spiritual* things. We perceive spiritual things, in the first place, by means of our *feelings*; these are our sense-organs upon the higher planes. Our emotions react to a spiritual stimulus, and lo the Lord is with us, for we have perceived Him . . .
>
> Yet all the time we live and move and have our being in a world of

spiritual realities just as the blind man moves in a world of light; it is *spiritual senses that are lacking to us,* not spiritual qualities to the universe. We might as well try to listen to a picture or to see a symphony. We are using the wrong sense-organs . . . It was the work of our Lord Jesus Christ to make the Kingdom of Heaven tangible to us so that there should be in human consciousness concepts of spiritual things, and He did it by translating spiritual ideas into *physical action* . . .

He caused the sick to be healed, the hungry to be fed, the sinful to be pardoned, the sorrowful to be comforted. These things are the fruit of the spirit and the emotions we feel when we contemplate our Lord's words is a *spiritual emotion.* Having felt it, we shall soon begin to arrive at some understanding of spiritual things.[29]

The Ordering of a Priest: The Orthodox Ritual

"The deacon who is to become ordained priest is led out by deacons into the middle of the church, before the Bishop, after the singing of the Cherubic Hymn, in order that he may on the same day take part in the celebration of the Eucharist. The circumambulation of the altar is conducted in token that he takes upon himself the greater ministry, and for that end is to receive the gift of priesthood. After the prayer of ordination, the Bishop gives to the newly ordained priest the vestments of his office: The Epitrachelion [stole], the girdle and the Phelonion [cape] and places in his hands the Book of Offices [manual of church services]. The newly ordained Priest then takes part in the further celebration of the Liturgy. After the transmutation of the Holy Gifts, the Bishop presents to him a portion of the Lamb, with the words: 'Receive this pledge and preserve it whole and intact unto the latest breath, for thou shalt be held to account for it at the second and dread coming of our Lord, and God, and Savior, Jesus Christ.' This ceremony indicates that the priest is the performer of the Holy Sacraments and that it is his duty to guard their sacredness, admitting to participate in them only them that are worthy. Before the exclamation 'The Holy to the holy', this pledge is returned to the Bishop. The newly ordained priest then receives Holy Communion and reads the prayer for which the celebrant descends from the Ambo."

An Esoteric Perspective

The ordination of a Priest focuses upon and opens up *Geburah*, the Right Shoulder Center, and activates his speech center (whence the custom of the "Roman collar" which draws our attention to and creates a light pressure on the throat center). This Ordination confers

upon him the power to bless people (with his right hand), to consecrate the Host, to absolve sins, and to preach and baptize. Again,
it is the Power of the Holy Spirit, conferred upon him by the Bishop,
that activates *Geburah* and enlightens his internal Tree of Life.

The Priest will strive to fashion the "living Temple of God" both
in himself and in others, through his words and deeds. Through the
Bishop's laying on of hands, the Priest's own powers of thinking,
feeling, willing, and intuition will be further stimulated by the
Power of the Holy Spirit, giving him the discernment to distinguish
good from evil. Here is how Leadbeater explains what happens at
the ordination of a Priest:

> The power of the Christ, the direct outflow from the Second Person of
> the Holy Trinity, comes always in the silence, for it has not yet
> descended sufficiently into materiality to manifest as sound; but the
> Holy Ghost came as a rushing, mighty wind and showed Himself in
> tongues of fire, conferring upon the apostles an unusual power of
> speech. So at the second imposition of hands later the word of power is
> employed as in the other Orders; but the tremendous gift of the first
> imposition descends in a silence that is felt. It is this act which actually
> makes the man a Priest and endows him with the power to celebrate the
> Holy Eucharist.[30]

Here, the Priest becomes the Tenth Hierarchy, linking the
divine, angelic, human, and physical worlds, "heaven and earth,"
and providing a double bridge, or pathway, through the various
planes of Creation so as to link the divine world to the physical
world, through the human world, and *Kether* to *Malkuth* through
Tipphereth.

The Priest becomes, in effect, the "incandescent filament"
wherein the Divine Light and Fire, and male and female polarities
of the Spiritual energies can be released in the world, radiating upon
all in their unconditional polarity, and vivifying all. The Priest,
therefore, becomes a great and living channel for the seven Sacraments, for the spiritual energies flowing through them, and for the
Power of the Holy Spirit to be poured forth in the world. It is also
something which we shall *all become* and *do consciously* after we have
undergone our spiritual Initiation. The Priest also blesses through
his *right hand*, the channel for the energies and Light of *Geburah*. In
the Catholic traditions, a man whose right hand has been amputated
cannot be a Priest.

The Ordering of a Bishop: The Exoteric Orthodox Ritual

"The consecration of a bishop takes place at the beginning of the Liturgy, since a bishop has the right not only of performing the Sacrament of the Eucharist, but also of ordaining deacons and priests; moreover it is performed not by one bishop but by several, i.e. by a convention of bishops. Before the beginning of the Liturgy, an arch-priest and a deacon conduct the candidate to an Ambo [or platform], placed in the middle of the church, where the bishops are seated. Here, standing on an Orlets ["Eaglet" or eagle-rug] he recites the Creed, expounds in detail the doctrine of the Holy Trinity and of the Incarnation of the Son of God, then pledges himself to observe the canons of the Apostles and Councils, the traditions of the Church, and to obey the Most Holy Synod, and, lastly, takes two oaths: the general state oath of allegiance and the single-hearted service to the throne and obedience to the emperor and the laws by him issued—and a special oath instituted for spiritual authorities, of fulfilling their duties in all conscience and the fear of God. Having taken both oaths, he receives the blessing of the eldest bishop present and kisses the hands of the other bishops who are to consecrate him.

"After the Introit with the Testament, the arch-priest and deacon conduct the bishop-elect before the Royal Gates. Here he is met by the bishops and kneels before the altar on both knees. The bishops lay an open Testament, text downward, upon his head, as though it were the hand of Christ Savior, and hold it there. During this time the oldest bishop says the prayer of consecration; after which the bishops chant 'Lord have mercy,' and lay their right hands upon the head of the bishop-elect. This ends the consecration, and the new bishop is forthwith robed in the Saccos and Omophorion, during which the word 'Axios' is uttered loudly. When the Liturgy is ended, the oldest of the bishops present the newly consecrated bishop with the crozier. This is done on the Ambo in the middle of the church."

An Esoteric Perspective

The episcopate is the highest of all the Holy Orders and corresponds to the third Spiritual Initiation, the opening of *Chesed*, the Left Shoulder Center. According to esoteric tradition, this is the highest initiation for a human being. For the actual, conscious opening of the next center, *Binah*, would cause his death and dematerialization. The ordination ceremony is, traditionally carried out by a minimum of three Bishops, who will awaken and stimulate the three aspects of the Holy Trinity (Light or Wisdom, Fire or Love, and Life or Creative Energies) in the Bishop-elect.

What are the specific functions of the Bishop? They are to consecrate churches, sanctuaries, and altars; to ordain clergy; to offer the sacrifice of the Mass and of the Eucharist; to bless with both hands; to baptize and confirm; to forgive sins and grant absolution; and, finally, to judge and interpret Church matters. The essential spiritual aspect of the ceremony comes when the Power of the Holy Spirit is invoked for the Bishop-elect and when, in his Tree of Life and auras, a particular channel is opened to connect his intuitional body and function with the Christ, both within his own being (in the microcosm) and in the world (the macrocosm)—but at the Superconscious level. As Leadbeater further explains:

> While all the spiritual powers of a Bishop are conferred simultaneously at the utterance of the words of power, it would be exceedingly difficult to bring them into practical operation without the aids which are given by this opening and by the anointing of head and hands . . .
>
> The consecrator now takes his seat and assumes his mitre, the head of the newly-made Bishop is then bound with a long napkin, and the consecrator with his thumb anoints the head with holy chrism, first in the form of a cross over the entire top of the head, then with a series of extending circles till all is covered with sacred oil . . .
>
> The anointing of the head is another important item in the ceremony, for the chrism is especially the vehicle of divine Fire. On the lower levels it is a powerful purifying influence, and on the higher it gives strength and clarity. When it is applied down here in the physical world, its effects extend far above into the unseen realms. The soul mirrors itself in the personality, and this reflection, like many others, is upside down. The higher mind or intellect is reflected in the lower mind, the intuition in the emotional or astral body, and the spirit itself down here in the physical vehicle. Ordinarily the triple spirit is so widely separated in man as we know him that there is no apparent result from this reflection; but in the Bishop this triple spirit has the opportunity of awakening, the application of chrism to the head intensifies the power of reflection, and makes the triple spirit glow most wonderfully, besides clearing the way down into the physical brain for the flow of the new forces . . .
>
> If he understands his business and uses his opportunities, every Bishop ought to be a veritable radiating sun, a lighthouse amid the stormy sea of life, a battery charged with almost unlimited power for good, so that he may be a fountain of strength, of love, and of peace, and his mere presence may itself be a benediction.[31]

One of the most important tasks of the newly consecrated Bishop is to unfold, coordinate, and activate genuine intuition, the ''knowledge

of the heart" and "the Wisdom of God." This is achieved by linking and integrating the lower with the higher mind, the emotions
with the inspirational vehicle (higher emotions), and the human
with the Divine Will. The Bishop should also balance and integrate
Severity with Mercy, *Geburah* (red) with *Chesed* (blue), which is why
he wears the *purple* color (the actual blending of red and blue), for he
should become a "psychotherapeute" (a healer of souls) blending
Wisdom and Love, Light and Fire. He should become a *conscious*
channel for the Love of Christ and for the Divine Spark—a radiating Sun in the Inner Worlds, spreading forth the spiritual Light and
Fire which engender the spiritual Life.

In the Holy Orders system of the Catholic traditions, we find (and
carried out above the threshold of the field of consciousness, at the
superliminal level) as it were, the whole Western initiation system and
journey up the Tree of Life and the Cross of Light. This leads to the
"Second Coming of Christ," the "Coming of the Messiah," and the
"Manifestation of the Mahdi": *union with the God within*, the very
Source and Essence of Life, Love, and Wisdom. What is done at the
"Briatic level" (the superconscious) must, eventually, be realized at
the "Yetziratic level" (the conscious). But, meanwhile, we have a
simple yet *operative* system to channel, radiate, and diffuse the spiritual
energies (the Divine Light, Fire, and Life) in the human and physical
worlds so as to guide, inspire, and accelerate the evolution of all those
who are ready for this, in this *exact measure* for which they are ready.
The energies that are so invoked and diffused can act both at the
unconditional objective level, radiating like the rays of the sun upon
all, good and evil, evolved and unevolved, and at the conditional subjective level, reaching those who are especially prepared and in tune
with them, to the exact measure of their openness and devotion.

Where could we find a more simple, practical, yet comprehensive
and subtle system to assist us in our slow growth and becoming?
The entire ancient Mystery tradition and arcane Initiation system
are embodied and conveyed through this Holy Orders system—
which is proof enough that it comes from the Spiritual Powers and
not merely from human beings, who adopt it and use it in different
ways, in different countries and times, in consonance with their own
levels of consciousness, affinities, unique needs, and aspirations.
The Christian Catholic Church is the institution which has preserved and brought forth this system, through the centuries, till it
could, once again, be used in a *conscious* and *fruitful* manner. For
then, this system will lead to *personal Spiritual Initiation* and to the
greatest of all "contacts"—that between God and Man, Spirit and
Matter, Heaven and Earth. And this time is NOW and YOU, WE,
are the Protagonists!

MATRIMONY

The Exoteric Perspective

"What is Matrimony? Matrimony is a Sacrament, in which, on the free promise of man and woman before the Priest and the Church to be true to each other, their conjugal union is blessed to be an image of Christ's union with the Church, and grace is asked for them to live together in godly love and honesty, to the procreation and Christian bringing up of children.

"Whence does it appear that Matrimony is a Sacrament? From the following words of the Apostle Paul: 'A man shall leave his father and mother, and shall be joined unto his wife, and they two shall be one flesh. This Sacrament is great: but I speak concerning Christ and the Church' (Eph. 5:31,32). Is it the duty of all to marry? No. Virginity is better than wedlock, if any have the gift to keep it undefiled. Of this Jesus Christ has said expressly: 'All men cannot receive this saying, save they to whom it is given. He that is able to receive it, let him receive it' (Matt. 19:11,12).

"Matrimony is a Sacrament, in which, in the image of the union of Christ with the Church, the conjugal union between a man and a woman is blessed, which means that the grace of a love as perfect as that which unites Christ and His Church is invoked on them for the blessed bearing and Christian rearing of children.

"As Matrimony can be entered into only by the mutual spontaneous consent of both parties, and they must receive the blessing of the Church on their conjugal life, the order of the Sacrament of Matrimony consists of two rites—that of betrothal and that of marriage. In the former, the man and the woman affirm their mutual engagement before God and the Church; the rings are the pledge of that engagement. In the rite of marriage, their union is blessed with prayers, invoking upon them the grace of the Holy Spirit; of that grace the crowns are the visible tokens . . . Both these rites must be performed in a church, in the presence of witnesses, and on certain days prescribed by the canons . . .

"*The rite of betrothal.* The priest, preceded by a lampadary, comes out of the sanctuary through the Royal Gates holding in his hands the cross and Testament, which he lays on a lectern in the middle of the church. Then he approaches the main entrance of the church, where the bride and the groom already stand, blesses them thrice with two lighted candles, which he then hands to them, conducts them into the church, walking before them and swinging the censer —the censing is expressly prescribed—and places them before the lectern, at a little distance from it. The betrothal begins with the

Great Ectenia and two brief prayers, with the addition of special petitions: for the salvation of the betrothed couple, the granting them of children, and peaceful and mutual affection, for their abiding in harmony, firm in the faith, and for a blessing on them, and that they may lead a blameless life. The prayers contain petitions for a blessing on the betrothed and on the betrothal . . .

"*The rite of marriage*. After the rite of betrothal the bride and groom approach nearer and nearer to the lectern, holding the lighted candles, and again preceded by the censing priest. This serves to remind them that they must live their lives in conformity with the commandments of the Lord, which the priest proclaims, that their good deeds must shine in the world and rise to Heaven like incense . . .

"This rite begins with the blessing of the Kingdom of the Most Holy Trinity and with the great *Ectenia*. To this *Ectenia* are added the petitions on behalf of the new consorts: that they may be granted a blessing upon their marriage, chastity, and well-favored children and joy in them, and a blameless life. Then the priest says three prayers, in which he asks that the Lord may grant to the consorts a peaceful life, length of days, chastity, mutual love, long life to their children, grace in their offspring, an unfading crown of glory in the heavens, and abundance of the good things of the earth so that they may be enabled to assist the needy; that the Lord may help the wife obey the husband, and the husband to be the head of the wife; that he may remember also the parents who reared them as parents' prayers make firm the foundation of houses. After these prayers the priest places a crown on the head of the groom, repeating thrice the words: 'The servant of God N. is crowned for the handmaid of God N. in the name of the Father and the Son and the Holy Spirit'. This he repeats, placing the other crown on the head of the bride, after which he blesses them thrice, saying 'O Lord, our God, with glory and honor crown them'. The crowns betoken their victory over their passions, as also the honor paid them for the chastity of their life before marriage, and reminds them that they must guard the purity of their lives after marriage also . . .

"After the ceremony of marriage and the blessing, a *Prokimenoi* is sung, in which the essence of the Sacrament of Matrimony is set forth: 'Thou has set upon their head crowns of precious stones; they asked life of Thee, and Thou gavest it them,' after which lessons from the Gospels and Epistle are read. The Epistle lesson speaks of the importance of the Sacrament of Matrimony and of the mutual duties of consorts; the Gospel Lesson tells of Christ's presence at the wedding at Cana in Galilee.

"The readings are followed by the Triple *Ectenia* and the *Ectenia* of Supplication, ending with the chanting of the Lord's Prayer; then a cup of wine is brought. The priest blesses the cup, and presents it alternatively to the husband and the wife to drink from, three times to each. This common cup signifies that they must live in an indissoluble union and share with each other joy and sorrow. The priest takes them by the hand and leads them three times around the lectern, while the sponsors follow holding the crowns above their heads. During this circumambulation the same hymns are sung as.at an ordination. This ceremony is symbolical of the solemnity and indissolubility of the conjugal union . . .

"The Orthodox Church allows widowers and widows, and also persons whose marriage has been dissolved for one of the legitimate reasons, to contract a second and third marriage; but this she considers as a condescension to human weakness and therefore the celebration of the second or third marriage does not take place with the same solemnity as that of a first marriage."

An Esoteric Perspective

Of the seven Sacraments, that of Matrimony is the highest because it focuses primarily on *Chesed*, the highest psychospiritual Center that can be activated consciously while a person is incarnate in the world of matter. As such, it is the one which is most hidden in symbolism that must be properly deciphered and interpreted. From the esoteric viewpoint, we can look at the Sacrament of Matrimony in three basic ways.

A. As a union between Man and Woman or persons of the opposite sex.

B. As coming in touch with and integrating the male and female polarities within oneself.

C. As a symbol of, and a step towards, the union of Christ with His Church, the Feast of Bridegroom with the Bride, the Marriage Feast of the Lamb. (We use throughout the ancient meaning of symbol as participating in a living experiential reality.)

A. Union between Man and Woman

The spiritual traditions of both East and West are quite clear and unequivocal about the question of homosexuality, yet one does not wish to show any less love to those who, by a complex of social, psychological, and karmic forces, find themselves struggling with this issue of our time. In the union between people of the same sex, two streams of force of the same type are called forth, finding no channels of return. The vehicles of the "higher bodies" are both of the same polarity, making it impossible to merge and fuse the two pluses or two minuses. Because this energy then cannot return to the Divine Source from whence it issues, it is "short-circuited," but, worse, it accumulates and thus can be used, as it has been, in dark magical practices—for the acquisition of power. From an esoteric perspective, those who enter into this act, it is true to say, "know not what they do," nor the harm and conflict that will accrue. Sexual energy derives from the Power of the Holy Spirit and the Sacred Fire; therefore, it is a most powerful force which must be grasped in enlightened thought, by an enlightened will, and expressed in enlightened ways—and this progressively so as one advances in initiation. If it is abused or misused, one is literally playing with fire, with very real and profound consequences on all levels of existence. Thus we see, too, as the records of ethnologists and historians show, that the practice of homosexuality occurs in all ages and races in the periods of their decay. All this must be carefully considered in what is brought forward to us daily on this question, but perhaps it can indicate why homosexuality has never been, nor will ever be, accepted by the authentic spiritual schools or the Church, and why sexual relations are to be confined to members to the opposite sex.

The struggle with the question of sexuality is endemic to our time, revealing now perhaps at least more openly what has been a perennial human challenge. The Catholic traditions have taken over the centuries the paradoxical position (so frequent in sacred traditions and writings) that intimate sexual relations between a man and a woman can be both a sin and a Sacrament. That is, that the same act or relationship can either further the evolution and growth, the health, creativity, and well-being of a person, or it can do the opposite. This also reflects the sociological insight that human interaction, the exchanges on various levels between human beings, can be both a medicine and a poison, a life-enhancing or a life-restricting experience.

For a long time, the position of the Church was that sexual relationships between married men and women were essentially for the procreation of children, though now this has been widened to include the goals of achieving and deepening their interpersonal union and emotional closeness. There are also signs of deepening the understanding of chastity, as not only abstinence from sexual relations, but also a virtue with a greater dimensionality—and, interestingly enough, this view is coming from both the esoteric and the exoteric perspectives. The esoteric view is stated by the anonymous author of *Meditations on the Tarot*:

The vow of *chastity* means to say the putting into practice of the resolution to live according to solar law, without covetousness and without
indifference . . . In other words, chastity is the state of the human being
where the center named in occidental esotericism as the "twelve-petaled
lotus" (*anahata* in Indian esotericism) is awakened and becomes the sun
of the microcosmic "planetary system." The three lotus-centers situ-
ated below it (the ten-petalled, the six-petalled and the four-petalled)
begin then to function in conformity with the life of the heart . . .
"according to solar law." When they do this the person is chaste, no
matter whether he or she is celibate or married. Thus there are "virgins" who are married and mothers of children, and there are physical
virgins who are not so in reality. The ideal of the Virgin-Mother that
the traditional Church (Catholic and Orthodox) puts forward is truly
worthy of reverence. It is the ideal of chastity which triumphs over
sterility and indifference.

The practice of chastity does not concern solely the domain of sex. It
bears equally on all other domains where there is choice between solar
law and all sorts of dulling intoxications. Thus, for example, all fanat-
icism sins against chastity, because there one is carried away by a dark
current. The French revolution was an orgy of perverse collective
intoxication, just as the revolution in Russia was . . .

The practice of chastity holds fast the leanings of the *hunter* in the
human being, of which the male side is inclined to pursue game and the
female side to set traps.[32]

There is another esoteric aspect of chastity which is that it also
involves a full concentration, or focusing one's attention (creative
energies); meditation, or focusing one's thoughts; devotion, or
focusing one's emotions; visualization, or focusing one's imagination—upon the Christ within, the Divine Spark. For this is the way
in which one intuits the balance between inner conscience and outer
authority. It is "being true to one's Self" (that Divine Spark within,
which is at one with, yet separate from, God), and being receptive
and responsive to the subtle "inner voice." Unchastity, on the other
hand, means to be dominated or overwhelmed by forces and factors
that are at odds with this Divine Spark—which can be people, passions, events, fears, desires, etc. Unchastity is then a fundamental
dishonesty to who one is in the deepest sense, to "lose one's Self,"
to become a stranger to one's Self, to become a "house divided
against itself"!

From a spiritual viewpoint, sex has not one but three functions: to
provide physical vehicles for incoming souls (procreation); to regenerate the vehicles of Life and Consciousness (the physical and
etheric, astral, mental, and spiritual bodies); and to express one's
self creatively (or "to create") on all four planes. In holding up the
"ideal" that sexual relations be used solely for procreation, the

Catholic Church was addressing itself to the "spiritual" men and women of tomorrow who have mastered their biopsychic drives or impulses, their emotions, imagination, and thoughts, and who have activated their psychospiritual Heart Center, transferring the center of their love-energies from the sexual to the heart, or solar, center.

Sexual energy derives, as we said, from the Power of the Holy Spirit, the creative Life-Force, flowing down through the seven planes of creation to manifest on the physical plane. It is a very powerful and sacred force which must be understood, contacted, and transmuted in a healthy and balanced way, guided by what our developed intuition on these levels tells us.

The symbol of the crown (which is put on the heads of the couple during the Orthodox marriage ceremony) also has several esoteric meanings, implications and applications. It is the symbol of *Kether*, the psychospiritual Head Center, and of its activation. It represents the achievement of self-mastery and control over one's psyche, its functions and energies—impulses, passions, fears, desires, emotions, imagination, and mind. It also indicates the linkage and proper integration, or "marriage" between Spirit and Matter, the Male and Female polarities, the human and the divine. Finally, it indicates the realization of spiritual consciousness—the halo of the Saints and the Crown of Glory of the true Initiates. Its repeated use, during the marriage ceremony, by the Orthodox Church is deliberate and has profound spiritual implications. It points to the work that must be done as a preparation for marriage and that can be done during marriage, as well as the ideals that can be striven for by the couple. For "crowning" points to the basic spiritual achievement for which we have come into this world and which literally *crowns* life on earth!

B. Integrating the Male-Female Polarities Within

From the point of view of psychosynthesis, there are three "marriages," or "unions," which take place on very different levels of our being, but with profound correspondences between them: personal (psychological), interpersonal (social), and transpersonal (spiritual) psychosynthesis, marriage, or union. Personal psychosynthesis is the marriage, or integration of the personality where all the elements of human consciousness and all the aspects and facets of the personality come together at the conscious level. This process leads to systematic self-knowledge, self-mastery, and self-integration, which are the essential objectives of this first type of marriage. Interpersonal psychosynthesis is the traditional marriage between a man and a woman. Transpersonal psychosynthesis is the marriage, or union and integration, between the Self and the Soul, and of the Higher Self with the lower self—the Mystical Marriage. Properly applied and understood, the activation and integration of the polarities on various levels of our being will bring about the greatest and most powerful stimulus to accelerate our evolution and becoming—which is why Matrimony is the highest and last of the seven Sacraments. And this for one very simple reason: it deals with LIFE and the flow of the life-force! In fact, Life, on any plane and in any polarization, can only flow and manifest itself through polarity, the connection and exchange between the male and the female principles.

But, where there is opportunity there is also danger! When the male and female polarities are brought together and life flows through them, this life will either create or destroy! In former times and in traditional societies, this principle was recognized—mainly on the physical plane. This is why it was so important for a woman to have children and why an unfertile woman could be left by her husband—because it was feared that if the union was not fertile or creative, it could become destructive. But the creative and destructive power of the life-force can manifest and express itself both within and between two people on the four levels of being, and not just on the physical level. Thus a couple can create and give birth not only to physical children, but also to new emotions, ideas, insights, intuitions, projects, and causes of various kinds. And union can occur not only between a man and a woman but also within each, between different aspects and functions of the psyche. For example, the lower mind can unite with the higher mind, the emotions with the lower spiritual principle, the physical body with the higher spiritual principle—thoughts with emotions, the imagination with the intuition, the will with behavior, etc. (The reader can find further details and analysis of this in my book *The Spiritual Dimension and Implications of Love, Sex, and Marriage*.) Leadbeater writes:

So great an opportunity necessarily brings with it its responsibility and its danger. The intimate connection which enables these two to help each other inevitably makes them abnormally sensitive each to the other's influence and feeling; so that if they allow disharmony to arise the link is as powerful for evil and for sorrow as it would otherwise be for good and for joy . . . A link so close and so strong is not broken by physical death; the power to influence and the susceptibility to that power reside not in the physical body, so they are not lost when it is dropped. Souls differ much in this respect; for their natures and their deserts are different; some rise quickly out of touch with earth, some are held against their will for many years in its immediate neighborhood, and some intentionally hold themselves back in order to remain nearer to those they love.[33]

C. The Union of Christ with His Church

While the union of man and woman contains tremendous possibilities for good or evil, it is an archetype—again, in the sense of living signs, participating in the reality—of the ultimate form of marriage or union. The ultimate form of marriage is between the Bridegroom who is Christ, both within and without (within as the Divine Spark, the Self, the part of God within each of us) and the Bride who is the Soul. Having arrived at a certain point, one must look for and find the Beloved. Having arrived at a certain point, one must look for and find one's own "inner fiancé." This is the true and final aim of human evolution on earth, represented by the final convergence of *self-actualization* and *Self-realization* the "personal Christmas," and the "Second Coming of Christ" or Spiritual Initiation bringing about the true underlying spiritual consciousness! We find all the core steps and processes symbolically represented by the ceremony of the Orthodox Church and its major symbols so that "he who has eyes" can see and "he who has ears" can hear.

All the ecstatic rapture of Solomon's Songs fills the consciousness, as does the lofty and enchanted "courtship" so well described in the *Spiritual Canticles* of St. John of the Cross and the visions of the Wedding Chamber in the accounts by the Blessed Anne Catherine Emmerich—all witnessing that the Spiritual Marriage proceeds with the infusion of radiant transport one has glimpsed if one has ever been in love, but this heightened, incomparably, in ardency, longing, and desire. Nor is it infatuation—though holy men are often called "God-intoxicated." For the Wedding to proceed, all the garments must be assembled and carefully prepared and all the Wedding preparations must be made, each with the care befitting the occasion, in the manner which reflects the Heart and Soul's unique Union. The Engagement can last years after the Betrothal, where one has been promised. And there can be tests and trials to be overcome, journeys to be made, dragons to be slain. The Marriage Feast is the crowning of the Quest, the true and ultimate "happy ending" in the drama of life and evolution on earth.

Charles Leadbeater, who observed the marriage ceremony from the "clairvoyant standpoint" and studied its deeper esoteric meanings, gives us the following core insights:

The general intention of the marriage Service is to open the natures of the bride and groom towards each other, especially at the *astral* and *mental* levels; and then, having done this, to draw *a ring around them*, separating them to a certain extent from the rest of the world. From the point of view of the inner life matrimony is a tremendous experiment, in which the parties agree to make certain sacrifices of individual freedom and preferences, in the hope and with the intention first, that through their mutual reaction each will *intensify the inner life of the other*, so that their joint output of spiritual force may be far greater than the sum of their separate efforts would be, and secondly, that they may have the privilege of providing suitable vehicles for souls who desire and deserve a good opportunity of rapid evolution . . .

As the bride-groom utters the troth-plight, his whole aura *shines and swells until it completely enfolds his bride*; and when her turn comes, she *surrounds him in the same way*, and the two greatly enlarged auras remain thus interpenetrating and of course strongly interacting. Into this *magic double-sphere comes the consecrated ring*, instantly lighting up both of them, and so raising their vibrations that they become *far more sensitive* than they usually are. While this condition of extended consciousness and high receptivity exists, the Priest pronounces the formula of marriage; and as he says the words a flood of light surges from him through the combined auras, and for the time *welds them into one*.

That light and that wondrous unity persist during the rest of the Service, and probably under favourable circumstances for some little time afterwards. Then gradually each settles back into again something like its previous form and condition; yet it is permanently enlarged and modified, and each retains a special *sympathy in vibration* with the other, so that it can far more readily be influenced by it than by any other stimulus from without. So the parties may continue indefinitely to react upon each other for good if they are able to preserve perfect harmony.[34]

One of the oldest marriage customs is that spouses exchange, and then wear, rings. What are rings and what do they symbolize in this case? A ring is the "signature" of the sacred circle, both as it represents the heavenly orbits and finds expression as well in the proportions of the human body. Magically, it is a special and bounded space, created as separate from what is without, which gathers within it attention and energies. It is the perfect symbol of the Infinite and Eternal that manifests its creative power in the finite and temporal world—where the energies and attention must be focused. Hence, in exchanging and wearing rings, the couple creates this sacred magical circle around themselves, to separate themselves from the rest of the world, and to concentrate their attentions and energies in creating or bringing something into manifestation. This sacred circle represents their united auras and the new life and consciousness body they fashion for each other. And it represents the esoteric core of their intimacy in marriage—the special links and focus that they share with each other and with no one else.

We find again this endlessness and timelessness of the circle in another tradition of the Orthodox Church which is that the ring of the groom should be made of gold while that of the bride should be made of silver. Gold represents the Sun, the Spirit, while silver represents the Moon, the Spirit and the Soul, Christ and His Church. This symbolism is carried further in the teaching of the Orthodox Church that the husband represents the Head and the wife, the Heart of the one being now formed in the Sacrament of Matrimony.

We find the same symbol repeated and physically enacted by the Priest who "takes them by the hand and leads them three times around the lectern," thus physically creating three circles. Each circle represents one magical circle on one of the three levels of the personality: the first in the etheric world, the second in the astral world, and the third in the mental world. This ritual thus links the couple's etheric, astral, and mental auras to form one common aura—at least on the astral and mental levels (and also at the etheric level when the auras are very near each other and touch each other physically.)

The same process is further repeated and reinforced when the Priest brings a cup of wine which be blesses and then gives to the bride and bridegroom to drink from three times. The cup is a symbol (a three-dimensional circle), sign, and living reality of the very gift of Love, the Holy Grail, the overflowing Chalice of Redemption given by the Hand of God through the Priest. The wine here partakes of all which we have gathered about this living sign in the previous Sacraments, but also represents, on the one hand, the astral body and, on the other, the lower spiritual body, the buddhic body, which are now joined and linked together by this ceremony. The exoteric meaning ascribed to this rite "signifies that they must live in an indissoluble union and share with each other joy and sorrow." Esoterically, it reinforces and deepens the strong connection and links that unite them on the subtle planes, especially at the emotional and higher emotional levels. For it is into this "home on the inner planes" that the incarnating souls will come and that establishes the inner heart of the marriage. The cup then, too, prefigures the cradle, the spiritual cradle which marriage is, a safe and warm haven for new life. After the marriage ceremony, the spouses both partake of Communion—which is the Life they now so deeply share together and will nurture together, their oneness united with God's, across the spectrum of the many planes of consciousness and creation.

The Priest also blesses the couple with two lighted candles three times. The two lighted candles represent Christ, in his Divine and Human Nature, the Divine Spark which, being recognized, will manifest itself at the physical level, as it already does at the spiritual level. It represents the union of Spirit and Matter which must now be realized on the three planes and bodies of the personality, that is, consciously at the etheric, astral, and mental levels. And this is the symbol of the "Union of Christ with His Church," of spiritual Initiation in the plenitude of fulfillment of all promises, both the Beginning and the End we have longed for in all our preparations of the Nuptials.

The Mystical Marriage is the true culminating point of the spiritual life. In fact, this is the true purpose for which all human beings incarnate on earth—to enter into this Union by completing and perfecting their being, that they may know, love, and serve Christ as Lord. We are completed and our being perfected through the fusion on the Spirit with its vehicles, the higher vehicle, the soul, and the lower, the personality. When the Christ within can indeed be Lord, be the ruling and integrating principle of our consciousness and behavior, then can the human self completely submit to God's Will —which will be clearly, consciously, and fully expressed in this world through the personality. Here the process is double: first, we must "build the Temple," actualize our personality and its faculties and potentialities; and then, invite the Christ to ensoul and indwell his Temple so that, together, they may fulfill their functions in this world. As Evelyn Underhill again perceptively elucidates it:

> The mystics find the basis of their method not in logic but in life: in the existence of a discoverable "real," a spark of true being, within the seeking subject which can, in that ineffable experience which they call the "act of union", fuse itself with and thus apprehend the reality of the sought Object. In theological language, their theory of knowledge is that the spirit of man, itself essentially divine, is capable of immediate communion with God, the One Reality . . . Where the philosopher guesses and argues, the mystic lives and looks; and speaks, consequently, the disconcerting language of first-hand experience, not the neat dialectic of the schools . . .
>
> Again, the great mystics tell us that the "vision of God in His own Light"—the direct contact of the soul's substance with the Absolute— to which awful experience you drew as near as the quality of your spirit would permit in the third degree of contemplation, is the prelude not to a further revelation of the eternal order given to you, but to an utter change, a vivid life springing up within you, which they sometimes call the "transformative union" or "birth of the Son in the Soul." By this they mean that the spark of spiritual stuff, that high special power or character of human nature, by which you first desired, then tended to, then achieved contact with Reality, is as it were fertilized by this

profound communion with its origin; becomes strong and vigorous, invades and transmutes the whole personality, and makes it not a "dreamy mystic" but an active and impassioned servant of the Eternal Wisdom.[35]

Finally, in the same vein, she concludes:

According to the measure of their strength and of their passion, these, the true lovers of the Absolute, have conformed here and now to the utmost tests of divine sonship, the final demands of life. They have not shrunk from the sufferings of the cross. They have faced the darkness of the tomb. Beauty and agony alike have called them; alike have awakened a heroic response. For them the winter is over: the time of the singing of the birds is come. From the deeps of the dewy garden, Life— new, unquenchable, and ever lovely—comes to meet them with the dawn.[36]

Let it be understood that Matrimony represents possibilities and potentialities, and does not necessarily confer any realizations at the conscious level—for example, a happy and healthy marriage, the proper integration of the male and female polarities within oneself, even less the Mystical Marriage between the Spirit and the Soul. In awakening and activating *Chesed*, it is both a promise and a model of what can be attained. And this is Matrimony as the Sacrament of the Bridal Chamber, realized both as an inner and outer reality; that which is Divine in us unites with what is Divine without in the most complete sense possible on earth. It can also explain many subtle and paradoxical aspects of human life and man-woman relationships, and offer a tremendous set of possibilities—a road map and a great stimulus to cooperate consciously at furthering our own evolution, that of humankind, and that of our planet.

In the summer of 1990, I went to Chartres to celebrate my first "spiritual marriage" for a couple belonging to a spiritual group I had established in the lovely city of Douce, France a few years ago. The couple in question had requested, in addition to the civil and religious ceremonies, a *spiritual celebration of their union*. For me, as for them, I think, and for all the people who participated, this was a unique and unforgettable experience: an experience in which each of us, according to his or her capacity and level of consciousness, experienced for a brief moment "a foretaste" of all three basic forms of marriage. First, of the intrapersonal marriage, where a person welds into conscious unity all the divergent and disparate parts, faculties, and potentialities of his own being. Then, of the interpersonal marriage, where two people who really love each other, and have tested their love, come together to cause more LIFE to flow through their being, for themselves and for the community in which they live—to marry the basic polarities of Spirit and Matter, Male and Female, joy and sorrow, in the circle of their union and being. Finally, of the transpersonal marriage, where the Divine Spark can marry the soul, which has prepared for it, as Christ married the Church, and about which nothing can be said other than "Come, taste and see" what the Creator has prepared for the Creature, what the joy and ecstasy of spiritual and *living union* really is like. This is what the mystics and all those who have awakened to spiritual consciousness and tasted of this union want for all of us, what they testify as being our destiny, and offer us as a living example of the ultimate human experience that bridges the finite and Infinite, the temporal and the Eternal!

Conclusion

Why did I write another book about Christianity when there are already many, and many fine ones at that? Well, the truth of the matter is that I did not set out to write a book about Christianity. At the beginning of my personal quest, nothing could have been further removed from my mind. Had anyone suggested it, I would have vigorously denied that I would ever do such a thing. At the time, I was not interested in religion in the least, and particularly not in Christianity—which I then identified with the Priests I had spoken to, observed, and been greatly disappointed in as a child. They disappointed me because they did not have the answers I was looking for—answers I thought they should have!—and because they were not the "living examples" of the Wisdom, Love, and Creative Energies I always associated with God, the Ultimate Reality.

One person, in fact, did tell me that I would, eventually, get back to religion and become quite involved with Christianity. That person was Padre Pio, and he told me this right in the middle of my "pilgrimage to the East," when my highest aspiration was to become a yogi and to articulate the various yogas on a "scientific," empirical-experimental basis. Of all the things he told me, and he did tell me many things, this was the hardest to understand and to accept at that time—even from someone like Padre Pio! For the first time, I really could not "resonate" with what he was telling me . . . but this was thirty-three years ago.

What I wanted, and wanted passionately, more than anything else, was to answer: Who was I? Where did I come from? Why was I in this world? And what was my purpose, duty, or the work I had come to undertake in this world? This work, or purpose, soon manifested itself clearly and imperatively to my awareness, overriding every other concern in my life. It was simply to *live Life*, to invite Life to flow at a more conscious and intense level through my consciousness and my being, to have a "Life more abundant"! And that Life more abundant clearly meant to me the basic trinity: *Know and understand more, expand my consciousness, and become more aware! Love and feel more passionately and intensely, be perpetually "in love"! Be more powerful, creative, and better able to express my self on all levels and in all ways, be more alive!*

To achieve this grand obsession and live Life more fully and consciously, what was needed was a science of Life and its basic laws, principles, and dynamics. I searched for this "science of Life" high and low, left and right, but I did not find it ready-made or on a silver platter anywhere. I did not find it in science (which was my first avenue into reality and truth) nor did I find it in philosophy, nor even (reluctantly!) in religion. I did not find it in Europe, in the Americas, or in the Orient. Thus, I set out to assemble it myself, single-handedly, or so I thought—for I had not yet realized that whatever one seeks in the world, one must first realize within himself. But, slowly, I was learning.

Following those before me (taking as an example, to mention one model, St. Augustine) and working along the same lines as others have (I can mention here Aster Barnwell, Thomas Legere, or John Rossner, three "brothers on the Path"), I set out on a course of systematic study and self-experimentation. From traditional science, philosophy, and religion, I moved on to the esoteric, sacred, and spiritual traditions: Alchemy, Hermeticism, Gnosticism, Rosicrucianism, Magic, Occultism, Mysticism, and many other "isms." I also sought to integrate (in good Renaissance tradition) the sacred traditions of the past with the very best of modern physics, humanistic sociology, transpersonal psychology, and the "new therapies," exoteric or esoteric.

After discovering Roberto Assagioli and Psychosynthesis (that came closest as a "system" to what I was seeking), I began to articulate the essential fragments of my own philosophy and art of living. These I organized, conceptualized, and published, first in the three books *Spiritual Man in the Modern World, Spiritual Perspective,* and *The Spiritual Dimension and Implications of Love, Sex, and Marriage*; then in three more books for Llewellyn Publications, *The Nature and Use of Ritual for Spiritual Attainment, The Invisible Temple,* and *Apocalypse Now*; and, finally, in the three volumes of my Italian work, *Lo Sviluppo dell'Uomo Nuovo*. Practicing and living this developing philosophy and art of life, I gathered more and more in way of results—results that naturally, organically, and imperatively led me to discover the spiritual and esoteric aspect of Christianity. This is what led to the birth of the present work; it is the synthesis of my own quest, of all my work and experimentation.

But, if one looks at the past and at the contemporary scene, one will soon discover that what happened to me was not all that unique. In fact, it is archetypal in many ways, because it bears the consequences of following a certain path, or course of action, in a spiritually logical progression—thus fully corroborating what Padre Pio had told me in San Giovanni Rotondo in 1958. In the past, this process can be seen in St. Paul, St. Augustine or, more recently, in Henri Bergson, Alexis

Carrel, and George Plummer, and in many others who have experienced much the same progression and have also written books about certain aspects, implications, and applications of the spiritual aspects of Christianity, exoteric or esoteric. This progression is also a convergence; insights, realizations, experiences, like rays on the circumference of a circle, converge at the center—at a central truth. These rays may bear different names, labels, traditions, approaches, but they do converge, however that convergence may be individually expressed. I would even go further and venture that all world religions, if properly understood, loved, and lived lead to the same "inner Temple," to the one God and God-Experience, which may have many names or none at all, and which is best realized in the silence of one's own consciousness and sanctuary.

At the very beginning of this work, I stated the central thesis, my personally lived conclusion that Christianity is the Ageless Wisdom, articulated in simple and practical, but symbolic and analogical terms which can lead those who live it to spiritual Initiation and authentic spiritual consciousness. I pointed out that it is composed of a body, a soul, and a spirit, and that it is the soul (that is, the meanings, implications and applications) that needs to be redefined to fit with our modern level of consciousness and world conditions.

In the next chapter, I pointed out that today, or roughly from 1950 to 2050, with the last decade of the twentieth century and the first decade of the twenty-first century as the epicenter, we are living in a very special time. We are privileged to witness and to participate in massive quantitative and qualitative changes. These bring with them extraordinary challenges, great dangers, and even greater opportunities. We are becoming more aware, more sensitive, and more powerful in creating or in the capacity for destroying, and can achieve great sorrows or great joys. All this means that we must now learn to live in a more conscious and responsible fashion. And this so that we may complete our own evolution, and become, as it were, the human father and mother of our soul and character . . . to help complete the creation process of God.

To accomplish this, more than ever, a comprehensive philosophy and integral art of living—leading to conscious growth and Initiation —is essential. Finally, of all the choices that are open to us to find such a philosophy and art of living, the one I have come to at the end of my quest (and at the beginning of mature and conscious living) is that of Catholic Christianity—but this was only when I was able to understand and "marry" its exoteric and esoteric, human and spiritual, past and present aspects. For in this tradition we can find, today, the Philosopher's Stone, the *Elixir Vitae*, and the *Panacea*—the Source and Essence of our Being and of Reality, of Life, Love, and

Wisdom. Drawing from my own life, adventures and misadventures, I explained how I came to this conclusion and realization.

This theme was then developed in the next chapter, showing what Christianity is, how it can grow and articulate itself, and what functions it might fulfill in the coming age. My fundamental argument, here, is simply that Catholic Christianity does contain all the theoretical knowledge and the practical exercises, as well as the social organization and the tools, to lead the mature and serious candidate to genuine spiritual Initiation.

At this point, I began to examine, in a systematic way, the esoteric structure and functions of Catholic Christianity. And this in the following manner:

1. By showing that the Church, the external, physical Temple, can be experienced as a visible blueprint and replica of our own inner anatomy and physiology—of our Tree of Life with its Centers, Bodies, and Auras. Thus, when we enter a Church, we can experience really entering into our own consciousness and Tree of Life. And what the Priest does at the altar, we can mirror in our own Heart Center (the altar of our living Temple).

2. I went on to examine the nature and relationship between the exoteric and the esoteric aspects of religion which are bound to exist in every authentic religion; in our case, with Christianity, this is because of a complex of historical, psychological, and sociological factors. The universal appeal of Christianity that reaches out to meet people where they are must coexist with the experiential vitality and potency of esoteric wisdom; the caution of inclusion into the norm of tradition must coexist with the experimental candor born of direct personal experience.

3. The language of the sacred traditions was seen to be not the normal language of everyday speech or of science, but rather a symbolic and analogical language which can be appropriately deciphered or decoded, replete with as many different meanings as there are different levels of consciousness and being.

4. Next, the seven Sacraments of the Catholic Christian traditions were seen first from the exoteric, then from an esoteric perspective, showing how each is related to a specific psychospiritual Center and how this can be awakened and activated, to integrate its activities with those of other Centers. Here can be found a complete program of Initiation, path-working, and human and spiritual realization. The heart of this program is the Eucharist, related to the Heart Center, as a way, if only temporarily at first, to commune with the Source and Essence of our Being and of Reality—to receive a transfusion of spiritual Light and Fire, engendering the spiritual Life. In other words, in consciously going to Communion, we can, momentarily,

reconnect ourself and our consciousness with the very Source and Essence of Life, Love, and Wisdom, thus achieving and living a "Life more abundant," a preview of things to come further ahead in our evolution—and we can help to bring it about! Finally, I also showed how Holy Orders and the Priestly tradition channel spiritual energy, or Grace, paralleling the conscious efforts achieved through Initiation but at the *superconscious level* and thus *outside* the awareness of the postulant, and without conferring the knowledge and powers that conscious Initiation bestows. And I showed how Matrimony is the highest of the seven Sacraments, affecting the last psychospiritual Center *Chesed*, the Left Shoulder Center that can be fully awakened while in an incarnate state. Matrimony also has three basic aspects: that of the union between man and woman, that of integrating the "male" and "female" polarities within oneself, and that of being a symbol of the union of Christ with His Church, of the Marriage Feast of the Divine Spark with the Soul. As such, it holds precious keys and treasures for becoming truly alive, for creative self-expression on all planes, and for the culminating experience of life on earth and of the spiritual life in particular: for becoming whole and consciously united with the divine within and without.

In the three appendices, I included materials derived from the perspective of Psychosynthesis that are very important for doing mature and effective spiritual work—for applying and living essential Christianity. Thus, I looked at the nature, structure, and functions of human consciousness. I developed an instrument, the "Consciousness Checklist," to monitor and evaluate quantitative and qualitative changes in human consciousness—so important when we practice any kind of discipline or exercises designed to affect and expand consciousness.

When we look at this work as a whole, we can readily see how it hangs together and presents an organic whole, drawing from the spiritual traditions of the past—Catholic Christianity in particular— as well as from the latest advances of modern science and from the most creative breakthroughs of our times. And this to lead modern men and women to live a fuller, more constructive and creative life. We can also see that it offers both a cognitive framework and a practical discipline and set of psychospiritual exercises to make sense of life, to answer the fundamental questions of life, to grow in a conscious and responsible fashion, and to find both Self and God— the Living Source and Essence of Life, Love, and Wisdom.

Its merit is to be, at the same time, simple and essential, practical and effective, sound and healthy, and to reconcile the past with the present and the future, the exoteric with the esoteric, theory with practice, and religion with science. As I have lived it and put it together (first, in my own life and being, then in the group work done with others, and, finally, in this book), it does contain a time-proven program and holistic approach, an approach that appeals to, trains, and integrates, in a meaningful synthesis of lived experiences, the most profound needs and the deepest aspirations of the human Mind, Heart, and Will. For these are necessary to establish a conscious and living communion with the spiritual Self, the Christ within, the ultimate Teacher and Initiator. And it does this by taking you right back to the living core and essence of our Western spiritual tradition and to the religion of your birth (which may or may not be Catholic Christianity). The same esoteric spiritual perspective, however, can equally be applied to other churches and religions—in their living essence!

The rest, the actual work, the realization of the Great Work, the Birth of genuine spiritual Consciousness, or the coming of the Savior, is now UP TO YOU, to your own readiness, training, aspirations, and personal experiences. For the ultimate Reality and Self we call "God" is, in the last analysis, always a personal lived experience, a passionate love and never an intellectual discussion like reading or writing a book. This is also the true meaning and implication of the authentic esoteric perspective—which can only be a personally realized and lived experience. Now you have a roadmap. Use it and share it with others that more Light, Love, and Joy may flow into your consciousness and being and thus into the world, so that you may consciously accomplish what you have come to do in this world. For, I suspect, this is really what Christianity was really meant to be and to do for its Founder and its living Examples!

Further aspects of living and practical esoteric Christianity will be discussed and analyzed, using the same perspective and methodology, in the next volume of *Divine Light and Fire*. From the first volume, you, the reader, should have a good enough understanding of the theoretical implications and practical applications of living and practical Christianity to apply them in your own life—to meditate and reflect on this and to "put it to work in your own life" in order to gather its first living and self-motivating fruits.

APPENDIX A

The Human Psyche

In the turbulent, bewildering, and fascinating era we live in, a transitional period when an old world is dying and a new world is being born, a fundamental consensus is slowly emerging amongst students of the human and social sciences as well as amongst students of the psychic and spiritual disciplines. This cognitive and crystallizing consensus asserts, briefly, that:

a Of all knowledge open to a human being, *self-knowledge* is both the most important and the indispensable prerequisite for any other kind of systematic knowledge.

b Of all mastery open to a human being, *self-mastery* is both the most important and the logical starting point lest a veritable box of Pandora be open with every new form of energy and control that man acquires.

c Of all quests open to a human being, the quest for *self-actualization* and the quest for *self-realization* are the most important ones and should precede the other manifold quests that the human adventure makes available.

At the foundation of self-knowledge, self-mastery, self-actualization and Self-realization and at their very core stands a *proper understanding of the human psyche*, its nature and structures, its functions and their dynamics, unfolding, and manifestation.

Another area of general consensus which is also slowly emerging and crystallizing today amongst concerned and mature thinkers is that the history of humanity is really *the biography of the unfolding and expression of human consciousness;* and that the *existential essence* of man is his *human consciousness* and not his biological organism or his Divine Spark. Finally, it is also more and more agreed upon by avant-garde thinkers that it is upon human consciousness and its quantitative and qualitative expansion and transformation that the thrust of the evolutionary forces is focused.

One of the most important and perennial questions that human beings have always asked and answered in different ways is: What is human consciousness and its matrix, the human psyche? The term *psyche* is the Greek word now generally used by the human and social sciences to designate what used to be called the "soul" of man's human nature. It is the matrix, the seat or structures, through which human consciousness emerges, flows, and manifests itself. The psyche is thus the "house," the "temple," or the composite vehicle of human consciousness. The sacred traditions generally subdivided it into the *animal, human,* and *spiritual* soul, body, or consciousness, which is made up of what the ancients called the four elements (Earth, Water, Air, and Fire) and that modern mystics and spiritual scientists call the *etheric, astral, mental,* and *spiritual* bodies. As these cannot be seen by the naked eye or through a microscope (though they can be seen by clairvoyant sight and are now seen through special screens and even photographed by the Kirlian method), they have not yet been studied by the human and social sciences which have, most of the time, denied their existence.

Since the second half of the nineteenth century, however, a number of independent and mystically or occultly oriented thinkers such as Helena Blavatsky, Rudolf Steiner, Max Heindel, George Plummer, George Gurdjieff, and others have again become vitally concerned with the question of the existence, the nature, and the manifestations of the human soul and have formulated unusual philosophies and methodologies to integrate the body of their studies and conclusions. A few great academicians such as Henri Bergson, Pitirim Sorokin, and Pierre Teilhard de Chardin have traveled along the same tracks and have come up with, basically, the same assumptions and conclusions. In the last three decades several humanistic and transpersonal psychologists have also become fascinated with the question of the human soul and its higher reaches and potentialities. Beginning with

Basic model: **Advanced model:**

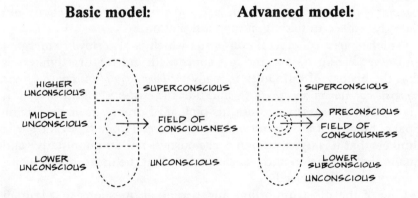

Figure A   The Structure of the Psyche
(Peter Roche de Coppens, *The Nature and Use of Ritual for Spiritual Attainment.* Llewellyn Publications, 1985.)

William James and Jung and continuing with Maslow and Assagioli, new models of the psyche, its nature, structures, and functions have been proposed. With the "rediscovery" and renewed emphasis upon the will, the superconscious, the inner spaces and latent energies of the psyche, and the transpersonal energies, the following model has finally crystallized, constituting the lastest and most sophisticated model of the psyche we have up to now.

Where the basic terms are defined as:

Superconscious: those levels and energies of human consciousness lying above the threshold of consciousness and deriving their being from the Spiritual Self. It is the seat and the source of intuitions, inspirations of a lofty religious, artistic, philosophic, or scientific nature, the creations of genius, sainthood, and heroism.

Higher Subconscious: those levels and energies of human consciousness that stand between and filter the materials between the Superconscious and the conscious.

Preconscious: those levels of human consciousness that stand on the very threshold of the conscious but which have not yet penetrated into its field.

Field of Consciousness: the stream of awareness made up of the "seven functions" which manifest through speaking and acting and which derive their energies from the human self.

Lower Subconscious: those levels and energies of human consciousness that stand and filter the materials between the conscious and the unconscious. Materials which have been forgotten and repressed and which are gathered from the entire range of human experience.

Unconscious: those levels and energies of human consciousness lying below the threshold of consciousness which derive their being from the biopsychic organism of man. The psychic energies that govern the organic life of the body: the seat of the basic instincts and drives such as sexuality, self-preservation, and aggressiveness. Here are also found complexes having strong emotional charges that are produced by traumas, psychic conflict, and very painful and threatening experiences.

Simply put, these various areas of the psyche represent the consciousness of the Spiritual Self (the Superconscious) which have not yet been brought into the field of consciousness and which theology called the personal "heaven"; the consciousness of the psyche, or human self (the subconscious, preconscious, and field of consciousness), which are partially within and partially without the field of consciousness and which theology called "purgatory" and "earth" respectively; and the consciousness of the biopsychic organism which lies outside the field of consciousness and which theology called "hell." Three major branches of contemporary psychology are now dealing specifically with each of these areas of consciousness. These are: psychoanalysis, or depth psychology, which focuses on the unconscious, existential psychology, which focuses on the conscious, preconscious, and subconscious, and finally "height" or transpersonal psychology, which focuses on the superconscious. The conscious, however, can be systematically expanded into the unconscious, and materials and energies coming from the unconscious, the subconscious, and the superconscious can find entry into the field of consciousness thus realizing *within* man the central injunction of science: from the known to the unknown.

The psyche   The functions of the psyche:

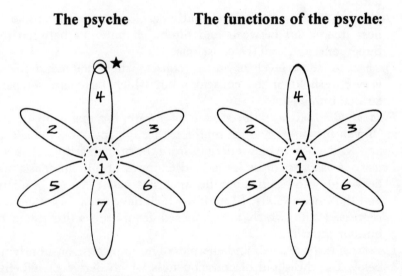

Figure B   The Functions of the Psyche
(Peter Roche de Coppens, *The Nature and Use of Ritual for Spiritual Attainment.* Llewellyn Publications, 1985.)

The basic terms are defined as:

*.   *The Spiritual Self,* the Divine Spark, the ontological essence of man.

A.   *The human self,* the conscious ego directing the seven functions of the psyche.

1.   *The will,* the focused energies of the human self which activate and propel all the other functions.

2.   *Thinking,* the mental process by which one grasps and makes sense of reality and of one's experiences in the world.

3. *Feeling,* energies issuing from the human self which impinge upon the field of consciousness and elicit a response. Example: joy, sorrow, surprise, awe, fear, excitement, etc.
4. *Intuition,* "seeing from within" or the "teaching from within," the spiritual function of the psyche through which a breakthrough of the superconscious takes place into the conscious.
5. *Imagination,* the image-making function which can reproduce any of the other functions within the field of consciousness and which is synthetic in nature. It has a receptive or female polarity and a creative or male polarity.
6. *Biopsychic drives, impulses-desires,* the basic drives of the body, such as hunger, thirst, fatigue, and of repressed instincts and painful experiences.
7. *Sensations,* external stimuli impinging upon the field of consciousness and eliciting a response. Example: seeing, hearing, tasting, smelling, and touching.

The first step, in exploring and analyzing the field of consciousness, is to have a map or a set of categories with which to denote the different energies and materials that flow through the field of consciousness. This map is provided by the seven functions aforementioned. The second step is to be able to identify, at any given moment, the operation of these seven functions, to recognize them experientially and to distinguish one from the other. The third step is to be able to deliberately train and further develop each function by a series of specific and efficient exercises. The fourth step is to coordinate and integrate these functions around the human self. The fifth and last step consists in having the Spiritual Self express Its energies and consciousness through the human self and through each of the seven functions.

After one has achieved a good theoretical and experiential grasp of the field of consciousness, one can continue and extend the exploration and analysis to the realms of the subconscious, the unconscious, and the superconscious.

To do so both productively and safely one should be very familiar with the seven functions of the psyche and have acquired a good control and coordination of them through various appropriate exercises. To provide an overall sense of timing, keep in mind that some schools dedicate one year's work for the proper exploration, analysis, development, and coordination of the field of consciousness after which another year is spent on the exploration and interpretation of the unconscious and another year yet for the exploration and interpretation of the superconscious. Thus it is only at the end of the three years' work that the truly serious and systematic work really begins!

While all seven functions are important and equally part of the psyche and of the personality, five of them are especially important for the inner work, both at the psychological and at the spiritual level. These, therefore, must be understood, consciously trained, and coordinated to begin the true work on the personality and the individuality (the lower consciousness and the higher consciousness). These are:

1. The *will* which must be understood in its nature and dynamics and experienced in its manifestations, and, naturally, properly trained and developed.
2. *Thinking* which must be understood in its nature and dynamics and experienced in its manifestations, and properly developed and trained.
3. *Feeling* which must be understood in its nature and dynamics and experienced in its manifestations, and cultivated and consciously directed.
4. *Imagination* which must be understood in its nature and dynamics, in its polarity and consequences, and which must be experienced and also properly developed and cultivated.
5. *Intuition* which must be understood in its nature and dynamics, in its polarity and "trigger mechanism," and which must be experienced, cultivated, and differentiated from emotion, impulse, and instinct.

The will is harnessed and applied through the process known as *concentration* and *affirmation;* thinking is harnessed and applied through the process known as *meditation* with its various stages; feeling is harnessed and applied through the process known as *devotion* and *adoration;* imagination is harnessed and applied through the process known as *visualization* and its various steps and degrees; and finally intuition is "triggered" and turned on through the process known as *invocation* and *evocation* which bring about a genuine breakthrough of the superconscious into the conscious, which opens up various "doors" and "layers" of the psyche through which different energies and materials can flow into the field of consciousness.

The inner work of man (work on the personality and on the self rather than action in the world) is based on the systematic and developmental use of these processes on all of the levels: *psychological* (development of the personality), *psychic* (exploration and use of the latent energies of the mind as in parapsychology, psychism, or witchcraft), and *spiritual* (exploration and alignment with the will and energies of the Spiritual Self). These, therefore, are the true *tools* or *instruments* that are used by the practical man, the scientist, and the artist, as well as by the magician, the occultist, and the mystic though, naturally, on different levels of operation and amplification. The three highest types of human beings known and venerated by human history, the Sage, the Saint, and the Hero, are actually personality types in which *thinking, feeling,* and *will* have been purified, organized, exalted, and properly aligned with the higher energies and will of the Spiritual Self.

To begin a genuine and sequential work on oneself and one's personality it is thus of paramount importance to understand, to work with, and to train these various functions. There is no substitute for this work and bypassing it or engaging in it in a haphazard or negligent fashion can be very detrimental and delusional for anyone.

The Tree of Life and the Psychospiritual Centers

In several chapters of this book, I have mentioned the psychospiritual Centers of man's energy and consciousness fields. These Centers, their nomenclature, nature, implications, and correspondences, constitute a very important and fascinating, albeit complex and controversial, subject matter that cannot adequately be covered in this work. To do justice to this subject, another book is the minimum that can be expected, which I already have in the planning stage for a later time. In the Western Spiritual Tradition, this subject is related mainly to the Qabalah and the Ten Sephiroth of the Tree of Life. In the East, on the other hand, it is related to the Chakras. Excellent works have been published on this topic and can be consulted by the interested reader. The ones that I am acquainted with and consider most reliable, both in theoretical and in practical terms are:

Dion Fortune, *The Mystical Qabalah*, London: Ernest Benn, 1963.

Gareth Knight, *A Practical Guide to Qabalistic Symbolism*, London: Helios Book, 1965.

Z'ev ben Shimon Halevi, *Tree of Life*, New York: Weiser, 1973.

Z'ev ben Shimon Halevi, *Adam and the Kabbalistic Tree*, New York: Weiser, 1974.

Israel Regardie, *The Tree of Life*, New York: Weiser, 1973.

William Gray, *The Ladder of Lights*, London: Helios Book, 1968.

R. G. Torrens, *The Golden Dawn*, New York: Weiser, 1973.

C. W. Leadbeater, *The Chakras*, London: Theosophical Press, 1938.

For the practical purposes of this work, I will include a basic diagram of the Tree of Life and list the Hebrew and English names of the Centers, together with their most important meanings and correspondences.

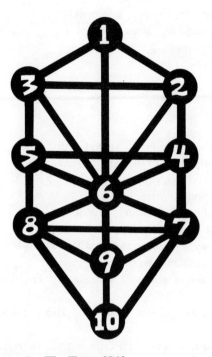

1. KETHER
2. CHOKMAH
3. BINAH
4. CHESED
5. GEBURAH
6. TIPHARETH
7. NETZACH
8. HOD
9. YESOD
10. MALKUTH

Figure A   The Tree of Life
(Peter Roche de Coppens, *The Nature and Use of Ritual for Spiritual Attainment*. Llewellyn Publications, 1985.)

Name of the Centers	Location on Human Body	Astrological Signs
1. Kether, The Crown	Head	Primum Mobile
2. Chockmah, Wisdom	Left Cheek	Zodiac
3. Binah, Understanding	Right Cheek	Saturn
4. Chesed, Mercy	Left Shoulder	Jupiter
5. Geburah, Severity or Strength	Right Shoulder	Mars
6. Tipphereth, Beauty or Equilibrium	Heart	Sun
7. Netzach, Victory	Left Hip	Venus
8. Hod, Splendor	Right Hip	Mercury
9. Yesod, Foundation	Genitals	Moon
10. Malkuth, Kingdom	Feet	Earth

Key Correspondences
1. Kether: Point of contact with the Divine Spark, Unity.
2. Chockmah: Eternal Masculine Principle, Expansion.

3. Binah: Eternal Feminine Principle, Contraction.
4. Chesed: Principle of expanding life, Energy, Enthusiasm.
5. Geburah: Principle of contracting life, Order, Discipline.
6. Tipphereth: Intuition, Equilibrium.
7. Netzach: Emotion, Combination.
8. Hod: Thought, Separation.
9. Yesod: Vitality, Creativity, Conception.
10. Malkuth: Behavior, Resolution.

Spiritual Experience, Virtue and Vice linked with given Center
1. Kether: Union with God; Completion of the Great Work; none.
2. Chockmah: Vision of God; Devotion, none.
3. Binah: Vision of Sorrow; Silence; Avarice.
4. Chesed: Vision of Love; Obedience; Tyranny, Hypocrisy.
5. Geburah: Vision of Power, Courage; Cruelty.
6. Tipphereth: Vision of Harmony; Devotion to Great Work; Pride.
7. Netzach: Vision of Beauty; Unselfishness; Lust.
8. Hod: Vision of Splendor, Illumination; Truthfulness; Falsehood, Dishonesty.
9. Yesod: Vision of the Machinery of the Universe; Independence; Idleness.
10. Malkuth: Vision of Holy Guardian Angel; Discrimination; Inertia.

The Tree of Life with its Ten Sephiroth has its roots and being in the Four Worlds of the Qabalists. These are:
Aziluth: Divine World; Divine Consciousness.
Briah: Mental World; Superconscious.
Yetzirah: Astral World; Conscious.
Assiah: Physical World; Unconscious.
The basic task of the student of the Mysteries is to become acquainted with the Tree of Life and each of its psychospiritual Centers; to cleanse, activate, and coordinate their energies so that these can be consciously used by the Self in man's consciousness and actions.

The Consciousness Checklist

The Consciousness Checklist described below is a practical instrument we have derived from Roberto Assagioli's *Egg of Psychosynthesis* which represents, diagrammatically, and describes the *structure* of the human Psyche. Its seven basic categories or questions are drawn directly from the Field of Consciousness and its seven functions: Willing, Thinking, Feeling, Intuition, Imagination, Biopsychic Drives, and Sensations. It is a most important psychological tool designed to enable the Candidate to develop his/her capacity for inner observation and to monitor what is really happening in his/her consciousness, to note and evaluate the qualitative and quantitative changes and psychospiritual transformations that might occur as the result of particular work being done, using Ritual or practicing other psychospiritual exercises.

It is the primary tool, operationalized from Psychosynthesis theory, for self-observation and consciousness-examination. As such, it should be properly understood in sequential order. Its proper use will enable the Candidate to systematically become aware of his/her inner state, of the processes and materials at work in his/her Field of Consciousness, and of possible transformations that will occur therein. These should then be noted mentally and/or in his/her workbook.

This is a tool that I have used not only for esoteric/spiritual work but also for psychological, human growth, and psychotherapeutic purposes, and that has yielded excellent results. Its merit is to be, at the same time, simple and practical, as well as systematic and exhaustive, tapping not only quantitative but also qualitative possible changes.

Consciousness Checklist

1. What *sensations* are you presently aware of in your field of consciousness?

a. Seeing
b. Hearing
c. Tasting
d. Smelling
e. Touching

What sensations are particularly strong, and which are weak?
Where do these sensations come from?
Realize that you are *not* these sensations, but that they are tools
for you to contact the physical world.

2. What *biopsychic drives* or *impulses* are you presently aware of in your
   field of consciousness?
   a. Hunger
   b. Thirst
   c. Fatigue
   d. Sexual Arousal
   e. Anger or Aggressiveness

3. What *emotions* and *feelings* are you presently aware of in your field
   of consciousness?
   a. Joy
   b. Sorrow
   c. Love
   d. Fear
   e. Excitement
   f. Depression
   g. Other

What emotions and feelings are particularly strong, and which
are weak? Where do these come from?
Realize that you are *not* these emotions and feelings, but that they
are tools for you to use, and that *you* control them, that they are
not really a part of your true being, but act as a source of great
energy and drive, joy or sorrow.

4. What *images* or *symbols* are presently activated in your
   imagination?
   a. Natural
   b. Human
   c. Spiritual

What images are particularly strong, and which are weak? Where
do these images and symbols come from?

Realize that you are *not* these images and symbols, but that they are tools for you to reproduce the other functions of the Psyche and experiences you have or could live.

Presently, is your image-making function strong or weak?

5. What *thoughts* or *ideas* are presently going through your mind?
   a. Of the Past
   b. Of the Present
   c. Of the Future

   What thoughts and ideas are particularly strong, and which are weak?

   Where do these thoughts and ideas originate?

   Realize that you are *not* these thoughts and ideas, but that they are tools for you to use to express yourself on the mental level, and that *you* can control them.

6. Is your *intuition* presently active in your Field of Consciousness?
   a. Spiritually
   b. Mentally
   c. Emotionally
   d. Physically

7. What are you presently willing, that is, directing your attention to?
   a. Physical objects
   b. Emotional objects
   c. Mental objects
   d. Spiritual objects

   How well can you presently use your will, the ability to direct your attention and concentrate upon the above objects? In your outer and inner work, are you able to do what you want to do and not to do what you do not want to do?

   What, if anything, is preventing you from presently using your will efficiently?

   How can you develop your will further?

Notes

Publication information not given in the notes will be found in the Bibliography.

Preface

1. Dante Alighieri, *The Divine Comedy: Paradise*, trans. James Cotter (Warwick, N.Y.: Amity House, 1986).

Chapter 2. The Christian Church

1. Plummer, *Rosicrucian Fundamentals*, 323–324.
2. Rolle, "Forms of Living," 182.

Chapter 3. The Christian Mystery Tradition

1. Clement of Alexandria, *Stromata*, vol. IV, bk. I, ch. 12 of Clarke's *Ante Nicene Library*.
2. Origen, *Origen against Celsus*, vol. X, bk. I, ch. 7 of Clarke's *Ante Nicene Library*.
3. Besant, *Esoteric Christianity*, 79.
4. Catherine of Genoa, 79–81.
5. Underhill, *Practical Mysticism*, 1–7.
6. Besant, *Esoteric Christianity*, 27.
7. Underhill, *Practical Mysticism*, 160–164.
8. Besant, *Esoteric Christianity*, 42–43.
9. Ignatius of Antioch, "Epistle to the Ephesians," ch. iii, xiii; "Epistle to the Trallians," ch. v; *The Martyrdom of Ignatius*, vol. I of Clarke's *Ante Nicene Library*.
10. Fortune, *Mystical Meditations*, 32.
11. Besant, *Esoteric Christianity*, 118.

Chapter 4. Sacred Language

1. Schneiders, *Christian Spirituality*, 1.

2. Ibid., 16–17.
3. Underhill, *Practical Mysticism*, 4.
4. Ibid., 168–169.

Chapter 5. The Seven Sacraments

1. Leadbeater, *Science of the Sacraments*, 25.
2. Ibid., *Christian Gnosis*, 251–252.
3. Ibid., 268–269.
4. Underhill, *Worship*, 42–43.
5. Ibid., 44.
6. Ibid., 45.
7. Leadbeater, *Science of the Sacraments*, 290.
8. Ibid., 291–292.
9. Ibid., 315.
10. Ibid., 318–320.
11. Ibid., 76.
12. Ibid., 78–83.
13. Anonymous Contemplative, *The Eucharist, A Christian Path*, Private manuscript, 1, 8–12.
14. Hodson, *Inner Side of Church Worship*, 66–68.
15. Leadbeater, *Christian Gnosis*, 257, 261–262, 265–267.
16. Underhill, *Worship*, 161–162, 341–343.
17. Ibid., 140.
18. Teresa of Avila, 240.
19. Underhill, *Worship*, 222.
20. Leadbeater, *Hidden Side of Things*, 163–168.
21. Underhill, *Practical Mysticism*, 148.
22. St. John of the Cross, 283.
23. Ibid., 323.
24. Underhill, *Practical Mysticism*, 136.
25. Leadbeater, *Science of the Sacraments*, 324.
26. Ibid., 345–346.
27. Ibid., 347–349.
28. Ibid., 351–354, 357.
29. Fortune, *Mystical Meditations*, 19–21.
30. Leadbeater, *Science of the Sacraments*, 380.
31. Ibid., 415–416.
32. Anonymous, *Meditations on the Tarot*, 113–114.
33. Leadbeater, *Science of the Sacraments*, 421–422.
34. Ibid., 420–421.
35. Underhill, *Practical Mysticism*, 15–17.
36. Underhill, *Mysticism*, 538–539.

Bibliography

Alighieri, Dante. *The Divine Comedy*. Translated by James Cotter. Warwick, N.Y.: Amity House, 1986.

Assagioli, Roberto. *La Vie dello Spirito*. Rome: G. Filipponio, 1974.

———. *Lo Sviluppo del Transpersonale*. Rome: Astrolabio, 1988.

Bailey, Alice. *The Soul and Its Mechanism*. London: Lucis Trust, 1971.

———. *From Intellect to Intuition*. London: Lucis Trust, 1971.

———. *From Bethlehem to Calvary*. London: Lucis Trust, 1981.

Barnwell, F. Aster. *The Meaning of Christ for Our Age*. St. Paul: Llewellyn, 1985.

———. *Meditations on the Apocalypse*. Rockport, Mass.: Element, 1992.

Bashir, Anthon, Archbishop. *Studies in the Greek Church*. New York: Syrian, Antiochian Archdiocese, 1960.

Bedrij, Orest. *One*. San Francisco: Strawberry Hill Press, 1977.

———. *You*. Warwick, N.Y.: Amity House, 1988.

Besant, Annie. *Esoteric Christianity*. New York: John Lane, 1911.

———. *Ancient Wisdom*. Wheaton, Ill.: Theosophical Publishing House, 1985.

Blanquart, Henri. *Les Mystères de la Nativité Christique*. Rennes, France: Editions Alrea, 1982.

Bucke, Richard. *Cosmic Consciousness*. New York: Dutton & Co., 1969.

Carrel, Alexis. *La Prière*. Paris: Librairie Plon, 1944.

Catherine of Genoa. *Purgation and Purgatory, The Spiritual Dialogue*. Classics of Western Spirituality. New York: Paulist Press, 1979.

Charpentier, Louis. *Les Mystères de la Cathédrale de Chartres*. Paris: Robert Laffont, 1966.

Eckhartshausen, Karl, von. *The Cloud Upon the Sanctuary*. New York: SRIA, 1952.

Emmanuel, R. *La Messe Vue Par les Yeux de l'Ame*. Paris: Dervy-Livres, 1976.

Ferrucci, Piero. *Inevitable Grace*. Los Angeles: Tarcher, 1990.

Fortune, Dion. *Mystical Meditations on the Collects*. London: Rider & Co., 1948.

———. *The Mystical Qabalah*. London: Ernest Benn, 1957.

Griffiths, Bede, Dom. *Return to the Center*. London: Collins Fontana, 1978.

Hani, Jean. *Le Symbolisme du Temple Chrétien*. Paris: Editions de la Maisne, 1978.

Harley, Christine. *The Western Mystery Tradition*. London: Aquarian Press, 1968.

Hodson, Geoffrey. *The Hidden Wisdom in the Holy Bible*. London: Theosophical Publishing House (TPH), 1930.

——. *The Inner Side of Church Worship*. Adyar, India: TPH, 1930.

——. *Man's Supersensory and Spiritual Powers*. Adyar, India: TPH, 1957.

——. *Clairvoyant Investigations into Christian Origins and Ceremonials*. Ojai, Calif.: St. Alban's Press, 1975.

——. *The Priestly Ideal*. Ojai, Calif.: St. Alban's Press, 1975.

——. *The Christ Life from Nativity to Ascension*. Wheaton, Ill.: Quest Books, 1975.

——. *The Brotherhood of Angels and Men*. Wheaton, Ill.: TPH, 1983.

John of the Cross. *Flame of Love, Spiritual Canticle*. Classics of Western Spirituality. New York: Paulist Press, 1984.

Jonas, Hans. *The Gnostic Religion*. Boston: Beacon Press, 1963.

Keating, Thomas. *Open Mind, Open Heart*. Warwick, N.Y.: Amity House, 1986.

Knight, Gareth. *A Practical Guide to Qabalistic Symbolism*. London: Helios, 1965.

Leadbeater, C.W. *The Hidden Side of Things*. Wheaton, Ill.: Theosophical Publishing House (TPH), 1974.

——. *The Science of the Sacraments*. Adyar, India: TPH, 1974.

——. *The Christian Gnosis*. Ojai, Calif.: St. Alban's Press, 1983.

——. *The Christian Creed*. Ojai, Calif.: St. Alban's Press, 1983.

——. *Invisible Helpers*. Wheaton, Ill.: TPH, 1985.

——. *Clairvoyance*. Wheaton, Ill.: TPH, 1985.

——. *The Inner Side of Christian Festivals*. Ojai, Calif.: St. Alban's Press, 1986.

Legere, Thomas. *Thoughts on the Run: Glimpses of Wholistic Spirituality*. Minneapolis: Winston Press, 1983.

——. *Your Spiritual Journey*. Liquori, Mo.: Liquori Publications, 1985.

Meditations on the Tarot. Rockport, Mass.: Element, 1991.

Meyendorff, John. *Byzantine Theology*. New York: Fordham University Press, 1978.

Needleman, Jacob. *Lost Christianity*. New York: Bantam Books, 1980.

Pagels, Elaine. *The Gnostic Gospels*. New York: Random House, 1980.

Parrish-Harra, Carol. *The Aquarian Rosary*. Tahlequah, Ok.: Village Press, 1987.

——. *The Book of Rituals: Personal and Planetary Transformation*. Santa Monica: IBS Press, 1980.

Peter Dieburg of Hildesheim. *Devotio Moderna*. Classics of Western Spirituality. New York: Paulist Press, 1988.

Plummer, George (Khei). *Rosicrucian Fundamentals*. New York: Flame Press, 1920.

——. *Instructions in Christian Mysticism*. New York: Mercury Publishing, 1926.

Richard of St. Victor. *The Twelve Patriarchs, The Mystical Ark, Book Three of the Trinity*. Classics of Western Spirituality. New York: Paulist Press, 1979.

Roche De Coppens, Peter. *Spiritual Man in the Modern World*. Washington: University Press of America (UPA), 1976.

——. *Spiritual Perspective*. Washington: UPA, 1980.

——. *Spiritual Perspective II: The Spiritual Dimension and Implications of Love, Sex, and Marriage*. Washington: UPA, 1981.

———. *The Nature and Use of Ritual for Spiritual Attainment*. St. Paul: Llewellyn, 1985.

———. *Apocalypse Now*. St. Paul: Llewellyn, 1988.

———. *The Sociological Adventure*. 2d ed. Dubuque, Iowa: Kendall-Hunt, 1990.

———. *The Art of Joyful Living*. Rockport, Mass.: Element, 1992.

Rolle, Richard. "The Forms of Living." *The English Writings*. Translated by Rosamund S. Allen. New York: Paulist Press, 1988.

Rossner, John. *From Ancient Magic to Future Technology*. Washington: University Press of America (UPA), 1978.

———. *From Ancient Religion to Future Science*. Washington: UPA, 1979.

———. *Religion, Science, and Psyche*. Washington: UPA, 1979.

———. *The Psychic Roots of Ancient Wisdom and Primitive Christian Gnosis*. Washington: UPA, 1983.

———. *In Search of the Primordial Tradition and Cosmic Christ*. St. Paul: Llewellyn, 1989.

Sadhu, Mouni. *Ways to Self-Realization*. New York: The Julian Press, 1962.

———. *Meditation*. London: George Allen & Unwin, 1965.

———. *Theurgy*. London: George Allen & Unwin, 1969.

Sedir, Paul. *Les Guérisons du Christ*. Paris: Bibliothèques des Amitiés Spirituelles (BAS), 1953.

Smith, Huston. *Forgotten Truth: The Primordial Tradition*. New York: Harper & Row, 1976.

Sofrony, Archimandrite. *The Undistorted Image*. London: The Faith Press, 1958.

Sorokin, Pitirim. *The Ways and Power of Love*. Boston: Beacon Press, 1950.

Swedenborg, Emmanuel. *Emmanuel Swedenborg*. Classics of Western Spirituality. New York: Paulist Press, 1984.

Teresa of Avila. *The Interior Castle*. Classics of Western Spirituality. New York: Paulist Press, 1979.

Underhill, Evelyn. *Mysticism*. New York: E.P. Dutton, 1919.

———. *Worship*. New York: Harper Brothers, 1937.

———. *Practical Mysticism*. New York: E.P. Dutton, 1943.

Yates, Frances. *Giordano Bruno and the Hermetic Tradition*. Chicago: University of Chicago Press, 1964.